Shambhala

Plate 1. *The Land of Shambhala. In the center are Mount Meru and the King's palace, surrounded by eight petal-shaped regions with their ninety-six principalities. The figures depicted around the mandala are a Kalachakric deity, Buddhas and the Third Panchen Lama.*

THE FASCINATING TRUTH BEHIND
THE MYTH OF SHANGRI-LA

VICTORIA LEPAGE

A publication supported by
THE KERN FOUNDATION

Quest Books
Theosophical Publishing House

Wheaton, Illinois ♦ Madras, India

The Theosophical Publishing House
P.O. Box 270
Wheaton, IL 60189-0270

A publication of the Theosophical Publishing House,
a department of the Theosophical Society in America

Library of Congress Cataloging-in-Publication Data

LePage, Victoria.
    Shambhala : the fascinating truth behind the myth of Shangri-la /
Victoria LePage.
        p.   cm.
    Includes index.
    ISBN 0–8356–0750–X
    1. Shambhala. 2. Legends—Himalaya Mountains.   I. Title.
GR940.L46   1996
398' .329496—dc20   96–18045
                                                              CIP

6   5   4   3   2   1   *   96   97   98   99   00   01   02

CONTENTS

ILLUSTRATIONS

Plate 1
The Land of Shambhala. (Tibetan painting, Musée Guimet, Paris.)
© Photo R.M.N.

Plate 2
The Immortals Visiting Xi Wang Mu. (Chinese painting.) Copyright British Museum.

Plate 3
The Bon Land of Olmolungring. (Drawing by Tenzin Namdak. From David L. Snellgrove, ed. and trans. *The Nine Ways of Bon,* 1967, by permission of the Oxford University Press. Reproduced here from Edwin Bernbaum, *The Way to Shambhala,* 1989, courtesy of Edwin Bernbaum and The Spieler Agency.)

Plate 4
Yggdrasil, the World-Ash. (Frontispiece of *Northern Antiquities,* Bishop Percy, 1847. 2500a 15.) By permission of the British Library.

Figure 1
The spinal chakric system. (Reproduced from *The Serpent Power,* by Arthur Avalon, Dover Publications, N.Y., 1974, with kind permission from the publisher.)

Figure 2
Map of Central Asia and India.

Figures 3 and 4
Two views of the Holy Place at Rennes-le-Chateau. (Reproduced from *The Holy Place,* Henry Lincoln, Jonathan Cape, London, 1991, pp. 93 and 122, with kind permission from the publisher.)

Figure 5
Tibetan system of mystical geography. (Drawing by Michael Young, based on Edwin Bernbaum, *The Way to Shambhala*, 1989, Fig. 3, p. 32, courtesy of Edwin Bernbaum and The Spieler Agency.)

Figures 6 and 7
Two clairvoyant views of the World Axis. (Drawing by Michael Young.)

Figure 8
A Syro-Hittite seal depicting Gilgamesh at the World Axis. (Reproduced from William Hayes Ward, *The Seal Cylinders of Western Asia*, 1910.) Copyright British Museum.

Figure 9
The Tree of Eternal Life on the Mycenean Ring of Nestor. (Reproduced from Sir Arthur Evans, *The Palace of Minos*, Vol. 3, p. 153.) Ashmolean Museum, University of Oxford.

Figure 10
Three variations of the Volute. (From Jurgen Spanuth, *Atlantis of the North*, Sidgwick and Jackson, 1979, p. 97.)

Figure 11
The Djed Pillar. (Papyrus of Ani.) Copyright British Museum.

Figure 12
Ancient Egyptian world-map, c. 1200 B.C. (From Jurgen Spanuth, *Atlantis of the North*, p. 29.)

Figure 13
Atlantis, laid out as a Troy Town. (Drawing by Michael Young.)

PREFACE

This book is primarily about Shambhala, said to be a hidden paradisial center of wisdom in the highlands of Central Asia; but it also entails an extremely ancient concept of the earth that is organically related to the central theme. This subtheme proposes that both the World Mountain and the World Tree of mythology are poetic images of a geophysical feature of the earth that can only be perceived clairvoyantly and that is unique to Shambhala. It envisions the planet as a living psychospiritual being whose body has an energetic structure our modern culture has not as yet recognized or understood, but which was once known to early races.

Clearly such a concept, which unites the physical and the psychic, cannot be validated through the usual channels of academic research or the amassing of factual information, but must rely on the more allusive methods that illuminate as best they can extremely new fields of psychospiritual study. But that limitation may soon be overcome.

Most scientific enquiry at present is restricted to a narrow band of thought whose parameters are tacitly defined and enforced by collective agreement, ensuring that the outcome never rises above a certain prescribed ceiling. But there is evidence of a growing countermovement, creative and idiosyncratic, which is determined to break the mold. Already some theoretical scientists are prepared to take seriously the phenomena of the psychic world, approaching them as a valid aspect of reality that may be included among the scientific possibilities to be rationally debated, even if it means working with radically new paradigms.

This is an important augury. It means that as a race we may be on the brink of a breakthrough into wider dimensions of thought that will transcend the old mental barriers, dimensions in which it is possible to ascend to transcendental levels without losing our scientific foothold. The day has not yet arrived but is surely approaching when it will be accepted that everything in the universe, including our planet, has its degree of life, consciousness and psychic potential, and that indeed this is the only basis on which human beings with their rich religious, cultural and social life can interact as they do with a physical world. The *credo* that conscious Life is sovereign in the universe is, I believe, already sounding its birth-note, and it is this *credo* that has inspired the following pages.

CREDO: A FORMAL STATEMENT OF BELIEF (RELIGIONS)

PART ONE

THE MOUNTAIN

There is a thing confusedly formed,
Born before heaven and earth.
Silent and void,
It stands alone and does not change,
Goes round and does not weary.
It is capable of being the mother
of the world.
I know not its name
So I style it "the way."

— *Tao Te Ching*

The Quest for Shambhala

There was a time when the universal order was stable, with God the Creator at the center and an assured place for humanity and all its works constellated about the divine Presence, safe from the outer darkness. In the natural order every community, however small, reflected the heavenly order in the pattern of its life, in its cycles of festivals and labor, its myths and rites, which all centered on some place of magnetic and energizing sanctity: a temple, a sacred spring, shrine or cave, a totem-house, the palace of a god-king, a chapel—all vital symbols of an ineffable Deity. It was precisely this centering process that brought repose, stability and a sense of certitude.

Today we are aware that that certitude has vanished. Now nothing is certain, and even the very concept of certainty is debatable. In a world in which all boundaries are dissolving, all values becoming ambiguous, all sign-posts illegible; in which centrifugal forces of destruction are flinging us outward, unwinding civilization; and in which change and instability are endemic—in such a world as ours is today the need for a new centering principle is paramount. In every conceivable context—spiritual, ecological, political, social—our need is for a magnetic center, for a zone of order within the primal chaos of possibilities; and in the search that has already begun for a saving new definition of self and cosmos the concept of the mandala provides the key.

Symbolically, the mandala is the embodiment *par excellence* of the centering principle, a device for focusing consciousness that has great transformative power. It is a diagram of perfect symmetry and balance, a mystical circle enclosing further boundaries of various shapes and values that draw the attention inward to the point of repose at the center. It is probable that the mind in its ordering operations is naturally mandalic, and that therefore a mandala is able to exercise over it a peculiarly regenerative, creative and stabilizing power, as yogis have always maintained. Certainly in traditional cultures the order humanity imposed on the cosmos was always of such a centralizing nature, with the zone of the divine presiding at its heart and radiating its unifying influence outward to the periphery of the universe. Ancient philosophies, religions and sciences have all conformed their worldview to this mandalic pattern as being the most in harmony with the natural contours of the mind.

"The Center," says Mircea Eliade, one of our foremost religious historians, "is preeminently the zone of the sacred, the zone of absolute reality."[1] The health-giving value of this realization is attested by the dominance of sacred mazes, labyrinths and "troy towns" in antiquity, as well as mandalic forms in space and movement such as the round dance, the spiralling ziggurat, the circumambulation of shrines—all of which were magical symbols of the Center that drew the mind inward to its deep creative core and activated the principle that renewed and stabilized the world. Today that world, that prophylaxis, has gone. We need new centering symbols. As the German physicist Werner Heisenberg warned, we have reached the limit of our exploration of the physical universe and need to find the path to what he called "the central order."[2] We need a new vision of the mandala of salvation, a new quest. And it is precisely that quest for the center that leads us to Shambhala.

For thousands of years rumors and reports have circulated among the *cognoscenti* of the nations suggesting that somewhere beyond Tibet, among the icy peaks and secluded valleys of Central Asia, there lies an inaccessible paradise, a place of universal wisdom and ineffable peace called Shambhala— although it is also known by other names. It is inhabited by adepts from every race and culture who form an inner circle of humanity secretly guiding its evolution. In that place, so the legends say, sages have existed since the beginning of human history in a valley of supreme beatitude that is sheltered from the icy arctic winds and where the climate is always warm and temperate, the sun always shines, the gentle airs are always beneficent and nature flowers luxuriantly.

There in a verdant oasis only the pure of heart can live, enjoying perfect ease and happiness and never knowing suffering, want or old age. Love and wisdom reign and injustice is unknown. "There is not even a sign of nonvirtue or evil in these lands," the Lama Garje K'am-trul Rinpoche has said. "Even the words *war* and *enmity* are unknown. The happiness and joy there can compete with that of the gods."[3] The inhabitants are long-lived, wear beautiful and perfect bodies and possess supernatural powers; their spiritual knowledge is deep, their technological level highly advanced, their laws mild and their study of the arts and sciences covers the full spectrum of cultural achievement, but on a far higher level than anything the outside world has attained.

Into this basic theme of a northern Utopia popular folklore has woven strange and wonderful features. The place is invisible; it is made of subtle matter; it is an island in a sea of nectar, a heaven-piercing mountain, forbidden territory. The ground is strewn with gold and silver, and precious jewels bedeck the trees—rubies, diamonds and garlands of jade; the place is guarded by great devas from another world and by walls as high as heaven; magic fountains, lakes of gems, of crystal and of the nectar of immortality, wish-fulfilling fruits and flying horses, stones that speak, subterranean caverns filled with all the treasures of the earth; these and many more wonders embellish the landscape of a primal paradise that seems to express the deepest yearnings of the human heart.[4]

But beneath these accretions of the popular imagination there is an underlying bedrock reality that has existed for as long as humanity has kept oral records. These testify to the love and reverence with which countless generations of Asiatic peoples have enshrined the mysterious Wisdom center in their folklore. Nor are these mythical accretions, as we shall see, as far from reality as one might think.

There are countless local versions of this wondrous place in the depths of Asia, but all agree that at every level the journey to it is difficult and dangerous. For those who have not been called and duly prepared the journey ends only in storms, landslides, fruitless wanderings and even death, among the pitiless wastes of snow and ice, for mighty natural forces conspire to guard the home of the Enlightened Ones from those who are not yet ready to enter. Even to those prepared for the dangers of the journey, the way is perilous and uncertain, psychically as well as physically. "The road leading to the Center is a 'difficult road,'" says Eliade again. It is "arduous, fraught with perils, because it is in fact a rite of passage from the profane to the sacred, from the ephemeral and illusory to reality and eternity, from death to life, from man to divinity."[5] His words can certainly be applied to Shambhala. The odyssey across the mountains, rivers and deserts of one of the most inhospitable parts of the world in search of the Land of the Bodhisattvas is described in Tibetan guidebooks as a contest with life and death—the goal, illumination.

For most people in the West, Shambhala, if it is known at all, is as remote from reality as Shangri-La, the mythical paradise that the novelist James Hilton immortalized in book and film. Nevertheless, Shambhala is gradually becoming known and taking tangible shape in the West as one author after another has attempted to outline its extraordinary supernatural contours. Their approach has varied. Some have been skeptical; some have dismissed it as an interesting fable, others as a guiding spiritual metaphor of value to the Hindu-Buddhist mystic in much the same way that Bunyan's *Pilgrim's Progress* is of value to the Christian's spiritual quest, but which cannot be taken literally. Finally, some have firmly and even passionately believed in it as a real place. This book falls into the latter category.

I believe the idea of Shambhala has not yet come to full flower, but that when it does it will have enormous power to reshape civilization. It is the sign of the future. The search for a new unifying principle that our civilization must now undertake will, I am convinced, lead it to this source of higher energies, and Shambhala will become the great icon of the new millennium. At the same time, I doubt we shall ever understand it as we understand other places on the earth. It will remain an enigma, one of those strange secrets that become stranger the more they are opened up. It is small wonder that the Russian traveler, Ferdinand Ossendowski, hearing about Shambhala on every side as he journeyed across Central Asia, declared that he could regard it as nothing less than "the mystery of mysteries."[6]

Others have named it in the same awestruck spirit. It has been called the Forbidden Land, the Land of White Waters (which may refer to the white salt deposits in the Tsaidam lakes east of the Takla Makan), the Land of Radiant Spirits, the Land of Living Fire, the Land of the Living Gods and the Land of Wonders. Hindus have known it as Aryavarsha, the land from which the Vedas came; the Chinese as Hsi Tien, the Western Paradise of Hsi Wang Mu, the Royal Mother of the West; the Russian Old Believers, a nineteenth-century Christian sect, knew it as Belovodye and the Kirghiz people as Janaidar. But throughout Asia it is best known by its Sanskrit name, Shambhala, meaning "the place of peace, of tranquillity," or as Chang Shambhala, northern Shambhala, the name Hindus use to distinguish it from an Indian town of the same name.[7]

Each of these peoples have had a tradition that Shambhala is the source of their own religion, whether it be Hinduism, shamanism, Buddhism, Taoism or other. Certain books of the pre-Buddhist Bon religion in Tibet, which knew the hidden kingdom as Olmolungring and Dejong as well as Shambhala, claimed that a kingdom called Shambhala had once actually covered most of Central Asia, from Lake Baikal to the Lob Nor and from Khotan almost to Beijing, and was the homeland of its cult. In the first century C.E. the Bonpo, the followers of Bon, mapped this country in its correct geographical relation to Persia, Bactria, Egypt, Judaea and other kingdoms of the then-known world and in the eighth century passed on the map and other documented information about Shambhala to the incoming Buddhists, although by then the kingdom had long since passed into myth.[8]

Tibetan Buddhism has taken much of its material on Shambhala from the Kalachakra texts. According to Buddhist tradition, the Kalachakra texts were originally taught to the King of Shambhala by the Buddha, where they were preserved over the centuries, until they were eventually returned to India. They were translated into Tibetan from the Sanskrit in the eleventh century, along with numerous commentaries. Many of these texts and other lamaist writings on the subject, such as the White Vaidurya, the Blue Annals, the Route to Shambhala, and the Sphere of Shambhala, have been translated and published in the West in the last few decades.

However, rumors about an earthly paradise in the heart of Asia have been reaching the West since Greco-Roman times, when the Greek Philostratus recorded the journey he took with the great magus of the Mysteries Apollonius of Tyana, into the Trans-Himalayan wilds of Tibet, which he knew as the Forbidden Land of the Gods. Intrepid Christian missionaries traveling

7

beyond the Himalayas were later to add their quota of information.

Shangri-la, the paradisial sanctuary of sages described in James Hilton's fictional work, *Lost Horizon,* and made famous throughout the world by the film of that name, was modeled on Shambhala and placed, not in the Himalayas, as might have been expected, but further north, in what seems to be the little-known Kunlun mountain range. Hilton having borrowed some of his material from the memoirs of Abbé Huc and other Catholic missionaries who explored Tibet and its lamaist culture in the nineteenth century.

THE SHAMBHALIC TRADITION IN THE WEST

Shambhala belongs to the most archaic stratum of Asiatic lore. A legend unfathomably old, it is the stuff of fable, of fairy tale, of romantic mythology, with the archetypal quality of a projection of the folk soul, which longs for just such an earthly paradise. Its true location has never been found, its hierarchy is invisible, its beginnings unknown, its existence unproven; and yet for those who care to look, evidence of its presence in the annals of human accomplishment is stubbornly substantial and undying. As alive today as it was thousands of years ago, it is regarded by most esoteric traditions as the true center of the planet, as the world's spiritual powerhouse and the heartland of a brotherhood of adepts from every race and country who have been influential in every major religion, every scientific advance and every social movement in history.

Ernest Scott, a Sufi member of a five-man team of researchers who delved into the origins of today's most notable cults, says that their findings were that every branch of esoteric tradition could be traced to a common parentage in Central Asia. Witchcraft, various western secret societies, Buddhist esoteric beliefs, Freemasonry, Sufism, Theosophy, alchemy and Vedanta—all, he implies, appear to have originated in Shambhala.[9] The Sufis, who can trace their Central Asian lineage back to prehistoric times, believe that the head of their hierarchy takes his directions from Shambhala; in Shambhala the Buddha is supposed to have received the Kalachakra, the great Buddhist doctrine of the Wheel of Time; at the end of his life the Chinese Taoist teacher Lao-Tzu, returned to Shambhala, although he called it Tebu Land. And it is from Shambhala that Hindus expect the coming of Sri Kalki Avatara, their future savior and the last King of Shambhala for this age.

Moreover, the ubiquitous nature of the Shambhalic influence is reflected in the universal symbology of esoteric doctrine, which is the same all over the world. Thus from the most remote past, says W. Y. Evans-Wentz, the Buddhist orientalist, "there has been a secret international symbol-code in common use among the initiates, which affords a key to the meaning of such occult doctrines as are still jealously guarded by religious fraternities in India, as in Tibet, and China, Mongolia and Japan."[10] Only in the western sphere with its impoverished esoteric tradition has the significance of this worldwide unity of initiatic language been lost. There the Shambhalic concept has remained very little known, although a garbled version of it seems to be contained in the medieval legends of the Holy Grail and the fabled kingdom of Prester John.

In the seventeenth century two Jesuit missionaries, Stephen Cacella and John Cabral, were stationed at Shigatse, the site of the Panchen Lama's monastery, and these were apparently the first Europeans in modern history to bring back informed accounts of the mysterious land of Shambhala that was ruled by the King of the World. The realm was even included in a map of Asia published by the Catholic authorities in Antwerp. Father Cabral wrote in 1625: "Shambhala is, in my opinion, not Cathay but what in our maps is called Great Tartaria."[11] And a hundred years later a Hungarian philologist called Csoma de Körös, who spent four years in a Tibetan monastery in the years 1827 to 1830, actually gave Shambhala's geographical bearings as forty-five degrees to fifty degrees north latitude, beyond the river Syr Darya.[12] But these rare firsthand forays into lamaist lore claimed little attention in the West, and it is to Helena Blavatsky, who founded the Theosophical Society in 1879, that the credit must be given for first alerting Western occult circles to the existence of the Central Asian sanctuary.

"Fabled Shambhallah," as she called it in her book *The Secret Doctrine,* was an etheric city in the Gobi Desert, the invisible headquarters of the Mahatmas, a brotherhood of great spiritual Masters who had moved there long ago after the submergence of the land of Mu under the Pacific Ocean. The heart of Mother Earth, Madame Blavatsky declared, "beats under the foot of the sacred Shambhallah."[13]   However, her account of it is brief, vague and confusing, and those interested scholars who began searching for the hidden kingdom—some, like the Buddhist explorers Alexandra David-Neel and Evans-Wentz, of considerable repute—were unsuccessful. Shambhala remained a rumor on the outermost fringe of credibility until the 1923-26 Roerich expedition was made across the Gobi Desert to the Altai Range.

Nicholas Roerich was a poet, artist and eminent man of learning who had emigrated from White Russia and settled in Paris. He was regarded as one of the most distinguished of the Theosophical elite of the period. Apart from searching for the home of the Mahatmas, the purpose of his scientific expedition across Tibet and Xinjiang to Altai was never made entirely clear in his diary, but appears to have been related to the return of a certain sacred stone to its rightful home in the King's Tower in the center of Shambhala.[14]

The stone was said to be part of a much larger meteorite possessed of occult properties called the Chintamani Stone, which was capable of giving telepathic inner guidance and effecting a transformation of consciousness to those in contact with it. The black stone of the Ka'aba at Mecca and that of the ancient shrine of Cybele, the Goddess-Mother of the Near East, are both believed by some occultists to be pieces of this magical meteorite, which is alleged to have come from a solar system in the constellation of Orion, probably Sirius. The Orion constellation, we may note, is a recurring motif in the Shambhalic story. According to lamaist lore, a fragment of this Chintamani Stone from what is probably the star Sirius is sent wherever a spiritual mission vital to humanity is set up, and is returned when that mission is completed. Such a stone was said to be in the possession of the failed League of Nations, its return being entrusted to Roerich.[15]

In the summer of 1926, Roerich reported a strange event in his travel diary, *Altai-Himalaya*, which was published soon after. He was encamped with his son, Dr. George Roerich, and a retinue of Mongolian guides in the Shara-gol valley near the Humboldt mountain chain between Mongolia and Tibet. At the time of the event in question, Roerich had returned from a trip to Altai and built a stupa, "a stately white structure," dedicated to Shambhala.

In August the shrine in the Shara-gol valley was consecrated in a solemn ceremony by a number of notable lamas invited to the site for the purpose, and after the event, writes Roerich, the Buriat guides forecast something auspicious impending. A day or two later, a large black bird was observed flying over the party. Beyond it, moving high in the cloudless sky, a huge, golden, spheroid body, whirling and shining brilliantly in the sun, was suddenly espied. Through three pairs of binoculars the travelers saw it fly rapidly from the north, from the direction of Altai, then veer sharply and vanish towards the southwest, behind the Humboldt mountains. The caravaneers pointed and shouted in great excitement. One of the lamas told Roerich that what he had seen was "the sign of Shambhala," signifying that his mission had been blessed by the Great Ones of Altai, the lords of Shambhala.

Later a lama asked him if he had been aware of a perfume on the air at the time, and on receiving an affirmative answer, said:

Ah—you are guarded by Shambhala. The huge black vulture is your enemy, who is eager to destroy your work, but the protecting force from Shambhala follows you in this Radiant form of Matter. This force is always near to you but you cannot always perceive it. Sometimes only, it is manifested for strengthening and directing you. Did you notice the direction in which this sphere moved? You must follow the same direction. You mentioned to me the sacred call—Kalagiya! When someone hears that imperative call, he must know that the way to Shambhala is open to him. He must remember when he was called, because from that time evermore, he is closely assisted by the blessed Rigden Jye-po [the Mongolian name for the King of Shambhala].[16]

Roerich then broke camp and traveled southwest in the wake of the flying craft towards western Tibet—towards Shambhala. He says in his diary that he stayed for a month in the holy place that is northwest of Tibet, although it is not known whether or not he returned the sacred stone.

Roerich was a man of unimpeachable credentials: a famous collaborator in Stravinsky's *Rite of Spring*, a colleague of the impresario Diaghilev and a highly talented and respected member of the League of Nations. His account of such a strange sighting—one of the first recorded sightings of a UFO—

aroused great interest in Europe and, corroborated as it was by George Roerich, brought to the West the first concrete evidence that there might be something present in Central Asia that defied understanding. In its vivid color and factuality, its bizarre but unarguable reference to an unknown golden aircraft that behaved as no ordinary airplane could, the Roerich story could rightly be called the first reliable intimation that the kingdom of Chang Shambhala was perhaps knowable as more than an intellectual curiosity, a popular Asian fable or one of the many phantasms dreamed up by the occult fringe groups then coming into fashion; and from about 1927 onward the world center in the northern mountains exerted on Western occult circles the fascination of an idea whose time has come.

Roerich believed Shambhala was the hidden principle uniting all religious traditions and their prophecies. He settled with his family in the Kulu valley in the Himalayan foothills, and thereafter devoted his life to the promotion of world peace through cultural and spiritual development. Today every major Russian city has a Roerich organization that puts forward his ideas for a new type of enlightened civilization based on the utopian principles of Shambhala. Roerich declared that enlightened people understood Shambhala to mean world regeneration, creativity, a coming New Era of cosmic energies and expanded consciousness. "All our latest discoveries are regarded by the East as signs of the era of Shambhala," he said. "Milliken's cosmic ray, Einstein's relativity, Teremin's music from the ether, are regarded in Asia as signs of the evolution of human consciousness, confirmed by Vedic and Buddhist traditions and the teachings of Shambhala."[17]

Roerich gave Shambhala a certain aura of credibility in the West. Andrew Tomas, a Russian brought up in the Far East and one of Roerich's staunchest admirers, also believed with all his heart in the holy place in Central Asia. In his book *Shambhala: Oasis of Light*, published in 1976 and the last of a number of his esoteric bestsellers no longer in print, Tomas presents the northern paradise as a world center or headquarters of the Greater Mysteries. For him Shambhala is primarily a gathering place of great scientific minds, a sanctuary for initiate scientists and philosophers who have been forced to take refuge there from the persecution of societies unable to understand or tolerate their advanced ideas. He claims that although hardly anything is known of "an invisible, scientific and philosophical society which pursues its studies in the majestic isolation of the Himalayas," from the earliest times there has been a steady exchange of knowledge between the widely separated groups of initiates in Asia and the Mediterranean Basin, despite the great distances involved, and that it is this knowledge that fed the Greater Mysteries of the ancient West.

Tomas claims the Vatican archives contain, for instance, many reports by Jesuit missionaries concerning deputations from the emperors of China to the Spirits of the Mountains in the Nan Shan and Kun Lun Ranges, usually in times of national crisis when the Chinese rulers could not reach a decision. The chronicles describing these missions of mandarins and priests from the court of the Celestial Emperor to the Genii of the Western Mountains speak of superbeings in artificially created bodies made of crystallized atomic matter. Tomas tentatively identifies them with the Hindu and Chinese legends of the "mind-born" gods who are actually adepts possessed of a highly advanced science as yet unknown to us. Tomas wrote:

> Certain details of these legends of China strike one with their concreteness. This secret place is inhabited by beings who were formerly ordinary men and women. They reached the sacred land because of their spiritual progression. What is more, the abode can actually be located by a worthy seeker after Truth who is devoid of selfish motives. . . . The Valley of the Immortals must have a basis of reality in spite of the imaginative characteristics by which it has been embellished in the course of countless generations.[18]

Tomas's conviction of the reality of Shambhala, fed by his meeting with Roerich in 1935, was shared by a growing metaphysical school in Europe in the first half of the century. Another strand to the story—one considerably more mystical and less accessible to the rational understanding—was provided by René Guénon. Guénon was one of the foremost Sufi scholars of the twentieth century and a skilled student of the Cabala, the ancient Jewish mystical system. In 1927, he published *Le Roi du Monde*, in which he gave unprecedented esoteric information about Shambhala—information that had apparently been hitherto part of the secret knowledge which the brotherhood jealously guarded from the uninitiated. Guénon accomplished this "leak" by veiling his information in a characteristically overcondensed and cryptic style that takes patience to unravel, and to which a large part of this book will be devoted to decoding.

According to Guénon, Shambhala is a center of high evolutionary energies in Central Asia. It is the source of all our religions and the home of Yoga Tantra, having a vital relationship to the kundalini science on which all our systems of self-transformation are based. Reflecting the changes in the aeonic cycles of the earth and the unfoldment of humanity's soul, it is the prototypic Holy Land of which all other Holy Lands such as Jerusalem, Delphi and Benares are or have been secondary reflections. "In the contemporary period of our terrestrial cycle," he stated, "—that is to say, during the Kali Yuga— this Holy Land, which is defended by guardians who keep it hidden from profane view while ensuring nevertheless a certain exterior communication, is to all intents and purposes inaccessible and invisible to all except those possessing the necessary qualifications for entry."[19] Once it was open and more or less accessible to all, and will be again with the closing of the Kali Yuga, but presently exists in a veiled state and is understood, if acknowledged at all, only in metaphorical and symbolic terms.

Guénon indicated that Shambhala exists both above and below ground. He enlarged on the vast underground network of caverns and tunnels running under the sacred center for hundreds of kilometers, attributing to these catacombs, as had Saint-Yves d'Alveydre before him in 1910, the function of an even more secret and advanced center of initiation called Agarttha.[20] Agarttha, he said, was the true center of world government. It was the impregnable storehouse of the world's wisdom, surviving the ebb and flow of civilizations and the catastrophes of the earth, and would shortly send forth its energies to create a new planetary culture.

In the same prophetic spirit, other occult writers saw Shambhala as the venue of the imminently returning Christ. The neo-Theosophist Alice Bailey, who was of the same era as Guénon, had nothing to say about Agarttha, but described Shambhala as "the vital centre in the planetary consciousness"[21] and the home of the great spiritual hierarchy of which the Christ was the head. She related it to the Second Coming, and through the writings of her disciple Vera Stanley Alder gave out many apocalyptic prophecies scheduled to be fulfilled in the latter part of the century. Other esotericists likened the mystical center to Campanella's City of the Sun and to Dante's Terrestrial Paradise. Like Tomas, they saw in it a significant likeness to the Rosicrucians' Invisible Academy of initiates so widely publicized in seventeenth-century Europe. That fraternity likewise was never found, but claimed to safeguard through the ages the highest spiritual and social ideals and promised the imminent coming of the New Jerusalem.[22]

THE CONTRIBUTION OF TIBETAN BUDDHISM

In the West the early wave of occult interest in Shambhala was notable for its high intellectual and Christian overtones, and remained largely unknown to the wider public, as indeed it still is. But Tibetan Buddhism, opportunely making its appearance during the sixties with a wealth of firsthand information gleaned from the mystical experiences of the lamas as well as the Bonpo texts, gave to the subject a more visionary and thaumaturgic dimension. Shambhala, said the Tibetans, was the source of the Kalachakra, the mystical system which, like Western Cabala, was based on secret kundalini practices, rendering it the most powerful spiritual discipline in the world. The monks brought with them written accounts of lamas who had gone to Shambhala in dreams and visions in search of the Kalachakric wisdom, traveling in bodies of finer matter, and had published mandalas, ancient mystical geographies and a number of guidebooks, both old and relatively modern, that gave detailed instructions for a physical journey there.

In the ensuing years Tibetan Buddhism has in large measure drawn Shambhala out of the shadowy realms of myth, adding such graphic and colorful details to the picture of the place as has given it a new aura of credibility, of material reality, as the habitat of a spiritual community that has managed to remain hidden from the outside world for thousands of years. Yet at the same time it has ostensibly done little to solve the mystery of its location. And so the same questions continue to be asked: Where is it? Why, if it exists, has it not been found already in these days of ubiquitous air travel, aerial surveys and increased population? Why is its very nature so enigmatic, so elusive, so pregnant with unearthly connotations? And why indeed has it taken such great pains to conceal itself?

These are pertinent questions for which a number of answers have been essayed, none of them really satisfactory. It is true that the great mountain ranges and vast deserts of Middle Asia offer optimum opportunities for concealment, and that there is in any case something inherently mysterious about a concentration of magico-mystical activity such as is Shambhala's keynote. But the pivotal question remains: why have such enormous pains been taken to hide its very existence from the outside world? And there is no doubt this is the case: travelers have persistently reported forbidden areas that their bearers will not enter, of tall, lightly clad guardians of the area who suddenly appear among the frozen peaks out of nowhere, of psychic vibrations at certain points that seem to discourage any further advance. Some have even suggested that the very skepticism and indifference habitually displayed towards Shambhala in the West has been deliberately fostered as a further deterrent to undue interest.

I believe this is very likely, for wherever a concentration of spiritual energies gathers there is power of a high order that can be misused in the wrong hands. Such a place is ringed with danger—not to its guardians, but to those who would seize its secrets in the wrong spirit. That the Nazi Party, for example, was aware to some small extent of Shambhala's potential for world dominance cannot be doubted. According to the French authors, Louis Pauwels and Jacques Bergier in *The Morning of the Magicians*,[23] as well as the British mystic and military intelligence agent Trevor Ravenscroft in *The Spear of Destiny*[24] and a number of other writers, the Central Asian mythos was behind the whole of the Nazi neo-occultist mystique. They state that the Nazis' attempts to contact the hidden center by sending emissaries to Tibet, where they believed Shambhala lay, were made in order to elicit (vainly, as it turned out) the secrets of a great "Ahrimanic" earth-force, unknown to science, that exerts power over all of material nature, and which they believed had its seat in Shambhala. This is clear enough evidence that wherever there is the smallest suspicion of such a thing there will always be men eager to seize on it for raw exploitation, unaware of the terrible price invariably paid. Although Shambhala's secret is of great value, it is a psychospiritual secret that cannot be taken by force or by guile, but can only be freely given—at the right time.

The inaccessibility of Shambhala and the questions raised by it have increasingly occupied the minds of Tibetan scholars. Edwin Bernbaum, whose book *The Way to Shambhala* is based on a deep study of Buddhism and interviews with numerous learned lamas, says that such questions have remained so intractable, despite the enormous amount of time, energy and enthusiasm Tibetans have expended in trying to answer them, that many younger Tibetans no longer believe Shambhala exists. How can it, they ask, when the Chinese have thoroughly explored Central Asia and have put down thousands of oil wells in the most likely areas to hold it? On the other hand, those lamaist scholars who still firmly believe in Shambhala's physical reality are now inclined to place it far north in Arctic Siberia or at the North Pole, or even beyond the earth altogether, on another planet or in another dimension.

The difficulty lies mainly with the Tibetan guidebooks, which promise much but actually lend their own special obscuration to the search. Compiled by Buddhist yogi-scholars of the past, some of them use outdated or unknown place-names that make the route impossible to follow, and all are in general notable for their bafflingly esoteric nature. Although they start out in a factual and geographically reliable manner, with descriptions of the various stages of the itinerary in terms of mountains, rivers and settled regions that can usually be identified, invariably they become more and more vague and abstract the nearer the goal is approached. A sense of dream supersedes reality; fantastic landscapes and mythical beings are encountered and demonic forces must be overcome; and the saga leads the reader on and on towards the North Pole and beyond and acquires the archetypal qualities of an inner journey of the soul, a mystical Grail search or Pilgrim's Progress towards a heavenly rather than an earthly destination, confounding all efforts to find it.

As Edwin Bernbaum says of these guidebooks:

As the traveller draws near the kingdom, their directions become increasingly mystical and difficult to correlate with the physical world. At least one lama has written that the vagueness of these books is deliberate and intended to keep Shambhala concealed from the barbarians who will take over the world.[25]

This may well be true and would be in line with traditional lore; but there is another explanation. In later chapters of this book the tendency for physical data on the subject to modulate imperceptibly into mystical abstractions leading out of this world will be found to recur in one context after another, encouraging us to conclude that it may be a characteristic and unavoidable feature of the enigma that is Shambhala. Tomas throws light on this phenomenon when he says of the sanctuary of the Immortals that there "the physical world joins the invisible realm of gods, and those who are privileged to be its dwellers are continually living in two worlds—the objective world of matter and the finer plane of spirit."[26]

In fact, to say that the hidden sanctuary of sages exists on two different levels of reality—that it is both visible and invisible—as is constantly affirmed, is simply to say that there is an aspect of the place that can only be seen in a heightened state of consciousness, clairvoyantly. It is to say that Shambhala is a real place with real geographical coordinates, but that it contains a feature that by its very nature reveals itself only to mystical vision. A set of directions to it would then exhibit precisely the dual reality, the shifting orientation towards the miraculous already noted, the nearer the destination is approached.

That this is the case is attested by the Tibetan mandalas, which include very old Kalachakric and Bonpo diagrams of the hidden kingdom. The best known is the eight-petalled lotus mandala (shown in Plate 1) that depicts it as enclosed in a circle of snow-tipped mountains and divided into an outer and an inner region by a further and even higher ring of snow mountains running within the first and surrounding the center. The outer region, which is subdivided into eight separate zones and lesser kingdoms, is populated by towns, temples and gardens in the usual earthly way, but the inner region at the center, sovereign over the whole, is a kingdom filled with mysterious symbols of transcendence: the magical radiations of the King's Tower, the mountain called Meru, the *axis mundi*, the tree of immortality, the King's throne surrounded by a throng of gods. These divine images tell us two planes of reality are indicated, the higher one at the center. They tell us that Shambhala's mystery and its power over the imagination lie primarily at the center, and that the way to the center is through the normal physical channels supplemented by paranormal abilities gained through spiritual training.

A similar message is metaphorically conveyed in a Chinese painting held in the British Museum, depicting the idyllic sanctuary of the Immortals situated on the heights of the Kunlun mountains, and evidently the Chinese equivalent of Shambhala (Plate 2). Three regions of increasing inwardness are shown in this beautiful painting, the third and inmost corresponding to the magical central realm in the Tibetan mandala. A group of long-lived men and women sit at their ease in the foreground, conversing and sipping tea in a flowering garden in the outer region, while steps lead up through the landscape to an inner sanctum, a kind of rocky cave in which a higher level of sanctity is indicated by means of the stillness of the contemplative figures standing in it. And higher still, almost hidden in the clouds, floats the palace of Hsi Wang Mu, the Queen Mother of the West who is also known as Kuan Yin, the Goddess of Mercy. From early Chinese records we know that her palace is built on the highest jade mountain in the Kunluns, and is surrounded by golden walls and flanked by a lake of gems; but in the painting the transcendence of the royal domain, in contrast to the mundane scene below, is emphasized by its ethereal elevation and by the flying deities that float upon the clouds.

Skillfully the scene informs us that ascending planes of consciousness must be scaled to arrive at an understanding of the spiritual meaning of the central myth, and that precisely that myth is the key to the legend of Shambhala. But the Tibetan Buddhist mandala and its commentaries are even more to the point. They clarify in the most masterly way the singular conditions and the baffling directions with which a traveler to Shambhala must necessarily comply if he is ever to reach the end of his search; for he is undertaking at one and the same time an inner mystical journey and an outer physical one through desolate and mountainous territory to a cosmic powerhouse hidden at the center of the earth. We shall see that in fact the lotus-mandala has given us, with perfect economy and clarity, the most valuable key that exists to the location of Shambhala, the meaning of Shambhala and the way to Shambhala.

Plate 2. *Immortals Visiting Xi Wang-Mu, the Goddess of the West, in the Kunlun mountains. Her palace is seen floating in the clouds in the upper left corner.*

The Mandalic Mirror

For millennia Shambhala has fulfilled a unifying function for Central Asia; wars have been fought under its banner, great spiritual movements founded: until the Chinese invasion it was the bonding agent for the whole culture. For Tibet it has been the center and ground of its religious life. The lamas have fixed the legend of Shambhala forever in the symbology of a mandala at whose heart lies the sacred mountain Meru, regarded by them as the ultimate unifying principle of the cosmos.

"Mandalas," says Edward Conze, a foremost authority on Buddhism,

> are a special form of an age-old diagram of the cosmos, considered as a vital process which develops from one essential principle and which rotates round one central axis, Mount Sumeru, the *axis mundi*. . . . Through them we can chain, dominate and dissolve the forces of the universe, effect a revulsion from all the illusory things of the samsaric world, and achieve reunion with the light of the one absolute Mind.[1]

Mandalic sand tracings and labyrinthine petroglyphs are a universal religious expression of early humanity found in all parts of the world, but the sophisticated and finely wrought works of art that Conze describes as ritual devices of Hindu-Buddhism evolved in Central Asia, a land whose prodigious depth of culture the West has still barely tapped. Countless forgotten cities, it is said, lie under its sands. From its heart ancient arts and handicrafts and rich veins of knowledge have fed the civilizations of India and China and made them great: but so old and vast is the region, so covered in the tracks of great migrations and the bones of dead races that its legacy is not easily read. Buddhism flourished there eight hundred years before it arrived in Tibet, and Taoism began in the Kunluns or perhaps in one of the oases that ring the Tarim Basin, its mystical metaphysic predating the Indus valley cities and the Shang dynasty of China. It is in the deepest and most esoteric stratum of that ancient cradle of civilization that the mandala began its history of development into a high art form.

The idea that such mystical devices are necessary for the continued maintenance of civilization is related to an early intuition that the world is built from the frozen mental energies of the race, and that our *belief* therefore sustains it. When *belief* changes, so does the world. When our *belief* crumbles, the world crumbles. Mandalas provided the yogi with a way of continually reconsecrating his mental energies to the work of creation. But they also provide a means of instruction, transmitting esoteric knowledge in a symbolic language that will remain opaque to the uninitiated, and in an economical form that is capable of illuminating all three of the reality planes—the spiritual, the psychic and the physical—at one and the same time. They offer the initiate in a single glance an overview of the whole that he can interpret in terms of any one of these three essential modes of being. The same principle of correspondence informed other such initiatic devices in antiquity. Thus Edouard Schuré, the French mystic of the nineteenth century, says the ancient Egyptian priests had a language that expressed their thoughts in three different ways simultaneously:

> The first was literal, the second symbolic and figurative, the third sacred and hieroglyphic. At their wish, the same work assumed a literal, a figurative or a transcendent meaning. . . . This language had a singular eloquence for the adept, for, by means of a single sign, it evoked the principles, causes and effects radiating from divinity into blind nature, into the human consciousness and into the world of pure spirit. Thanks to this writing, the initiate embraced the three worlds in a single glance.[2]

In the same way the Tibetan Buddhist eight-petalled lotus-mandala depicting the hidden kingdom has a multilayered function and can be interpreted in three different ways, as having either a geographical meaning, a psychosomatic meaning or a metaphysical meaning. Meditating on the diagram with the aid of the Kalachakric texts and the various guidebooks compiled by lamas of the past, the yogi finds it is like a magic mirror reflecting the same truth on three different planes. These three dimensions are united by Meru, the World Axis, which intersects them all at the center of the diagram and is the key to the whole mythology of Shambhala. Generally speaking, the yogi's approach to the lotus-mandala is on the middle plane, viewing it as a psychosomatic metaphor that enriches and illuminates the practice.

THE LANDSCAPE OF THE MYTHIC KINGDOM

As Mount Meru unifies the three planes of existence so also does the King of Shambhala, reigning from his palace at the center of his kingdom. In the Kalachakra his is a Hindu-Buddhist monarchy, the two traditions being so intertwined that sometimes the Hindu or Buddhist sovereigns are interchangeable. Hindus know the king as Indra, the king of the gods, while in the Tibetan Buddhist lexicon each king, reigning for a hundred years, is the incarnation of a well-known Bodhisattva. In the latter tradition, the first Buddhist king was Sucandra, who journeyed to India to receive the Kalachakra doctrine from Gautama Buddha and then returned to Shambhala to teach it to his people. But the more popular variant of the story is that the Kalachakra is indigenous to Shambhala and each Buddha travels there to receive the primordial teachings.

According to the myth, the kingdom is laid out in precisely the same form as an eight-petalled lotus blossom, with the sacred mountain rising in the center of a circle of snow mountains, themselves surrounded by a further chain of snow mountains that have turned to ice and glow with a supernal light. And within the sacred mountain, in a cave or sometimes on its summit, lies the pagoda palace of the King of Shambhala, protected by the two rings of mountains and surrounded by the habitats of millions of gods and devas, his immediate courtiers. The monarch's palace is in the capital of Shambhala in a city called Kalapa, which is flanked on the east and the west by two lakes filled with jewels; one is shaped like a crescent moon, the other like a half-moon. To the north are the shrines of saints and deities, and to the south, in a beautiful parkland filled with sandalwood trees, the first king built an enormous mandala for the purpose of giving Kalachakric initiations.[3]

Within this mystic circle is a three-dimensional model of the mandala embodying the essential meaning of the Kalachakric doctrine of nonduality, which in Buddhism is known as Advaita. Advaita teaches that inner and outer are not in opposition, as we erroneously suppose; rather it is the case that Kundala Shakti, the creative energy of the universe, generates both mind and matter, and so binds in one transcendental unity humanity's soul and the material universe. This corpus of Advaitic wisdom abides at the center of Shambhala and is revealed only there, say the commentaries, for the key to it is under the guardianship of the king himself; not even those in the outer regions possess that key.

In some texts the Kalachakric teachings are said to be kept in a ring of such three-dimensional mandalas built around Shambhala's inner zone, again for the purpose of conducting initiations. Thus a Tibetan prayer for rebirth in Shambhala says that "each year at the new moon of the black month, the great King, who has the power of accomplishment, manifests the body of the all-pervading lord, the glorious teacher, the Kalachakra himself; and with initiations he ripens the minds of his disciples."[4] The lesser kings of the outer region of the kingdom have magic rods called "possessors of the Power of Mind" which enable them to remain in telepathic communication with the central command and with their own subjects, and over all lies the luminous disembodied presence of the main tutelary deity of the Kalachakra, "the all-pervading lord." He is represented in the center of the lotus-mandala by the sacred syllables known as the Ten of Power: Om ha sva ha ksha ma la va ra yam.[5]

The Ten of Power is an important emblem in Tibetan iconography that is painted over the entrance of Buddhist monasteries as a good luck symbol. It embodies the sonic principle of manifestation that generates the visible universe, and is the equivalent of the creative Word or Logos of Western metaphysics. Bernbaum says that in the Tibetan Buddhist practice of visualizing the mandala, its various features usually issue from the central syllable and constellate around it. "At the end of the meditation, they dissolve back into this syllable, which vanishes back into the void from which it came. The mandala therefore displays in vivid detail all that lies concealed and latent in its center."[6]

In this case the sacred syllable represents, as has been said, the Kalachakra deity, who is in Buddhist lore a glorious Spirit, a cosmic Being from beyond the earth for whom the King of Shambhala acts as regent. From all this it is evident that the mountain, the king and the Kalachakra are components of a single transcendental complex situated at the very center of the hidden country and are the last to yield to the seeker's understanding.

Each king reigns with the help of two counselors and is revered as the ruler of this world and the next, with power over the fate of all men and women on earth, from the mightiest potentate to the least of beggars. That is why he is also called the King of the World. Surrounded by a host of incarnated gods who help him in his work, he knows the secrets of life on other stars and solar systems, and has at his disposal aircraft "made of stone" as well as other kinds of powered vehicles. His palace is a place of magic that shines by day and night with a diamondlike glow and is festooned with jewels; and from that citadel on Mount Meru the king, enthroned in wisdom and power, never departs, for the well-being of the whole kingdom depends on his continuing office. He and his counselors are perfectly enlightened, the inhabitants of the outer region not completely so; yet they are well on the way to perfection and are able to live harmoniously in two worlds, on the plane of material reality and at the same time on a higher spiritualized one, by virtue of the supernatural powers they have attained.

Each of the eight outer zones holds twelve principalities, making ninety-six in all, which are ruled by lesser kings and princes; and each zone specializes in a particular branch of learning, such as medicine, music, physics, psychology, philosophy, astronomy and so on. And indeed Tibetans claim to have received most of their medical and calendrical knowledge from Shambhala, as well as their occult arts of alchemy, astrology, control of the elemental forces of nature and other facets of their culture. There is thus considerable cultural diversity in the outer regions, but it is based on unity, for all the inhabitants study the Kalachakra and practice its yoga, and all ninety-six of the minor kings and princes give their allegiance to the great king in his central domain.[7]

Lamaist lore claims that twenty-seven Buddhist kings have reigned in Shambhala, the current one having ascended the throne in 1927 as a reincarnation of Manjushri, the Bodhisattva of Wisdom. The expectation is that he will rule until 2027. During his reign, in accordance with prophecy, Buddhism and the Kalachakra have greatly declined in Tibet, China, Mongolia and other parts of Asia due to the invasion, first, of Islam and then of Chinese communism. But Shambhala, say the lamas, has preserved the pure teachings of the Buddha untroubled by these calamitous outside events. In the reign of the thirty-second king, the great savior-warrior Rudra Cakrin, "the wrathful one with the wheel," will come to power, the last of his line. With his armies and with the power of the Wheel of Truth he will defeat the enemies of Buddhism who have meanwhile overrun Shambhala, and will establish a golden age throughout the world. This is supposed to take place in 2327 C.E., but most lamas believe not all the kings have reigned for a hundred years and that therefore this apocalyptic event may take place quite soon.[8]

According to the followers of the Bon religion, the first king was called Shenrab. In 16,027 B.C. he ascended the throne of Olmolungring, a country also known as Shambhala that the Bonpo believe lies northwest of Tibet, somewhere in the mountains between Samarkand and Alma Ata. Shenrab then took the sacred teaching of the land across mountains and deserts to Mount Kailas in Tibet, where a great Bon school was formed, of which a surviving lamaist form is the shamanistic cemetery-cult of Dzog Chen. After that he returned to his own country and there established a spiritual lineage of kings that has continued to preserve the secret teachings to the present day.[9]

In contrast to the Buddhist version, the Bonpo diagram of Olmolungring is laid out in a square, with eight rectangles comprising the outer region (Plate 3). Moreover, in the Buddhist mandala there are only the two regions, the outer and the central one, and the king and his courtiers dominate the sacred inner region to such an extent that sometimes Meru is hardly visible at all. But in the Bon mandala, derived as it is from an older iconographic tradition, there are three distinct regions, one within the other, and Meru rises alone and majestic in the third, at the very inmost heart of the kingdom, a mountain of nine levels that symbolize the nine planes in the cosmic spec-

Plate 3. *Olmolungring, the sacred Bon kingdom, showing nine-storied Mount Meru in the center, the whole surrounded by a square of snow-covered mountains. The inscription at the bottom includes Shambhala as one of Olmolungring's names.*

trum of Being. Thus the Bon diagram expresses somewhat more closely than the other the threefold nature of the cosmos that divides it into three realms, that of the spiritual, the psychic and the physical, and makes clear why the King of Shambhala is also called the King of the Three Worlds.

SHAMBHALA AND TANTRIC YOGA

What is most interesting about the above legends are their descriptions of the hidden paradisial kingdom in terms directly borrowed from the iconography of kundalini yoga, the system that has given the Kalachakra the reputation of being the most powerful and the most secret tantric discipline in the world. What relationship, we may ask, can tantric yoga have to the landscape of Shambhala? Yet clearly there is one, for we find that the latter's nomenclature and imagery—indeed, its very layout—closely conforms to the psychosomatic circuits that the yogi clairvoyantly maps in his own body. This interrelationship is a most curious discovery, and is one that suggests Shambhala cannot be understood in depth without an understanding of the basic concepts of the kundalini science—itself said to have had its source in the hidden kingdom.

The spinal chakric system (Figure 1) that mirrors the physical glandular system in human beings is now so well known that it needs little introduction. Discovered and clairvoyantly studied in very remote times, it was probably systematized by Central Asian shaman masters long before the literate civilizations arose.

Countless generations of adepts have subsequently elaborated and perfected its iconography and veiled its secrets in a closely woven system of symbols now for the first time being opened to our understanding. Barbara Ann Brennan, a clairvoyant healer trained as a physicist and psychotherapist, describes the chakras as spinning cone-shaped vortices of energy made up of a number of smaller cones of energy (the so-called petals of the lotus) and situated within a multilayered energy field that surrounds and permeates the physical body. This all-encompassing field is composed of seven levels of vibrations corresponding to the seven major chakras, each one as highly structured as the physical body and all seven occupying the same space at the same time. Each one extends out beyond the last to two or three feet beyond the surface of the body.

In this auric field, says Brennan, "there is a vertical flow of energy that pulses up and down the field in the spinal cord. It extends out beyond the physical body above the head and below the coccyx."[10] The tips of the swirling cone-shaped chakras point in to this main vertical power current, and their open ends extend to the edge of each layer of the field they are located in. The number of petals in each chakra signifies its relative position and value within the whole and at once discloses the qualities inherent in that particular energy center.

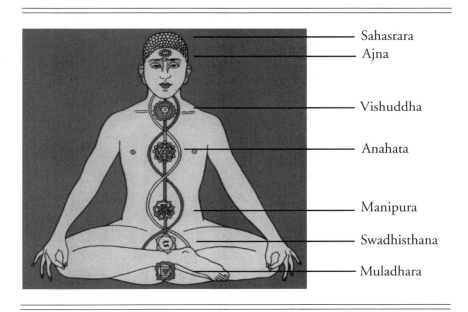

Figure 1. *The Spinal Chakric System.*

The four-petalled root lotus at the base of the spine, the *muladhara* chakra, is called the earth center. There the universal creative energy that Hindu-Buddhists call *kundalini shakti* sleeps at the chthonic level, coiled about itself like a snake until awakened by yogic practices, when it rises up the spine, piercing as it goes the various lotuses and activating the higher levels one after another. In the process each center liberates to the personality its own peculiar qualities. The personal ego governs the three lower centers; when kundalini reaches the heart-center, the *anahata*, the soul awakens and embarks on the spiritual Path proper. From then on the yogi's higher self operates to release his latent powers until the highest lotus of all is pierced, the *sahasrara* in the crown of the head, which has a thousand petals. In the sahasrara, the heaven center, the bliss of supreme consciousness is won. An exhaustive study of this subtle energy system that lies within the physical body, but separate from it, is contained in *The Serpent Power* by Arthur Avalon (Sir John Woodroffe).[11]

Now we find that the meanings and designations of Shambhala are those of this same yoga. Kalapa's two lakes, Bernbaum tells us, have the crescent or half-moon shape of the cross section of *nadis* or nerve channels that the yogi apprehends in his own body in meditation; and likewise the polarity of his physiology, in which the lower part is the seat of fertility and life-energies, the upper part that of the cognitive faculties, is exactly mirrored in Shambhala by the groves of sandalwood trees to the south and the shrines of the gods to the north. Again, the layout of the kingdom as a whole is that of the lotus blossom, which is the flower by whose name the chakras of the yogi's spinal energy system are known; and like the latter, the kingdom has a number of smaller lotuses arranged within it.

The lotus, as is well known, was probably chosen to represent the chakras because of its purity, its narcotic property and its similarity to their petalled and wheel-like structure, and also because, again like the chakras, it opens and closes in unusually sensitive response to stimuli. In Tibetan and Chinese art Buddhas and Bodhisattvas are sometimes depicted seated or standing on lotus flowers to show they are untainted by the world's passions, even as the lotus flower is unsullied by the mud and slime from which it grows. According to Iamblicus, a philosopher-magus of the fourth century, the lotus is a figure of perfection since its leaves, flowers and fruit form the figure of a circle, as do the chakras as they open and close. All these characteristics also are attributed to Shambhala.

Furthermore, the eight-petalled lotus is a symbol of the heart chakra (though sometimes represented with twelve petals)[12] and is regarded by most Tantras, and by the Kalachakra in particular, as the most important center in the psychosomatic system and as the seat of the soul. The Upanishads say that the divine Self, "who understands all, and whose glory is manifest in the universe, lives within the lotus of the heart."[13] In the anahata chakra the Inner Teacher, the Higher Self itself, is activated by the rising of kundalini and establishes the spirit of wisdom, compassion, truth and benevolence in the life of the individual. Likewise in Shambhala all the human virtues flower; it too is known as the seat of the World Soul, the habitation of the great Teacher and as the true entrance to the spiritual Path.

Lastly, the name of the sacred mountain is borrowed from yogic physiology. In Sanskrit *meru*, sometimes called *merudanda*, is the cerebrospinal axis of the human body, the backbone or staff of power through which kundalini passes, connecting all the chakras like the thread through a string of beads.[14] And since kundalini is regarded in tantric yoga as the cosmic life force that generates and maintains everything, meru, besides being the body's central structural support, is its creative center and source of life. This idea has also been transferred in toto to Shambhala's topography.

The summit of the cosmic mountain, says Mircea Eliade,

> is not only the highest point of the earth, it is also the earth's navel, the point at which the Creation began. There are in early societies even instances in which cosmological traditions explain the symbolism of the Center in terms which might well have been borrowed from embryology. The Holy One created the world like an embryo. As the embryo proceeds from the navel onwards, so God began to create the world from its navel onwards and from there it spread out in all directions.[15]

Tibetan yoga applies the same symbology in respect of Shambhala. Mount Meru is conceived of as its navel as well as its central staff, its source of life, power and government spreading out from the central region to the eight outer zones, and from thence to the world.

From all this the conclusion is inescapable that Shambhala must be a place with most unusual properties. Or is it simply an imaginery construct of lamaist devising as an aid to meditation? Lest we jump too hastily to the latter conclusion it should be noted that in a later chapter we learn that, according to René Guénon, ancient Hebrew esoteric lore assigned to the sacred place precisely the same yogic meanings. This can hardly be a coincidence.

Tibetan Buddhist teachings throw little light on the puzzle. Since the accession to power of the Reformed Yellow Hat sect in Tibet in the sixteenth century, these identifications and correspondences as applied to Shambhala have immensely proliferated, but at the same time the Tibetan Buddhist yogi has tended to disengage himself from Shambhala's physical reality and to interest himself mainly in the psychic dimension of the mandala to the exclusion of its physical and metaphysical meanings. Although in theory he believes that by visualizing Shambhala's eight-petalled diagram in meditation he may be led to the homeland of the Kalachakra and hence to the very essence of its teachings, in practice his orientation has become primarily psychological. Bernbaum outlines the underlying rationale to this approach:

> In order to uncover the hidden meaning of Shambhala, we need to see how the physical version described in the texts reflects the nature of the other two [i.e. the psychic and the spiritual] versions. The inner [or psychic] kingdom is thought to be the most important of the three: If a yogi can find it through the practice of the Kalachakra, then he will possess the awareness needed to see the physical and the spiritual kingdoms.[16]

For this reason, whether valid or no, Bernbaum takes the orthodox psychological approach in laying greatest stress on the interior kingdom; and in fact any other interpretation of the lotus diagram has become quite rare.

Regarding his body as a microcosm of the universe, the yogi may imagine the mandala laid out in his body and Shambhala as residing in the heart chakra in the center of the spinal energy system. There, and in each of the psychic energy centers visualized as lotus-shaped mandalas, the tutelary deities of the cosmos may appear to him in the meditative state; and it is from these deities, in accordance with the laws of correspondence, that the divine power comes that awakens the deeper levels of his mind leading to illumination.

In this view the sovereign all-conquering Self is symbolized by the myth of a great king ruling over a hidden kingdom. In the center of the lotus of the inner Shambhala, as in a citadel, lies concealed the jewel of the innermost mind unclouded by ignorance, undimmed by the passions, "gleaming with the diamond-like clarity of the deepest awareness of all—the awareness of the absolute nature of reality itself."[17] By the same token the lamas regard the eight outer zones of the kingdom as representing the eight stages of mind or eight states of consciousness whereby meditation progressively, and often with great pain and conflict, draws inward to the dharma chakra of the heart in the course of the yogi's *sadhana*, uncovering at last the radiant mind of enlightenment. Thus, interpreted as a diagram of the anahata chakra, the mandala reveals that the only way to Shambhala is through practices that radically purify the heart, but sheds little light on Shambhala itself as a real place on the earth's surface. The mandala serves as little more than a useful metaphor for the ruling Self that abides within the yogi's own body.

But the earlier Red Hat sect, a line of Nyingmapa lamas founded by Guru Padma Sambhava, who first brought Buddhism to Tibet, has helped to preserve in their original purity the pre-Buddhist Bon doctrines, in which Shambhala's literal, geographical reality was one of the most important givens. The mystical wisdom of these Ancient Ones, as they are often called, is proverbial in Tibet and Mongolia, and many knowledgable Tibetans believe that they even form an adjunct to Shambhala itself, so close are their connections supposed to be. However, all Tibetan Buddhist schools, including the Yellow Hat sect of the Dalai Lama, honor the Shambhala teachings and their mystico-magical belief system.

A Lama's Journey to Shambhala

Bernbaum records in his book an account of an amazing dream or vision about a journey to the sacred kingdom given to him by one Garje Khamtul Rinpoche, an incarnate lama of the Nyingmapa sect presently living in India. Khamtul himself firmly believes his nocturnal experience was not so much a psychic one as an actual flight in his inner body to an actual place whose name, he was told, was Shambhala. The lama, who now works in the Council of Religious and Cultural Affairs of the Dalai Lama in Dharamsala, told Bernbaum that the event occurred in 1948, when he was a young monk of twenty-one.

He was asleep one night on a holy mountain in Tibet after a period of retreat when he received the call to Shambhala, although he did not then guess that was what it was. His guide appeared in the guise of a young Indian girl who told him to wake up and come with her, because his lama wished to speak with him. Khamtul was surprised and said he had no wish to go with her. "You're an ordinary lady wearing only cotton clothing, nothing special. You don't impress me," he replied. However, when she had shown him magical signs on her hands, feet and face he consented to accompany her. Instantly she snapped her fingers, and at the same time he felt his physical body melting away, although he could still think. Then the girl took him in her hand and swallowed him.

The first part of the journey Khamtul then undertook did in a sense take place on the psychic plane, for he was conscious of being drawn into the body of the saviouress Tara and there being progressively purified by initiations in each of the goddess's chakras in turn. After passing through all Tara's energy centers and coming out through her sexual organ, he said that at that point he felt very unusual, as if he had no body at all. "My mind was comfortable, clear, and without thoughts. At the time it seemed I could go anywhere I wanted without walking." This strange purificatory and empowering experience apparently prepared him for the rest of the journey.

After he had been ejected from the body of Tara in a new state of heightened awareness, his guide took him by the hand and they flew into the sky, where she directed his attention to the various countries below. He who had never traveled outside Tibet or studied maps now saw for the first time the shape of India, Ceylon, China, Japan, Nepal and other smaller countries spread out beneath him. Flying north beyond Tibet, they passed over snow mountains and saw lands and mountains of different colors which were filled with gold and precious jewels, with diamonds, rubies, emeralds and sapphires; for evidently with the spiritual energizing of Khamtul's perceptions, mythical and transcendental elements had now entered into the landscape.

Finally they came to a country ringed by snow mountains and containing many towns separated from each other by lakes and rivers. This was their destination, although Khamtul still did not know its name or why they were going there. The rocks were of crystal, silver, coral and other precious substances, and flowers he had never seen before bloomed in the meadows. In the center of the land was a great lake and on the other side of it was a palace, its golden roof shining. After various rituals of an initiatory nature, Khamtul and his guide entered the palace on its eastern side, as initiates do when entering a mandala in meditation. Inside, it was immense, a secret world everywhere colored turquoise, with natural features stretching into the distance. "In some places there was sand, in others springs," said Khamtul.

Far off he saw a great blue horse standing patiently. This was Tamchog Mahabala, an emanation of Buddhahood, waiting for his rider, the next king of Shambhala. Some prophecies said that the great savior and avatar, Rudra Cakrin, would soon ride forth from Shambhala on his supernatural horse, whose name means Great Willpower, to wage the last great battle against the forces of evil.

Passing over the west side of the palace, the monk at last came upon his lama's palace. He described this building as looking more or less like a Tibetan monastery, with a big courtyard like those used for religious debates in his own country. He climbed up a flight of black and white marble stairs, and on reaching the top entered the palace. There was a great hall and at the far end a shrine room, in the middle of which was a golden throne resting on eight lions, just as in Tibet. On the throne sat a lama Khamtul had never seen before.

The lama was brown-skinned and old; he was holding a rosary and reciting Om Mani Padme Hum. But when Khamtul expressed doubts about his credentials the old man turned into the Bodhisattva Avalokiteshvara with four hands. The two middle ones were folded in prayer, and of the other two, the right one held a crystal rosary and the left a lotus. In this divine and reassuring form, the lama then instructed the young monk in the full meditation of Avalokiteshvara, from the beginning practices to those that would finally grant enlightenment, and gave him a special mantra to repeat, besides many other spiritual teachings and advice about his life. The lama then prophesied in a kind of poetry the end of Buddhism in Tibet, the uprising against the Chinese that would soon take place in its eastern region, and the changes that would occur as a consequence in all three regions. He said that when Khamtul was thirty years old he would have to leave his homeland, and he wanted the young man to take back with him news of all these things in order to prepare others for the end. Nevertheless, he was also to tell his brothers that the war of Shambhala would come, and that one day Tibet would regain its freedom.

At last the old man blessed Khamtul with both hands placed on his head and said: "Now go around and see this land, and then you must return. Then, when you are sixty or seventy you will be reborn here. Pray for that, and I will pray for it too."

Khamtul then asked him: "Where is this land?"

And the other replied: "This is Shambhala. All that I have told you here, you must remember. Do not forget any of it."

And then Khamtul was led back the way he had come and was absorbed back into his body, after which he woke up.[18]

As Bernbaum points out, in any assessment of the objective reality of the monk's experience, it must be borne in mind that he had been versed in Shambhalic lore since childhood and was thoroughly familiar with the guidebooks to the hidden sanctuary in the mountains, so that his mind in fact had all the material needed to produce the dream, if dream it was, in all its incredible detail. But later on, in Chapter 6, we shall hear of a vision comparable to Khamtul's that was experienced by a young Western woman with a churchgoing Protestant background who had initially never heard of Shambhala, but who also spoke of it as a real place among the mountains north of Tibet, a place to which she often flew at night in a state of consciousness very different from that of dream. And other episodes like Khamtul's, though less dramatic, accompanied the birth of the New Age movement during the sixties, when large numbers of young Americans reported being transported in a visionary nighttime state of consciousness to Shambhala, or a place like Shambhala, where they received spiritual initiations. These young people were of various religious faiths or sometimes none at all, and were unschooled in Tibetan lore, yet they too spoke of being taken to a center of spiritual training with a definite location in Asia, and of being told that it had a role to play in the course of future world events.[19]

I believe that many people all over the planet may be similarly undertaking such spiritual journeys while asleep without necessarily remembering them or ever becoming aware of their vital link with an Asiatic center of initiation; and that this may have been happening all through history, particularly at times of sudden evolutionary change. Khamtul Rinpoche, being a trained initiate, was fully conscious of his experience in extraordinarily vivid detail, whereas most of us may not be. And yet that unconscious schooling under the guidance of advanced teachers may be at the back of the seemingly spontaneous accessions of knowledge, of prophecy, of new powers and a sense of unaccountable spiritual awakening that so many people are experiencing today. It is possible, as this book theorizes, that some such collective nighttime programming is actually responsible for the kind of sudden and inexplicable cultural metamorphosis that began in the sixties as a worldwide phenomenon, and which is still going on.

Putting Shambhala on the Map

The above idea is in line with the multilayered symbology of the Shambhala mandala, which is traditionally believed to have a very real geographical-occult meaning hidden within it. For example, the thirteenth-century Kanjour text, the earliest of all the Tibetan Buddhist commentaries on the subject, speaks of Shambhala only as a round center from which eight roads fan out to all points of the compass like the spokes of a wheel with guardians posted at each of the eight terminals, and may well have been referring to an old regional map drawn by the Bonpo. This literal interpretation is not incompatible with the religious symbology displayed in the eight-rayed figure.

Studies of megalithic art disclose that the eight-rayed wheel was once a symbol for the sun and was related to a Neolithic calendar that divided the year by solar observation into eight parts.[20] The art demonstrates that this type of wheel was an important part of the worldwide iconography of the Sun religion that spread from Central Asia, and from which Buddhist symbolism is directly derived. We have only to consider how strictly the architecture of sacred places like cathedrals, mosques and Hindu temples express the spiritual principles of their respective religions to realize how likely it was for the architects of Shambhala to follow the same procedure.

In the Kalachakric texts a mandala of world geography shows Mount Meru at the center of the world surrounded by four continents. One way of interpreting this diagram, as Bernbaum shows, is for the yogi to visualize the mandala in his body, identifying Meru with his spine and the four surrounding continents with his four limbs. But we must go beyond such psychic correspondences to plumb the full significance of the eight-petalled diagram; for despite its yogic symbolism, it projects a direct geographical import that was probably its original intention. It is certainly no coincidence that on the most pragmatic level the lotus-shaped mandala, whether of eight petals or four, has implications that render it a faithful abstract of the ethno-religious topography of High Asia, with its convoluted system of snowcapped mountain ranges and great river systems and its encircling border of eight ethnic culture-areas: Siberia, Mongolia, China, Tibet, Kashmir/India, Afghanistan, Turkestan and Kazakhstan (the latter a part of the old Scythian hegemony); all of which are in general separately defined by the natural formation of the land.

Furthermore, although each ethnic area has preserved its own religious beliefs and culture, if we go beneath these we find evidence of a commonly held ideology regarded by all of them as having its source in Shambhala, their shared center. Thus Nicholas Roerich has described a rare banner he saw hanging in a Tibetan monastery which showed the King of Shambhala, Rigden Jye-po, seated in the center, and encircling him representatives of the various religions of the surrounding nations. "There was a Ladakhi in his high black hat; Chinese, in their round headgear with the red ball on top; here, in his white garments, was a Hindu; there a Muslim in a white turban. Here Kirghiz, Buryats, Kalmuks; and there Mongolians in their characteristic dress." All were paying the king homage, said Roerich. All revered him as the centerpiece of their faith and "offered him the best gifts of their lands."[21]

He found that the teachings of Shambhala infused the religions of all these cultures to an astonishing degree, imbuing them with an inner mystical meaning that transcended them all. The prophecies of Shambhala, the common legends and lore of Shambhala and the aspirations connected with finding it preoccupied peoples of every faith to a degree that Roerich found truly impressive as he journeyed through Asia. Around the nightly campfires, the vast and perilous darkness of the desert all about them, Shambhala and its divine king were an ongoing and endlessly fascinating topic. The song of Shambhala was constantly heard intermingling with the songs of all the religions; and as Roerich's bearers guarded the camp each night the password was Shambhala. He had not the least doubt that Shambhala's authority over all these diverse races was real, and that its esoteric mystique had woven them into a rosary of faiths encircling the Asiatic heights precisely as the eight-petalled mandala suggests.

The religions of the East have become more familiar to us over the last two or three centuries, and yet, so little do we know about the Shambhalic tradition that few ever realize the extent to which its spiritual lore is a substratum underlying all of them. In this respect as in many others, the lotus-mandala depicting the hidden kingdom gives us encoded information that fits the geographical-cultural entirety of Asia's inner region to a remarkable degree—even taking into account the shifting boundaries and cultural changes imposed on it by Russian and Chinese communism and the extensive infiltration of a homogenous Islamic culture since the mandala was conceived.

A Wreath of Religions

Over the centuries travelers through the interior of Asia have commented on the spellbinding spirit of place that haunts the whole of that territory. In the desolate winds of high altitude and the harshness of the stony never-ending plains, hundreds of miles from habitation, unseen forces are always abroad. A nineteenth-century Chinese traveler said: "You hear almost always shrill whistlings or loud shouts; and when you try to discover whence they come, you are terrified at finding nothing."[1] The mountains, declared Roerich, give out long lingering calls of the conch shell, though no monastery is near; beyond the campfires at night hundreds of dark presences press. Some people have sensed with terror or awe a mysterious numinous presence which they have attributed to the invisible influence of Shambhala.

Writing in the early part of the century, Ferdinand Ossendowski said he noticed there were times in his Mongolian travels when men and beasts paused, silent and immobile, as though listening. The herds of horses, the sheep and cattle, stood fixed to attention or crouched close to the ground. The birds did not fly, the marmots did not run and the dogs did not bark. "Earth and sky ceased breathing. The wind did not blow and the sun did not move. . . . All living beings in fear were involuntarily thrown into prayer and waiting for their fate."[2]

"Thus it has always been," explained an old Mongol shepherd and hunter, "whenever the King of the World in his subterranean palace prays and searches out the destiny of all peoples on the earth." For in Shambhala, he said, live the invisible rulers of all pious people, the King of the World or Brahatma, who can speak with God as I speak with you, and his two assistants: Mahatma, knowing the purposes of future events, and Mahinga, ruling the causes of those events. . . . He knows all the forces of the world and reads all the souls of mankind and the great book of their destiny. Invisibly he rules eight hundred million men on the surface of the earth and they will accomplish his every order.[3]

Not only in Mongolia but in every part of Central Asia, Shambhala, even today in the secular era of post-Communism, exerts a very real influence that transcends all differences of place, race and religion. Particularly in the more desolate mountainous region of High Asia, which has barely come into the modern age, the stories and songs of Shambhala and the many tales about the King of the World, his prophecies and his armies, his divine helpers and his sacred ceremonies conducted in subterranean caverns that run, so it is said, under the whole of Central Asia, are told and sung endlessly among the people and merge with the legends about Maitreya and the warrior-savior Gesar-Khan, the hero-king of the Mongols. Great world-changing myths have been born in that rarified environment and they still endure.

High Asia has been called the navel of the world, the cockpit of Asia. There are still huge areas that have never been explored; secret valleys fed by hot springs that lie like verdant paradisial oases among the icy wastes of glaciers and snowfields; unmapped passes and perilous high routes that give glimpses between rifts in the clouds of green meadows, rivers and flowering jungles far below. A bird's-eye view reveals that the land has a curiously ridged formation like a clenched fist, due to the crushing effect of the Indian subcontinental plate impacting on that of northern Asia (Figure 2), while beyond the Trans-Himalayas and the Tibetan plateau a vast waste of deserts and more mountain ranges, the highest in the world, stretch north to the great Siberian forests in roughly elliptoid formation. Along the northern border of Tibet rear the Kunlun mountains, and beyond them the Altyn Tagh Ridge curves north on its eastern flank to the Nan Shan mountains and the Gobi Desert. Further north again is the Altai Range in southern Siberia, and to the west of Altai are the Tien Shan mountains in Turkestan; while southward again the circular knot of the Pamirs overlooks Afghanistan and is met by the Hindu Kush, the Karakorum Range north of Kashmir and the western end of the Kunluns.

Figure 2. *Map of Central Asia and India.*

Within the arms of these great mountain masses are further ranges broken by river systems, the whole compacted arrangement enclosing the Tarim Basin and the Takla Makan, the forbidding desert of the Xinjiang Province in western China, as well as the Dzungaria Basin, the Turfan Depression and part of the Gobi Desert. According to the majority of reliable sources Shambhala, if it exists at all, exists within this ambience. For as Bernbaum says: "Sparsely populated and cut off by geographical and political barriers, this vast region remains the most mysterious part of Asia, an empty immensity in which almost anything could be lost and waiting to be found."[4]

He refers also to hidden valleys regarded as sacred by the Tibetans and closely associated with Shambhala; sheltered valleys congenial to human settlement but isolated, uninhabited and almost inaccessible, tucked away in crevices between towering mountain peaks that plunge down to unimaginable depths to the valley floor, and almost totally concealed from observers above by a dense curtain of treetops. A lama told Roerich:

> In the midst of high mountains there are unsuspected enclosed valleys. Many hot springs nourish the rich vegetation. Many rare plants and medicinal herbs are able to flourish on this unusual volcanic soil. Perhaps you have noticed hot geysers on the uplands. Perhaps you have heard that only two days away from Nagchu, where there is not a tree or plant to be seen, there is one valley with trees and grass and warm water. Who may know the labyrinths of these mountains?[5]

Bernbaum was told that whole networks of such unknown valleys are strung throughout the region awaiting discovery by settlers, and that long ago, when the Indian missionary Padma Sambhava first brought the teachings of the Buddha to Tibet, he set the gods to watch over these idyllic places and keep them hidden from the world. Only the true followers of Guru Padma Sambhava, said the lama, the ones who really practice his teaching, can find them, but if the wrong kind of people try, snow leopards will attack them at the mountain passes and drive them away.

Among the Sherpas and other people of the region, these beautiful verdant places have many legends attached to them. Such guidebooks as exist set out the same requirements for their successful discovery as are needed for Shambhala: the searcher must in both cases be of good character and skilled in meditation, he must wait until he is called, and he must pursue his quest at the right time, for the sacred places are closed to the profane. However, the guidebooks to Shambhala are written for the lone pilgrim, while those to these hidden valleys are written for quite large groups of travelers, people who will wish to colonize the secret terrain if they are successful in finding it. And so Bernbaum concludes that the valley sanctuaries lie on the outskirts of Shambhala, approaching it but not of it, and that the instructions for finding Shambhala are for the more advanced seeker, the single intrepid traveler who has left behind kith and kin to essay alone the more perilous path into the interior.

The hidden-valley legends seem to be in a spiritual genre of their own. They belong to the mysterious tradition of *termas* or "concealed treasures," usually sacred texts or magical objects which are hidden in the valleys and then discovered by a *terton* perhaps hundreds of years later. A *terton* is the special person destined to find the treasure as prophesied at the time of its concealment and is the only person able to do so; he alone will be divinely guided to the right place at the right time. The terma tradition has been known to most races, from the ancient Egyptians to the Celts and the Aztecs, but it is from the Tibetans that we learn most about it.

According to the Ancient Ones of the Nyingmapa sect, their founder Padma Sambhava and his consort Yeshe Tsogyel, herself a spiritual adept, hid many such termas for future generations. Usually Yeshe Tsogyel took the master's teachings and hid them in "diamond rocks, in mysterious lakes and unchanging boxes"[6] in sacred valleys which were then magically closed; and, so that they could not be discovered by inappropriate people, spirits called *tetsung* were set to guard them until the time of the destined terton. The texts thus hidden in rocks, streams, trees and even the sky by Padma Sambhava's supernatural power form the basis of many of the religious teachings and practices of the Nyingmapa sect. Among them is the Tibetan Book of the Dead, the *Bardo Thodol*.

Moreover, the hidden valleys themselves are believed to be concealed treasures, some of which, according to Padma Sambhava's own prophecies, he set aside as sanctuaries for Tibetan people in times of war or conquest; and these too had to be opened up by a special person, a named terton, before it could be used. "Each valley," Bernbaum reports, "has a particular time when it is supposed to shelter people from turmoil outside. . . . Although some valleys have already fulfilled their destinies, others await the future when wars will destroy all traces of religion."[7] And in fact in periods of foreign invasion and civic strife, Tibetans in the past have found safety in remote mountain valleys said to have been sealed off for that purpose by Padma Sambhava, and may still be doing so.

In Search of Nine-Storied Mount Meru

The terma tradition that points the way into Shambhala is only one of the many mysteries associated with Central Asia. The region has been a migratory staging-post and a melting pot of cultures from time immemorial. Races and civilizations have come and gone in deserts that were once fertile tracts; world religions have been cradled among its mountains, their holy places guarding the deepest secrets of the spirit, and from that cultural crucible the Sons of the Sun are said by many traditions to have gone forth on their civilizing missions, spreading the Sun religion to every corner of the globe. Here, on the steppes of present-day Kazakhstan and southern Siberia, an old shamanic culture that goes back to the Ice Ages carved the first-known mandala on mammoth ivory and, according to Ivar Lissner, a well-known Russian ethnologist, evolved in a prehistoric heartland in the Altai mountains. In a world dominated by the mythology of mountains, by soaring peaks of snow and basalt where the gods dwell, the Altaic shaman's cosmology enshrines a sacred world mountain whose name, in certain versions of the myth, is like the Sumeru variant of Meru—Sumyr, Sumbyr or Subur.[8]

And here too in Inner Asia, lost in antiquity, was the locale of the heroic Mahabharata and Ramayana epics of India. In the Tarim Basin, so scholars believe, lay Uttarakuru or northern Kuru, a version of Shambhala which the Mahabharata describes as the blissful land of the sages towards which Arjuna, the warrior-prince of the Bhagavad-Gita, traveled in search of enlightenment.

Northern Kuru, a place of marvels where magical fruit trees yield the nectar of immortality, is said to be one of four regions that surround Mount Meru like the four petals of a lotus and to be the homeland of the Siddhas, enlightened Indian yogis famed for their miraculous tantric powers. "The people of that country," says the Mahabharata, "are free from illness and are always cheerful. Ten thousand and ten hundred years they live, O king, and never abandon one another."[9]

To a nearby mountain paradise at the eastern end of the Kunluns the Chinese philosopher Lao-Tzu traveled twenty-five hundred years ago, after a lifetime spent in the distant Chinese empire. He was returning to the source of the Taoist religion and indeed of his very race and civilization. For there is a legend that the primordial pair, Nu and Ku, the Chinese equivalents of Adam and Eve, were born there in the land of Hsi Wang Mu, the Queen Mother of the West, and that in the third millennium B.C. the Sons of Heaven brought their culture to China from that place of supreme enlightenment.[10]

The nine-storied jewelled palace of Hsi Wang Mu is said to stand on the summit of a jade mountain in the Kunluns that legend identifies with Meru; and there in the palace gardens grows the peach tree of immortality that blossoms only once in every six thousand years. Those sages like Lao-Tzu who are permitted to eat of its fruit are men and women of great virtue and knowledge who, thereby becoming immortal, reside in that sanctuary in perfect happiness. "Music from invisible instruments can be heard in the air and one can drink the elixir of youth at the fountain of eternal life," says Chinese folklore. "In this place are the Fields of Satisfaction. Phoenix eggs are the people's food and sweet dew their drink; everything that they desire is always ready for them."[11]

Each of the Asiatic religious traditions tends to identify Mount Meru with a different mountain and not necessarily one in its own ethnic area. The Chinese, for example, revere a peak in the Kunluns that is utterly remote from their own empire, and Hindu yogis likewise look north, beyond India, for their sacred mountain. Again, although some Tibetan yogis believe Mount Kailas, rising alone and majestic as the highest peak in the Trans-Himalayan chain, may be mythical Meru, most believe it lies beyond Tibet. One in the former category, however, was the third Panchen Lama, who saw in Mount

Kailas all the unique features classically ascribed to Meru.

Kailas is a perfectly symmetrical, pyramidal mountain of cemented gravel and snow whose four faces match the four quarters of the compass, and which has a great natural swastika, symbol of the pole, emblazoned on its southern face. Revered by the Bonpo as the sacred "nine-storied swastika mountain," it has unique geographical and geological properties and is the legendary source of the four great rivers that Hindus believe purify the world: the Indus, the Sutlej, the Ganges and the Brahmaputra.[12] It has been the Mecca of countless Hindu, Buddhist and Jain pilgrims who call it Kang Rinpoche, the Jewel of the Snows, and consider it the abode of Shiva, for which reason its sides were honeycombed with the caves of meditating yogis before the Chinese invasion.

Another who identified Kailas with Meru was Lama Anagarika Govinda, a well-known Western scholar of Buddhism:

Whether Kailash is spoken of as "throne of the gods" and the "Abode of Siva and Paravati" or as the "Mandala of Dhyani-Buddhas and Bodhisattvas," or as "Meru," the spiritual and phenomenal centre of the world, the fact which is expressed in the symbolic languages of different traditions is the experience of a higher reality, which is conveyed through a strange combination of natural and spiritual phenomena, which even those who are unaffected by religious beliefs cannot escape. Like a gigantic temple rising in regular tiers of horizontal ledges and in perfect symmetry, Kailash marks the centre of the "Roof of the World," the heart of the biggest temple, the seat of cosmic powers, the axis which connects the earth with the universe, the super-antenna for the inflow and outflow of the spiritual energies of our planet.[13]

But however closely the transcendental qualities imputed to Kailas resemble those of Meru, the directions given in the guidebooks to the holy kingdom point almost without exception to a region northwest of Kailas, beyond Tibet's northern border. S. M. Ali, the author of a substantial study of Puranic geography, argues for the great Pamir Knot of Asia as the site of Mount Meru, the Kirghiz people having selected for the role Muztagh Ata, a huge pyramidal mountain of cemented gravel and snow like Mount Kailas, but towering above all others in the Pamirs;[14] while Siberian shamans revere Mount Belukha, the highest mountain in the Altai Range, as a similarly sacred dwelling place of gods. Nevertheless the claim of any of these peaks to be legendary Meru is debatable.

AN OASIS OF RELIGIOUS PEACE

The richly varied tapestry of faiths surrounding Shambhala has been woven in a land outstanding for its tradition of unique spiritual prowess on the part of its holy men. Lines of great adepts of godlike powers, mysterious miracle-working figures, have risen again and again around the mountainous rim of the Central Asian interior, their sages, saints and magicians creating deathless legends among the people: the Siddha and Shaivite yogis from India, the Taoist *hsien-jen* or mystical mountain men from China, the Sufi Khwajagan from Turkestan, the Nyingmapa and Dzog Chen yogis from Tibet and Mongolia, and the Magi from Afghanistan no less than the shaman-khans from southern Siberia. Legends deifying these august fraternities have been carried through the ages, surviving the rise and fall of countless secular kingdoms, and their hidden centers of initiation have been sought out by aspirants from every land and mythologized in the folkways of the world. Nowhere else on earth has such an aristocracy of the spirit flowered so persistently or in such deep isolation as here in Inner Asia, and it is here we must look for the ultimate answers to the riddle of Shambhala.

Throughout the territory monasteries and religious settlements of various denominations, often hundreds of miles apart, lie hidden in the folds of mountain crags, in warm fertile valleys and oases, their training centers so closed to the outside world that their very existence is unsuspected. "In the past twenty-five years China has been thoroughly explored," says Andrew Tomas. "The formerly desolate Chinghai Province is now covered by thousands of oil wells. In the Lob Nor Lake area Chinese nuclear tests have taken place. Both of these sites are included in the territory of Shambhala. However, the world's first scientists are capable of protecting themselves from these perils by retreating into their mountain catacombs."[15] Tomas, well informed on the topic of Shambhala by his years of living in the Far East, is referring to the vast system of caverns known to stretch for hundreds of kilometers inside the mountain ranges, as well as to the unsuspected valleys lost among colossal snowy mountains on the Tibetan plateau.

Here communities of adepts of many different traditions have lived for centuries in seclusion, unmolested by outside interference: shamans, Buddhists, Taoists, Hindus, Magi, Bonpo, Manicheans, Zoroastrians, Gnostics, Nestorian Christians, Sufis; all have been able to pursue together their spiritual, philosophic or scientific objectives in peaceful cohabitation. According to esoteric tradition they have even amalgamated themselves into a permanent body that, in the words of the eighteenth-century mystic, Karl Eckartshausen, "is hidden from the world and submissive solely to Divine Government."[16]

Of the groups of initiates who once formed the Mystery schools of antiquity, Tomas says:

> Sometimes they were within the confines of the recognized religion of the land where they belonged as an elite. On other occasions they were outside of its sphere, completely unknown initiates. . . . There was a chain of their centres all over the world and when a certain civilization was to receive a stimulus, assistance immediately arrived from other branches of this worldwide brotherhood. This explains the sudden rise of new ideas in certain historical periods and the radical changes following their acceptance.[17]

This chain of centers, Tomas contends, was connected to the great School of Wisdom which still exists in Central Asia, where it abides as an island of goodwill and cooperation in a global sea of ceaseless religious warfare and interfaith persecution.

From the seventeenth century onward, lamaist texts referring to the onslaughts of the "barbarians" have given some indication of the religious strife raging in Asia as the advances of the Muslims, and to a lesser extent the Nestorian Christians and others, destroyed Buddhism wherever they went. The same texts have proclaimed the punishment in store for these godless barbarians when the Great Warrior Gesar rides forth from Shambhala with his mighty hordes to vanquish the demonic forces of evil.[18] Yet in support of Tomas's assertion, the British philosopher and mathematician J. G. Bennett says that in Xinjiang, the heart of Inner Asia, Muslim Sufis have lived for centuries in harmony with the lamas, sharing many of their doctrines and deeper tantric techniques; and in Altai, Roerich visited a group of Old Believers, a mystical Christian sect persecuted at home by the Russian Orthodox Church, who lived amicably with their shaman neighbors. Jews, Zoroastrians and Gnostics have likewise found friendly asylum in the foothills of the Asiatic mountains among communities of other faiths.

This oasis of peace is reported as still existing. The various small spiritual communities hidden within it express the highest ideals of religious brotherhood and are widely respected for their clemency, their tolerance, their humanity and their joint preservation of occult techniques that seem to depend on a knowledge of physical laws unknown to science. While each one remains faithful to its own religious tradition, following its own hallowed communal rules, doctrinal precepts and liturgical usages, esotericists believe that all share, at least in part, a secret inner ideology and identity never disclosed to the world at large. As has been said, they contend that secretly these fraternities are constituted as cadres in an invisible hierarchy and that they work together in the world's service under a single central command. Thus they correspond to Shambhala's eight outer kingdoms, each with its separate tradition and chain of command, yet affiliated under one spiritual authority that is higher than the authority of any one of them.

Attempts have been made to identify the hidden paradise with one or other of the little kingdoms, now forgotten and in ruins, that have flourished in various parts of Inner Asia; perhaps one of the Greek kingdoms of Bactria left behind by Alexander the Great, or the Kushan empire that followed the Greeks, or the Uighur kingdom, Kocho, established by the Turks in the Turfan Depression south of the Tien Shan mountains. Another possibility that has been entertained is the ring of little kingdoms, among them Kashgar, Yarkand and Khotan, that once flowered in the fertile oases around the Tarim Basin and which, say some, might have provided a model for the Shambhalic myth. And yet another possibility, suggested by the Western orientalist Helmut Hoffman, is a forgotten kingdom in the Ferghana valley near the Pamirs, in the same general direction as Olmolun-gring.[19] Wolfgang Bauer, another Western scholar, thinks that the mythical kingdom of Hsi Wang Mu may well have been inspired by a small Chinese country, now vanished, that once bore the same name.[20]

But it must be remembered that Shambhala is not only still alive and active, but is also described again and again as a historically unique religious reserve from which all the usual trappings of the world have been excluded. It can never have corresponded to an ordinary, politically inspired secular king-dom. Rather its outer region corresponds, as has been said, to the network of spiritual orders that stretches to this day across the whole of High Asia, an affiliation of semiautonomous bodies under a single mystical directive. Bern-baum suggests something of the sort when he says:

> Perhaps the historical site of Shambhala lies hidden right on the map as the most obvious and overlooked spot of all—the entire region of Central Asia. . . . It could be a secret society with mem-bers scattered all over Asia.[21]

If the inhabitants of Shambhala are indeed so scattered, no contradic-tion is involved in the fact that pilgrims claiming to have visited it point in so many different directions or that the findings of explorers and theorists are so much at variance with each other. The fact that Professor Guiseppe Tucci, the eminent Buddhist scholar and explorer, believed Shambhala would be found in the Altyn Tagh district would no longer conflict with Alexandra David-Neel's equally firm opinion, stated after extensive travels in Central Asia and shared by the Afghan Sufi Idries Shah, that it was synonymous with Balkh, the ancient "mother of cities" in Afghanistan that had been destroyed by Geng-his Khan, nor with Geoffrey Ashe's closely reasoned conclusion in his book *The Ancient Wisdom* that it was situated on or near Mount Belukha in the Altai mountains. Rather it would seem that the Taoist monastery in the east-ern Kunluns, the Sufi Sarmoun settlement in Afghanistan, the Dzog Chen school on the slopes of Mount Kailas or Muztagh Ata, the Buddhist monas-tery in an oasis of the Tarim Basin, and the Manichean center in the Ferghana valley are all part of the secret kingdom. The Muslim who has been called may go to a dervish stronghold, perhaps in the Hindu Kush or the Tien Shan mountains, the Hindu yogi to a monastery in the western Kunluns, the shaman to Altai; but all go to Shambhala. For Shambhala lies within the walls of the brotherhoods.

Furthermore, contemporary Sufi publications indicate that one day we shall find that the settlements exist in a pattern of distribution that is not random but ordered hierarchically along the lines of a vast mandala, thus bringing High Asia even closer to the traditional mandalic conception of Shambhala. In 1960 an American travel author, Peter King, noted in his book *Afghanistan: Cockpit of High Asia*, that in the area of Afghanistan called Nuristan (formerly Kafiristan), which is close to the Hindu Kush, there are Sufi monasteries almost impenetrable to outsiders. They have been built in a circle around an even more inaccessible core circle of monasteries or training centers belonging to a people about whom almost nothing is known, but who are connected with the Sufis. In the most inaccessible place of all is the Markaz or powerhouse of these inner masters, although what its nature is no one will say.[22]

Afghans assert that the celebrated Armenian magus and spiritual teacher George Gurdjieff was the only outsider permitted to penetrate the outer ring of Sufi centers, where he was trained by Bahauddin Nakshband, one of the outer masters; but that as for the initiates in the central strongholds, "no one will tell an outsider anything more," says King, "than that their monasteries exist."[23] They are called by Afghans the People of the Tradition and are supposed to be in touch with extraterrestrial intelligences and to be the custodians of the secret traditions that are the basis of all religions and all human development. J. G. Bennett, who was closely associated with Sufism, believed they formed an inner circle of humanity and coined for them the name of the Hidden Directorate.

In Peter King's account we are clearly being presented with something very like a great mandala in three dimensions expressive of the Sufi hierarchy, reminding us of the three-dimensional mandala that was built by the first King of Shambhala in a park to the south of the mythical city of Kapala. That mandala too embodied the essence of the most spiritual teachings known to humanity, and it too converged on a transcendental center inhabited by deities. The Sufi hierarchy, which is headed by the Qutub or Axis and his two assistants, has many features in common with those of Shambhala and may be similar in its structure to other ethno-religious orders in Inner Asia, as the Sufi author Ernest Scott suggests.[24]

SHAMBHALA: A RING OF SPIRITUAL POWER CENTERS?

Can it be that the Kalachakra describes Shambhala in yogic terms because it is literally laid out according to yogic principles? It is not beyond the bounds of possibility that the monastic circle Peter King found in Afghanistan is duplicated by other esoteric fraternities in each of the other ethnic zones, and that all are constellated around a ring of spiritual "power points" situated on special mountains, the whole configuration composing Shambhala. We know such special mountains exist and that they are centers of initiation highly magnetic to mystics: holy Mount Kailas for one has been ringed for centuries by Buddhist monasteries and little seasonal settlements of Dzog Chen practitioners. And to the Kirghiz people who inhabit the uplands west of the Pamirs, holy Muztagh Ata is another such Mecca, as is Mount Belukha to the nomad races of southern Siberia. May not these spiritual power points and others like them constitute a circle of beacons alerting the attuned seeker to the boundaries of Shambhala?

The possibility of a vast natural mandala being laid out deliberately over the whole of this great region may seem scarcely credible, yet it is in the spirit of the traditional societies of antiquity. All settlements, says the English Cabalist and author John Michell, develop as cosmological schemes that represent in microcosm the order of the heavens as these correspond to the order of life and the pattern of the human mind. "The marks people make on the ground reflect the philosophy of the time."[25] So everywhere on earth we find evidence of cities, palaces and temples laid out in mandalic form according to metaphysical principles as then understood and for extremely practical purposes connected with the control and augmentation of earthly and celestial forces.

Usually these living mandalas were planned as an image of the spherical universe of ancient cosmology, in which the civic center was a great citadel rock or artificial mound, the seat of oracular and law-giving power that represented the heavenly mountain, the axis of the universe and the canon of eternal law. For in metaphysical language, says Michell, "the mountain represents the state of vision; in terms of dynamics it is a generator of the energy that inspires the high state of madness or prophecy; and so, following the law of correspondence, it provides an appropriate rostrum for prophets and preachers."[26]

Such a sacred ground plan is found in Firuzabad, an Iranian citadel town of the third century C.E. Many other ancient towns, villages and cities have been built on the principles of the Celtic Cross or the Solar Wheel. With the spread of the Sun religion that civilized most of the known world, temples and palaces conformed to solar principles. To solar societies, says Michell, "a palace retains the solar power of the emperor and, like all centres of government throughout the world, is approached by long straight avenues which conduct the power throughout the kingdom, and at the same time draw into the center the tribute of the countryside and the people."[27] Thus Versailles, the seat of the French Sun King, was laid out like a wheel to function as a solar center. And in fact the sacred monarch, charged with solar power which he transmitted to the people, was once a universal institution known in the Far East and Africa. In the Americas, he reigned as the Great Sun from an observatory temple on the mound or pyramid in the center of his Mayan kingdom.

But of even deeper significance is the discovery that has recently been made in Rennes-le-Chateau, in southern France, of a vast architectural construction across miles of countryside based on a perfect pentagon of mountain peaks, a sixth mountain at its center. Unfolding from this regular natural pentagon with consummate surveying skill is a maze of far more complex designs in dazzling constellations of interlocking circles, triangles and hexagons; these figures, some of which are of deep occult significance, being delineated by the positioning of churches, shrines, calvaires, castles and natural features of the landscape, such as springs and grottoes (Figures 3 and 4). The whole is structured on an underlying grid fixed in the first place by the pentagon of mountains and formed by parallel lines that intersect in perfect ninety-degree angles on the sites of churches, castles and so on. The grid extends for an indefinite distance beyond the environs of Rennes-le-Chateau and is reminiscent of the ley lines of Britain.

Henry Lincoln, who has made an exhaustive study of the site, calls it the eighth wonder of the world, a holy place, an immense man-made temple incredible in its complexity of design, control of measure, distance and alignment and sophistication of surveying techniques, and says it was built by the Knights Templar in the twelfth century but superimposed on an earlier megalithic construction that was no doubt dedicated to the Great Goddess. Henry Lincoln, who is co-author with Michael Baigent and Richard Leigh of *The Holy Blood and the Holy Grail* and *The Messianic Legacy*, believes it is of far greater engineering and geometrical skill than that needed to build the great pyramid of Giza.

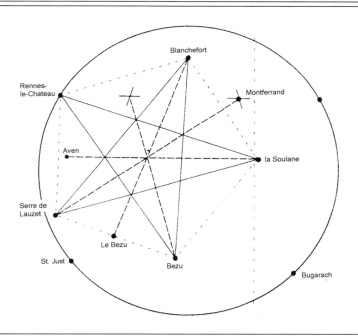

Figure 3. *A view of the Holy Place at Rennes-leChateau showing the basic pentagon of mountains defined by the position of the churches etc. and aligned to the Paris Zero Meridian.*

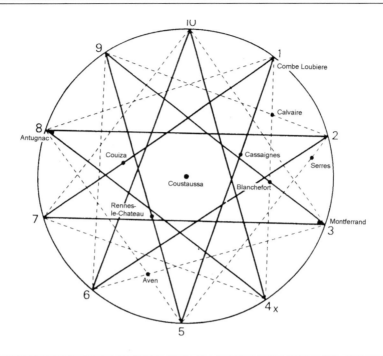

Figure 4. *Another view of the Holy Place at Rennes-le-Chateau showing a ten pointed star made up of two interlaced pentacles. The measurement used throughout is the universal mile. "One must wonder," Lincoln says, "at the incredibly sophisticated culture of its creators. The Temple, I suspect, would never have been discovered without the extremely accurate maps which we are only now, in the twentieth century, capable of producing."*

"Unlike other great works of early civilization," he writes, "this Temple has not fallen into ruin and decay. It is still as real and tangible as it was on the day of its completion—and yet, for all that, it is invisible. . . . The Temple is invisible simply because it is too vast to be seen."[28]

The Rennes-le-Chateau discovery was made as a consequence of cryptic clues leaked to him by an old and prestigious French occult society, the Prioré de Sion, which claims a direct descent from the Templar Order, and is evidently part of a small initiated circle that has preserved many secrets about the Rennes-le-Chateau complex and its builders. In a postscript to Henry Lincoln's book, he reports the discovery of yet another such temple of astonishing geometrical subtlety and complexity on the island of Bornholm in the Baltic Sea. Bornholm lies, with Scotland, on the fifty-fifth parallel, in a due line with Pliny's land of the Hyperboreans, of whom we shall hear more later. The ruined churches, castles and commanderies that define this holy place in southern Scandinavia were constructed by the Teutonic Knights, the heirs of the Templars, towards the northernmost limits of their activities. But the great temple on Bornholm may have been only one of several such holy places that they constructed on their way north. In Scandinavia, as in the Languedoc in southern France, these temple complexes were built by the Templar Orders on the sites of earlier megaliths. Bornholm may have been only one of several such holy places that they reconstructed on their way north.

One thing Lincoln became certain of as he continued his astonishing researches in southern France was that Rennes-le-Chateau was only a small part of a greater wonder. He writes:

> Whatever culture created the Temple was undeniably and amazingly skilled in geometry, mathematics and surveying. Some, and perhaps all of the necessary skills were clearly possessed by the Neolithic communities which produced the Megalithic Stone Circles. The few traces of such communities—standing stones and dolmens— all appear in the alignments. . . . It is my suspicion that the builders of the Temple of Rennes-le-Chateau will indeed prove to be part of that culture which produced Stonehenge and Carnac, and to date from approximately the same period, i.e., c. 1500 B.C.[29]

But John Michell, who has demonstrated the existence of a similar holy place laid out on the Glastonbury countryside but based on a six-sided geometry, says that in an even more remote period an unknown pre-Celtic race built a worldwide network of such temples aligned to the earth chakras around the globe, and that the network still exists beneath the surface of our modern civilization.

Its purpose, he says, was to invoke powerful terrestrial and stellar forces of a magnetic and even subtler nature and to induce them by various forms of natural magic, such as numerical proportions, sounds and patterns laid out on the earth, to work to the benefit of humanity. According to the law of correspondence, the earth could be rendered by art a reflection of the heavens and so draw down the celestial energies. "As the earth's nervous system is reflected in the body of God and in the body of a man," Michell says, "so were the paths that link the terrestrial magnetic centres marked out across the earth, following the pattern of those luminous streams of energy between the stars which are sometimes perceived in dreams and visions."[30] In this way the power-base of an ancient civilization was created of which we have lost all trace and memory. Michell comments furthermore that such an energy network demanded a center onto which all local holy places converged, a kind of religious capital of the world.

He tentatively nominates to the position the great pyramid of Giza, a construction that has recently been subjected to the researches of Robert Bauval, a construction engineer with a long-standing interest in Egyptology, and Adrian Gilbert, a publisher specializing in the Egyptian Hermetic tradition among other gnostic traditions, and who has been researching ancient Egypt for more than twenty years. In *The Orion Mystery* they suggest that the Giza pyramid may be one component of a pyramidal complex whose pattern laid out on the Egyptian sands mirrors the pattern in the heavens of the Orion constellation.[31] But although the Giza pyramid-complex has important occult connotations, Shambhala, situated as it is in the center of the Eurasian landmass, is more highly qualified still to fill the role envisaged by Michell. On all counts it is hard to imagine a place better suited to be the still-surviving geographical center and supreme seat of government of a cultural system once operational around the globe and now fallen into disuse.

And so it is possible that Shambhala is laid out according to the same geometrical principles as the holy places of Rennes-le-Chateau, Glastonbury and Bornholm—but on the basis of an octagon rather than either a pentagon or a hexagon, since an octagonal form is indicated by both the Buddhist and Bon mandalas. The octagon, with a ninth point in the center, is also central to the mystical symbology of Sufism. It is the seal or design which Ernest Scott says "reaches for the innermost secrets of man."[32] Meaning wholeness, power and perfection, this primary geometrical symbol is one which Sufis associate with Shambhala, and is an archetype of universal significance in primitive as well as advanced societies, as mythologist Joseph Campbell tells us:

> The hogan or mud hut of the Navahos of New Mexico and Arizona is constructed on the plan of the Navaho image of the cosmos. The entrance faces east. The eight sides represent the four directions and the points between. Every beam and joist corresponds to an element in the great hogan of the all-embracing earth and sky. And since the soul of man itself is regarded as identical in form with the universe, the mud hut is a representation of the basic harmony of man and the world, and a reminder of the hidden lifeway of perfection.[33]

For the Navahos and archaic humanity in general—or at least for its spiritual adepts—the vision of reality was evidently not only unitary and transcendental, but also hierarchical, as Mircea Eliade makes clear again and again in his studies. Not only did they conform every earthly construction to a celestial prototype which took precedence in all creative undertakings, being regarded as far more important than the hard facts we so much value today, but the nearer they drew to the center the more complex became the validating symbolism and the higher its geometrical value, until the center itself was assigned the ultimate number of power or its geometrical equivalent.

Thus Shambhala, which would certainly have been contemporaneous with the forgotten epoch of magical landscaping that Michell describes, may well have a ground plan conceived along cosmological lines as a temple enclosure, a vast working shrine to the Most High whose architectural symbolism is meant to convey its supremacy as the mystic center of the world. But if that is the case, it has been constructed on a cyclopean scale unprecedented elsewhere, dwarfing even the great Rennes-le-Chateau holy place and capable of sending out its tentacles of influence to the whole of Central Asia. Who could have had the resources and expertise for surveying on such a scale? When could it have been done? And how could we know nothing about it in the outside world?

Lincoln has already provided some of the answers. A man-made structure of such titanic proportions could lie undetected for millennia among the towering peaks of Inner Asia, its secrets hidden forever unless we were to find the key to a special kind of knowledge apparently long lost to us. Yet whatever the organizing intelligence that may have impressed itself on a terrain as vast and dangerous as High Asia, we are left, like Lincoln, with many more questions unanswered. Indeed, if we are to take Shambhala seriously as a real place, it is necessary to admit at the outset that every aspect of it—and not least the riddle of its central feature, Meru, a mountain not found on any map in the world—conveys a sense of intractable mystery that only deepens as we penetrate further, revealing vista upon vista of unknown territory.

THE COSMIC MOUNTAIN

It would seem unlikely that the cosmic mountain, one of the most ubiquitous images in the repertoire of mythology, should symbolize a central element in tantric yoga and have a literal meaning as well; but so I believe. We in the West whose culture is becoming increasingly impregnated by eastern yoga must accustom ourselves to reading in a new light our old inheritance of myth, discovering in it a subtle multiform doorway to new realizations on more than one plane. "It would not be too much to say," writes Joseph Campbell, "that myth is the secret opening through which the inexhaustible energies of the cosmos pour into human cultural manifestation. Religions, philosophies, arts, the social forms of primitive and historic man, prime discoveries in science and technology, the very dreams that blister sleep, boil up from the basic magic ring of myth."[1] And in doing so myth can support a wide spectrum of meanings—even those directly relevant to modern physics.

Within the magic ring of myth the cosmic mountain image is preeminent, both for its universality and its spiritual resonance. As the meeting-place of heaven, earth and hell and the axle of the revolving firmament, it has figured in the mythology of nearly every race on earth and has been revered even in lands where there are no mountains. It is always pictured as the Axis Mundi and as bearing the habitats of sages, saints or gods upon its sides, as four-sided or six-sided and eighty miles high, with the heavens rotating about its peak and the pole star shining above. It is said by all accounts to be so high that it pierces the firmament, while its roots descend into the abyss beneath the earth where chaos reigns. It has seven levels, believed by some races to be nine,[2] and these correspond to the seven or nine inner worlds and also to the ascending stations of consciousness traversed by the initiate on his purgatorial pilgrimage to heaven.

In Nordic mythology the cosmic mountain is made of glass, and the hero must climb it to win the king's daughter imprisoned on the summit; but it is also Mount Sinai, terrible in darkness and storm, on which Moses received the tablets of the law from God. In the medieval Grail tradition it is called Montsalvat, and in the Icelandic Eddas Himinbjorg, where Bifrost, the rainbow, reaches to the zenith. Even among the prehistoric Semang pygmies of Malaysia, an immense rock called Batu-Ribn was thought to rise at the center of the world, from whence a magic tree-trunk soared into the sky. And in the center of Palestine the Israelites called holy Mount Gerizim the navel of the earth, the *gymbal* or binding post that united the earthly and the celestial spheres. Circumpolar peoples such as the Altaic and Scandinavian races knew of the World Mountain as the center of the universe, and so too did early Sumer, symbolizing it in its seven-tiered ziggurats, on the top of which were the sacred bridal chambers of the gods. The Arabs had a like belief that centerd on Qaf, "the mount of saints," and the Iranians held that the sacred mountain Haraberesaitiz (El-burz) was located at the center of the world and was joined to heaven.

In all these varied myths of the cosmic mountain, one glimpses connotations of a supreme spiritual power that transmits its beneficence to the world around and was once, when the world was younger, ardently sought by culture-heroes and kings as life's most precious boon. Thus Anne Baring and Jules Cashford, two analytical psychologists who are also mythologists and historians, say in *The Myth of the Goddess* that in antiquity the cosmic mountain myth was treasured as symbolically making manifest a divine power that moved in the primal order of the Creation:

> for in its shape lies the original mound, the "High Hill," which first emerged from the waters as habitable land; and in many cultures the hill was the image of the goddess as earth. In Sumeria the mountain was also the underworld—Kur—the womb of the Moth-

er, and in Crete the goddess stands upon her mountain, flanked by lions and holding her sceptre of rule.[3]

According to this symbolism the mountain was correlated with the throne of kings, and it was said that the throne made the king, bestowing on him the qualities of a ruler, for it was never forgotten that what was thus manifested in throne, mound or hill was actually a heavenly power, an underlying force, itself invisible, that created and ordered the visible world. For this very reason the Egyptian goddess Isis wore a throne upon her head.

To the early Hindus, Mount Meru was the apotheosis of this causal principle. From Central Asia they brought into India the legend of a paradisial mountain to the north which, as the Mahabharata declares, "stands carrying the worlds above, below and transversely,"[4] and which Hindus believe to this day is the prototype of all other mythic mountains. This northern mountain was inhabited by seven great Rishis who appeared in the world whenever a new spiritual revelation was required. Eliade catches the inner meaning of the legend when he states that the cosmic mountain symbolizes the highest pinnacle of mystical exaltation, of enlightenment. Hence in antiquity, he says, every religious center partook of the meaning of the sacred mountain: the temple was the highest point of the land, the center of the world, the gateway to revelation, to prophecy, to heavenly gifts and to the human laws received from the gods. Where there was no mountain the people built one; a mound, a pyramid, a ziggurat.

Babylon was a *Bab-ilani*, a "gate of the gods," for here the gods descended to earth in order to bless it, the temples and sacred towers of the city being consecrated to the cosmic mountain and known by such names as "Mount of the House," "House of the Mount of all Lands," "Mount of Tempests," "Link between Heaven and Earth" and so on.[5] Similarly the Javanese temple of Borobodur was built as an image of the cosmos, an artificial mountain at the center of the world up whose seven levels the Buddhist pilgrim moves, passing from one plane to another, until on the highest terrace he transcends profane space altogether and enters a pure region, a zone of paradisial peace and enlightenment. And Dante's Mount of Purgatory may be thought of as a Christian Meru. It is represented as a kind of ziggurat with seven spiralling levels, seven stages of purgation of souls and a divine bridal chamber at its summit, from which Beatrice leads Dante upwards through the stars to the throne of God.[6]

Yet although everywhere in the ancient world there has prevailed this same system of pictorial symbolism summed up in the cosmic mountain myth, some researchers are in accord with the Hindu cosmology and believe the universality of the theme is not due to accidental factors or to parallel cultural development, as might be supposed from a superficial reading. Rather, the myth has spread from a single source somewhere in the depths of northern Asia, from an original Eden, and from thence has infused all later cultures. René Guénon is one eminent author who holds this view. He claims that every sacred center in antiquity has looked to Shambhala-Agarttha as its northern prototype and has imitated or reflected in a secondary way the mystique of its sacred mountain.

THE FIRST TERRESTRIAL PARADISE

Guénon calls Mount Meru the Pole or the polar mountain because it is the axis around which all other spiritual centers turn and from which they derive their initiatic knowledge. He states that once Agarttha was above ground and had a different name, that of Paradesha, which in Sanskrit means "supreme country." From Paradesha he traces the Chaldeans' Pardes and the Judeo-Christian Paradise, and points out that Meru, the mountain of the Terrestrial Paradise, therefore means the same as the Pardes of the Hebrew Cabala. And so for Eastern and Western traditions alike, for Hindu, Muslim and Jew, Buddhist and Christian, Meru is the original "supreme country" which "according to certain Vedic and Avestan texts," says Guénon, "was originally sited towards the north pole, even in the literal sense of the word. Although it may change its localization according to the different phases of human history, it still remains polar in a symbolic sense because essentially it represents the fixed axis around which everything revolves."[7]

In *The Ancient Wisdom*, the well-known British author Geoffrey Ashe arrives at a similar conclusion. With meticulous care he has put together a common myth that can be construed as drifting down from a (possibly) Altaic center to the temples and royal courts of Egypt, India, Greece and China, where it has fragmented into many different mythological forms. "In the far north," his scenario runs,

> there is a high and paradisial place, peopled by an assembly of beings of superhuman longevity and wisdom. They have associates and contacts at lower levels. Access is difficult. This is the place where earth rises to join the celestial center, the pole of heaven. Here is the axle of the sky, and above is the power that keeps it turning. The visible and sovereign sign of that power is the great constellation of seven stars [Ursa Major] which possess a divine life, and circle in the centre without setting. Our disc-shaped earth has a sacred center which is in union with this center where the heavens are pivoted.[8]

And that sacred center on earth, Ashe postulates, is Shambhala-Agarttha. He points out that, curiously, support for the idea of a common center is concealed in the scriptural texts of the world religions, in which traditional peoples frequently located their sacred mountain not in their own land but in the far north. In equatorial Egypt, for example, Set and Horus were gods of the north star; and according to the Koran, the highest place on earth is the Ka'aba because "the Pole Star bears witness that it faces the center of heaven."[9] And in Psalm 48:2 of the Bible, Mount Zion is unaccountably called "Mount Zion in the far north." Ashe states:

> The holy mountain seems to have acquired stature through being mystically identified with another, much higher one, which was not in Palestine at all. The same northern mountain figures in related myths of the Canaanites. They called it "Safon" and said it had an earthly paradise on it. "Safon" occurs in the Bible as a synonym for Zion, and Ezekiel places "Eden, the garden of God" on a "holy mountain of God" which cannot possibly be the mundane hill of Jerusalem (Ezek. 28:11-16).[10]

The Babylonians, too, seemed to look to a holy mountain in the far north. In Isaiah 14:13, Isaiah, denouncing the hubris of the king of Babylon, declares: "You have said in your heart, 'I will ascend to heaven; above the stars of God I will set my throne on high; I will sit on the mount of assembly in the far north.'" And Ezekiel, captive in Babylonia, saw in a vision the Lord's chariot coming not from Zion in the Holy Land to the south, but out of the north on a storm-wind (Ezekiel 1:4).

The ancient Greeks also had their northern Elysium in defiance of the local cult. To them Delphi was the center of the world; yet Apollo, god of the Delphic sanctuary, was a foreign shamanic newcomer to the Greek pantheon and was believed to be the god of a secret land far to the north, where stood the cosmic axle supporting the seven-star constellation that the Greeks called Helice, "That Which Turns." It was the home of a semi-deified race of sages called Hyperboreans, among whose blessed assembly Apollo spent three months every year as their ritually returning deity, riding the sky in a chariot drawn by swans. Geoffrey Ashe comments that Apollo's "chariot-drawing swans recall a 'road of birds' that leads to the celestial realms in northern folklore—that of Lithuania, for instance."[11]

The Greeks located this circumpolar race of wise beings, whom we shall meet again later, anywhere from Britain to the borders of China. But the scholar W. K. C. Guthrie maintains that the Hyperboreans were originally Siberian and Mongolian shamans and medicine men and that Apollo, whose name means "god of the assembly," began his career long ago in the Altai mountains, his teachings and ecstatic practices, so foreign to the Greeks, gradually drifting southward through Asia Minor to the Aegean.[12] Quoting Guthrie, Ashe argues that the cosmic mountain concept almost certainly had its source in the shamanism of southern Siberia and that the idea of Shambhala likewise grew up around the semi-mythical magicians and pole-lords of Altai.

He cites a Mongolian legend full of esoteric symbolism related by Nicholas Roerich in *Altai-Himalaya* that tells of seven blacksmiths who became the seven stars of the Great Bear constellation; and since smiths and shamans are closely related in Siberian lore, a smith being proverbially the elder brother of the shaman, Ashe is persuaded that the seven Rishis of Hindu mythology may be identifiable as master shamans connected with the Altaic Great Bear cult.

"Both this Mongol story and the Rishi myth of the Hindus could be rooted in a single Altaic concept of the seven stars [of Ursa Major] as seven undifferentiated Wise Ones—smith-shamans," he observes.[13]

He further links this idea of a Siberian assembly of shaman adepts with Roerich's comments on Altai as a sacred region. "Roerich refers, with some wonderment," he writes, "to the 'general reverence for Altai' and to 'the coming of the Blessed Ones to Altai' and 'the true significance of Altai.' In another entry he records . . . that the mountain Belukha, the principal peak of the Altai range, has a name meaning 'Orion-dwelling-of-gods'—which, he says, correlates it with the world-mountain of other mythologies."[14] And so, Ashe adds, it looks as if the Hyperborean paradise could have been the same one which other myths placed on top of the northern mountain, and as if its semi-divine inhabitants were the beings imagined elsewhere as Rishis or Gods.

All these allusions to a prehistoric center of high spirituality in southern Siberia are corroborated by the field researches of Ivar Lissner, who has traced the migrations of the stargazing Altaic race from northeastern Asia to the steppes of Central Asia during the seventh millennium B.C., bringing with them a sophisticated knowledge of the polar heavens and unparalleled trance techniques.[15] The same allusions have led Ashe to hypothesize a Siberian seed-bed of civilization, now long-forgotten, that can be equated with Shambhala. Infused with the star lore of the Great Bear, Shambhala's background, he believes, is rooted in the astral wisdom of a center of high magic in the Altai mountains.

Like Guénon, he interprets the myth of Mount Meru as having a basis in reality; like Guénon, he asserts that our inheritance of Greek learning and science, and indeed the entire Mediterranean Mystery tradition, may have stemmed originally from a circumpolar culture now lost in the mists of time whose center was Shambhala; but that Shambhala itself may be still active somewhere in southern Siberia, still populated by initiates whom Stone Age hunters would have called Immortals, Gods or the Sky-born.

"We might venture to wonder," Ashe writes,

> about a real outflow of myth and cult from a real northern centre, a literal Siberian or Mongolian Meru. . . . The Altaic Wisdom may

be imagined spreading out into lower latitudes, taking various forms
. . . but always with some of the reconstructed essence present—
ideas about the cosmic centre, the circling heavens ruled by the
Bear, the heptadic linkage of above-and-below, the mountain, the
paradisial assembly, and so forth.[16]

But Ashe, while acknowledging the ambiguity of the cosmic mountain
concept, is inclined to accept it at face value as referring to Mount Belukha.
Guénon is not. And it is to Guénon's work that we must now turn for an
interpretation of Meru unparalleled anywhere in the literature. He assigns to
it the literal Sanskrit meaning of a spine or backbone, which he associates, as
does kundalini yoga, with a subtle inhering psychospiritual energy system.
Meru, he indicates, is accordingly not a mountain but a metaphor for a conduit of terrestrial energy constituting the earth's primary power source whose
nature, location and function is presently unknown to us. He suggests that
the knowledge of this fact belongs to a most arcane and little-known branch
of the tantric science that is concerned with cosmic Shakti and the building of
worlds, and which for that reason has been jealously guarded from the public
view for many thousands of years.

TERRESTRIAL KUNDALINI AND THE WORLD AXIS

Since Guénon published his metaphysical works touching on this subject, a vast amount of new material has been released in the West giving information about kundalini shakti in the context of the human body. But for
most of us the concept of *terrestrial* kundalini is still an unfamiliar one, never
directly addressed.

In examining this once-secret department of Indian metaphysics, however, we should remember that kundalini shakti has always had relevance to
many areas of knowledge other than the personal yogic. The kundalini science has been at the core of all the Hindu philosophies and these have been as
much concerned with the study of the earth and its forces as with religion, for
it is a science that strives to comprehend the cosmos in its entirety. Acknowledging this fact, some quantum physicists and biologists are already seeking

inspiration in the subtle byways of Tantra and it well may be that one day geophysicists interested in the constitution of the planet will do the same.

In the meantime, a brief recapitulation of general tantric doctrine and its central principles may be helpful to an understanding of Guénon's more specialized and esoteric thesis regarding terrestrial kundalini, for it is doubtful whether we can understand his concept of the World Axis without it.

As is now widely known, kundalini yoga is based on the premise that in human beings a spiritual body of finer matter interpenetrates the physical and extends beyond it. "According to the highest tantra," Lama Thubten Yeshe explains, "our body and mind exist not only on the gross level we are normally familiar with but also on subtle levels about which most of us are completely unaware. . . . Within the boundaries or atmosphere of this physical body is another far more subtle body; the so-called *vajra* body, '*vajra*' having the connotation of indestructible."[17] Within this conscious vajra body of light there circulates a primal nonphysical vibration called kundalini that actually underlies all the coarser vibrations of the physical system and is so intimately connected with the nervous system that it is often incorrectly identified with it.

Indian cosmology calls the primal formative energy of the universe in its static state *Maha-kundali*, "the great coiled power," of which, strictly speaking, kundalini is the diminutive form applied to the same energy when found in individual bodies. This unmanifested primal energy is an all-pervasive, all-nurturing, all-organizing life-principle filling all space and matter and forever inaccessible to us except through its manifested forms, be they gross or subtle. It is found in a highly concentrated form in the chakras of the human spinal system, which distributes the energy throughout the body. When amplified by spiritual techniques, kundalini intensifies the activity of the chakras, thus expanding consciousness, opening up the intuition to the subtle energy body that underlies the physical, increasing intelligence and the capacity for love, and maintaining the physical body in a highly augmented state of health and vitality.

The subtle chakric system on which kundalini depends for its permeation and maintenance of the body gave birth to the symbol of the Egyptian caduceus or Hermetic staff of the medical profession.

"The two serpents in a double helix around a central rod are known in yogic terms as Ida—related to the Moon, the female or negative polarity, magnetic in nature—and Pingala, related to the Sun, the male or positive polarity, electrical in nature," says a widely read researcher on the subject, Mark Balfour, in *The Sign of the Serpent*. "They represent two of the major Nadis or conduits through which polarised Bioenergy (life-force, kundalini or serpent force) is normally conducted throughout the biophysical system."[18] The central rod is known as the *sushumna*, within which is the hair-thin central duct, the Brahma Nadi, which carries the awakened kundalini to the crown of the head, a stage of evolution that represents the effective conquest of the higher states of being.

Dr. Hiroshi Motoyama of Tokyo has thoroughly documented this energy distribution system in human beings. A yogi and a highly qualified scientist trained in empirical methodology, Dr. Motoyama was chosen by UNESCO (the United Nations Educational, Scientific and Cultural Organization) in 1974 as one of the world's ten foremost researchers in parapsychology. He says:

> The Chakra-Nadi system bears striking resemblances to the layout of the autonomic nervous system. This is remarkable in that the yogic model was developed before the anatomical constituents of the nervous system were understood. The Sushumna seems to be in the exact place occupied by the spinal chord and the Ida and Pingala are similarly located along the main sympathetic nerves. Each chakra appears to have a corresponding nerve plexus (bundles of nerve tissue which control respective areas of the body and the internal organs they contain).[19]

Dr. Motoyama summarizes:

> We have proved conclusively that the human is more than a body and a limited intellect. He possesses non-physical properties and energies that are still largely unknown and uncharted by traditional science. Man has three bodies, the physical, the astral and the causal, which overlie and interpenetrate each other. Each level of

the human's three beings is sustained by the energy of that dimension. More refined matter is to be found in the higher dimensions. . . . The forces we are dealing with are so far removed from what we regard as the material world that they will completely revolutionize physics and philosophy and bring about a profound change in humanity's perception of reality.[20]

René Guénon was fully aware of these forces and of Vedanta's tantric teachings on the role of kundalini in the higher evolution of human beings. But in extending his understanding to cover a far wider field of enquiry—the spiritual nature and evolution of the planet itself—he was well before his time. Not only did he anticipate the revolutionary changes in understanding of which Dr. Motoyama speaks and that are now rapidly escalating, but he has been able to sow seeds in what is today still virgin ground in the earth sciences.

A Frenchman who died in Cairo in 1957, Guénon moved in Parisian intellectual circles contemporaneously with George Gurdjieff and Nicholas Roerich at the height of the great revival of French occultism, and entered Islam at the age of twenty-six. Steeped in Islamic and Sufi mysticism, he later settled in Egypt and married into the family of a Sufi sheik. His breadth of esoteric learning was immense and catholic, for he was also deeply versed in the Cabalistic-Hermetic tradition of the European post-Renaissance and has added considerably to our understanding of the symbology underlying not only Islamic teachings but those of all the major religious traditions. He did not disclose his sources, but since Northern Africa is the site of a very old and prestigious center of tantric Sufism based on practical Cabala, which has led to the establishment there of a modern school of Sufi symbology, presumably access to the secrets of the Egyptian tradition contributed to his deep and unusual insights. Certainly as an elitist and traditionalist who had studied great French esotericists like Fabre d'Olivet he owed little to Theosophy, which in his critique of the movement he disavowed as a parvenu "pseudo-religion," declaring somewhat testily that Madame Blavatsky's conception of the "Great White Lodge" in Asia was "quite simply a caricature or imaginary parody of Agarttha."[21]

Both in France and Egypt, Guénon moved among members of old

esoteric societies that had kept alive the small flame of enlightenment in the Western hemisphere throughout centuries of persecution, and shared their dedication to the ideal of a brotherhood and community of religions free of intolerance. For although Sufism was affiliated with Islam from the time of Muhammad onward, it was far older than Islam and was, as Lady Drower says in her study of an Iraqi dervish sect, "always suspected of pantheism and of cherishing ancient faiths."[22] In its more esoteric quarters it does indeed contend that mystical experience transcends all the religions, going beyond them and uniting all in a brotherhood of the spirit.

Accordingly, Guénon believed the proper function of Sufism was one of synthesis, and in his exposé of Shambhala-Agarttha called into play the symbolism of all the religions, drawing especially on the Taoist and Hindu-Buddhist tantric conceptions of the Axis Mundi as the uniting principle of the cosmos. All religions, he said, arise out of one primordial and universal wisdom preserved in its uncorrupted state in Shambhala, and all lead back to that source, which itself owes its being to an ultimate energy not yet discovered by science. He called it the Eternal Light, an energy that is outside space and time but that manifests in this terrestrial world as kundalini shakti, and that in its terrestrial form abides at the center of Shambhala as Meru, the World Axis.

Guénon made clear his reluctance to publicize his ideas, but wrote that the urgency of the times must be his justification for lifting at least a corner of the veil on the mystery of Shambhala—a mystery that has been compounded by the secrecy cast over the very existence of this Asiatic Wisdom center. Because of the dangerous potential of ultimate energy, he judged that concealment of its existence has always been necessary, but nevertheless foresaw that a collective awakening of the race was imminent and must be prepared for. In making his disclosures to prepare humanity for its awakening, he put forward what must surely be one of the most astonishing theories of modern times: that besides the two axes of the earth of which we are aware, the spin axis and the magnetic axis, there may be a third that we have not yet discovered which traditional societies knew as the World Axis.

Guénon considers the principles governing the organization of the human body to apply equally to the planet and the whole of the universe. The earth too has a spiritual energy body subtending the physical one and circuits of kundalini analogous to those in the human body. It too has a chakric system, a spinal axis and a central conduit of primal energy running through it in concentrated form. He likens Shambhala-Agarttha to a major earth chakra, and describes it as a subtle accumulator or magazine of immense spiritual power locked in the earth's center in the same way that kundalini in its latent state is locked into the root chakra at the base of the human spine. And precisely as the subtle central path of kundalini, the sushumna, runs within the human spinal cord from the root chakra to the supreme plexus in the crown of the head, so Mount Meru represents the central duct called the Brahma Nadi that carries within the earth's sushumna its great current of life-energy.

Moreover, the nature of this primal energy that feeds the human system from its lowest chthonic centers to its highest centers of wisdom and altruism is the same as that found in the earth, according to Guénon. Terrestrial kundalini is not a blind mechanical force like electromagnetism. It lies behind electromagnetism, an intelligent and purposive psychospiritual power that seeks to express itself in every dimension of the forms it creates, potentiating both the life of the body and the life of the soul. It is, so to speak, the common root of all the physical, biological, psychic and parapsychical forces in the universe; it gives rise to all of them. Mount Meru, then, symbolizes a kind of generative organ in the body of the earth, a reservoir of concentrated psychospiritual life-force presently hidden in Asia under conditions that are proof against depredation, even as the muladhara chakra is hidden in the human body, and has the same creative and potentiating function. In his own extremely condensed and cautious fashion, Guénon strove to convey this ancient metaphysic in much of his work.

He redefined the nature of the planet away from the matter-dominated philosophy of the nineteenth century, and in this again he was before his time. Like some of our foremost modern physicists, for him gross material reality is figurative, a mere facade of signs and symbols denoting underlying energy patterns that constitute the deeper reality, and the earth as we know it is therefore merely symbolic of the earth as it really is. It is not simply a rotating mass of rock and plasma, but Gaia herself, a living astral being essentially spiritual, intelligent, nurturing and in some sense sentient, with an inner energy body like our own, having a similar bipolar structure, a similar system of energy vortices or chakras extending beyond the physical frame, and in general all the properties, propensities and laws pertaining to its human counterpart.

The Amerindian Medicine Wheel: The Seventh Gate

The medicine wheel of the Amerindian shaman is in effect a microcosm of Shambhala that illustrates in a primitive way its relationship to the psychospiritual central principle. Lesley Crossingham is a North American Indian who has been taught the use of the medicine wheel in the Cree and Blackfoot tribes of Alberta. She says that "the little star-people," small, three-fingered, large-eyed folk, brought all the North American peoples the gift of the medicine wheel, and that archaeologists, digging down, have found these ancient stone circles superimposed on each other to a great depth in the earth, showing they have been in continuous use for thousands of years, a source of wisdom and natural knowledge to the tribes throughout that time. Other scientists, she claims, have studied the wheels and say they indicate the rising patterns of stars and constellations.[23]

The shaman is well aware that kundalini exists in the energy body of the earth as it does in his own chakras and employs the principle of correspondence to create in an entranced state a vortex of terrestrial kundalini that will put him in touch with the cosmos. He does so by first of all marking out on the ground a medicine wheel consisting of two circles, one within the other, and the four quarters of the globe: north, south, east, west. Next, by invoking the energies of the tutelary gods of the four directions, he is empowered to move from the outer circle into the inner, where he next invokes the energies of the vertical axis of his mandala: that is, the two further directions of space, one upwards towards the heavens, the other downwards into the depths of the earth. This centering ritual enables him to activate the wheel by appropriate shamanistic invocations which align his consciousness to the seventh gate, the sacred spiral in the center.

The sacred spiral winds around the vertical axis. The source of healings, oracles and psychophysical manifestations, it is terrestrial kundalini in a concentrated form, a shaktic phenomenon; a pillar of primal energy, of invisible light shaped like a cone or a mountain, which unites the shaman's inner world to the outer cosmos. Connecting his entranced consciousness to the entire cosmic spectrum, it puts him in touch with the energies of the stars above, the earth beneath and his own deeper psyche. It is in fact the same dynamic principle in miniature that is found at the center of Shambhala.

The Amerindian mandala with its six gates—the seventh being the shaman's heightened consciousness, the key to the activation of the whole—is a universal archetype that was once endlessly repeated throughout the religious centers of the ancient world. The peripheral details might differ, but everywhere the underlying configuration has been the same, of which the crucial feature is Meru, the vertical dynamo at the center. Thus wherever temples were erected, the prayers and invocations of the priesthood established the seventh coordinate, the mystical means whereby a sacred pillar of light was maintained above the altar in the middle of the temple. This was the omphalos, which was always situated over a spring of sweet water.

Invisible to all except those with clairvoyance, the pillar of light was regarded as the seed of life in concentrated form, the holy spirit that brought everything into manifestation and right organization, and therefore the essential center of every human enterprise. Accordingly, every settlement, city, temple and nation was ceremonially founded by reference to the sacred "mountain" at its center, which was duly symbolized by a navel stone, menhir, or perpetually burning torch.

The above examples of traditional religious and animistic customs entailing the conjuration of magical power are almost all we have to help us visualize a feature of Shambhala that has never been openly declared. As has been said, the energizing principle at the center that "makes the wheel turn" has always been a taboo subject, permitted into the public domain only when veiled in metaphor. Hence until the most recent decades the mass of mythological literature on the subject of the cosmic mountain and humanity's endless search for it remained a puzzle for which no key was ever found until Guénon offered it.

He was the first occultist to break the taboo and put forward the concept of terrestrial kundalini as the real meaning of Mount Meru, although he did so cautiously and with due safeguards. He evidently wrestled with his conscience over disclosing in print as much as he did of what was at the time of writing, over sixty years ago, forbidden esoteric material because of its potential abuse by militaristic powers. But he believed the end of the age was in sight, bringing with it a period of optimal instability for the planet, and that humanity would therefore soon be in need of a greater understanding of its world.

His presentiment has been fully borne out. Sixty years on, our need for spiritual information, particularly about the planet, has become urgent as ecological problems multiply. As though in response, pioneers of the New Age movement like David Spangler and John Michell, freed from the trammels of occult security, have been able to bring the earth's energy body into much sharper focus.

Thus Spangler, the Findhorn philosopher of the seventies, says that the earth is surrounded by its etheric field or vital body, which can receive energies flowing through the cosmos or from higher dimensions of vibration and transform these energies into qualities capable of nourishing and vitalizing the denser matter of the physical level. The etheric field, then, is the source of the basic, primal creative energy from which the physical forms are built and from which they are sustained in being.[24] He is in fact describing what a Buddhist sage would call more generally the earth's vajra body or light body. Spangler believes that psychospiritual energy is not confined to the human body, but that the individual body is analogous to the etheric field around the earth. The latter also possesses cosmic energy centers as does the human body.

"This field," he says, "is criss-crossed with lines of power flow, just as a country may be criss-crossed by high-tension electric lines. Seen clairvoyantly, from one level, this network of lines gives the impression of being a web, hence the phrase, 'the etheric web of power'. . . Cosmic Power Points receive energy from universal sources and transform them to planetary requirements."[25] And because of the correspondence between human and planetary etheric fields, ancient adepts and initiates who had knowledge concerning them were able to use the cosmic power points to establish their own centers of spiritual radiance.

So much is now becoming more widely accepted. Yet the revelation that the earth is limned by lines and loci of subtle power flow is surely but the beginning of its hidden story. The many allusions found in occult literature to the magnetic currents and chakric power points in the earth have said nothing about a unifying arterial system of which they are a part; nor have they related such a system to the mysterious *Axis Mundi* so often cited without further qualification. And so if we are to grasp the meaning of the latter and its relation to Shambhala, we must return again and again to René Guénon and to the traditional sources, some of great antiquity, on which he has drawn. For Guénon is not so much an innovator as an expositor and interpreter of a system of thought so old, so abstract and so well guarded that few have known of its existence. As a consequence, there is possibly no ancient doctrine so little understood today.

A TRAFFICWAY OF ANGELS

According to the Hindu Kurma Purana, an island called Sweta-dvepa, or White Island, lay in the northern sea, the paradisial homeland of great yogis possessed of supreme wisdom and learning. The Gobi Desert, says Tomas, is the bottom of this inland sea and the island is now a cluster of high mountains rearing up from the barren and stony seafloor. A Russian explorer named N. M. Prjevalsky recounted more than a century ago an old Mongolian legend regarding this Isle of Shambhala. "Another very, very interesting tale," he said, "concerns Shambhaling—an island lying far away in the northern sea. Gold abounds in it [as it does in the Altai mountains], corn grows to an enormous height there. Poverty is unknown in that country; in fact Shambhaling flows with milk and honey."[1] Since the Gobi Desert must have been formed, and the inland sea drained, many millennia ago when a cataclysmic climate change throughout Central Asia transformed much of it into the desert and arid steppe known today, the legend of the Isle of Shambhala must be extremely ancient, circulating before the rise of the literate civilizations.

As already noted, Ashe considers the broadly Altaic zone that takes in the Gobi Desert as the most likely one in which to look for an Ancient Wisdom whose rational principles might have later been passed on to India, Greece, China and Egypt. "If we wish to picture Masters or alien visitors, teaching prehistoric humanity and leaving legends behind, this is the most promising place to locate their earthly headquarters,"[2] he asserts. Here in southern Siberia, as indicated by Mesopotamian and Greek sources, may best be found a

Shambhalic or Hyperborean body of doctrine that might have given birth to humanity's intellectual development, providing its earliest conceptions of number, natural law and an ordered and intelligible cosmos: a cosmos, Ashe reminds us, on which all science and rational thought still depend.

He turns to Greece and one of its greatest geniuses, Pythagoras, to illustrate his thesis. Pythagoras, as Ashe says, was the chief founder of Greek philosophy and science, a mathematician of the highest order who taught that "all things are numbers." By this he meant that "by the use of numerical methods—measurement and calculation—we can build up an intelligible, harmonious system of the universe."[3] He discovered the numerical basis of musical octaves and put forward the idea of the atomic basis of matter, which again could be numerically defined. "With this sense of exactitude in nature," says Ashe, "attained by no Greek before, he was able to arrive at the first clear notions of proof, in geometry for instance."[4] There is little doubt that Pythagoras received much of this seminal knowledge from an Altaic source, for he was a devotee of Apollo and was instructed by a Hyperborean teacher called Abaris, who was said to ride through the air on a golden arrow. Arrows as magical vehicles or emblems of magical astral flight are part of Siberian lore to this day.

"Is it absurd," Ashe asks,

> to see these forward strides of the mind as Hyperborean-inspired, whether through continuing actual contact or through the rediscovery of the implications? After all, even a modern shaman . . . has a Cosmos of sorts. His key numbers anatomize the heavens and hells. His central world-tree unifies the realms above and below, bringing everything within the scope of his superior knowledge.[5]

And indeed this prime insight into an ordered universe could have come most readily to a race of shamans who at one and the same time were able to observe, enumerate and record the ordered pattern of the polar stars and the equally ordered and centralized pattern of the human chakric system, and to synthesize their data in what would one day be known as the basis of the Kalachakric science.

Lissner's researches in Siberia have confirmed the truth of the legends that abound concerning the knowledge of astronomy and many other secrets of Nature possessed by the Altaic shaman masters and pole-lords of prehistoric times. He believes that, however degenerate today, the Siberian shaman is heir to a formerly great tradition in which number has always been an integral part of the exploration of the ascending planes of being within and the heavens without. In depictions of him or her in traditional regalia, numerical and zodiacal symbols made of iron are shown dangling from the shaman's costume. But it is the immemorial conception of a cosmic axis, represented by a World Mountain or a World Tree, that is the crucial element in the complex of ideas that regulate the shamanic art and that prompts Ashe to theorize that the shaman's remote Hyperborean ancestors were the true founders of civilization.

WHAT IS THE WORLD AXIS?

In the literature of antiquity the World Axis is never explained in a way that makes sense to the modern mind. We usually assume it to be an attempt by earlier and more primitive cultures to signify the spin axis of the earth, imaginatively extending it to the apex of the sky, where it props up the apparently circling heavens. But this is purely an assumption on our part. The same literature frequently asserts that the World Axis is associated with the center of Shambhala, and therefore it cannot possibly coincide with the earth's spin axis unless Shambhala lies at the North Pole. Nor does its vertical relation to the pole star help us very much, for the pole star shines directly over the North Pole for only a relatively short period in thousands of years. It is scarcely credible either to identify it with the magnetic axis, whose wandering northern pole is currently in Canada and whose electromagnetic currents stream backward towards the earth before the solar wind and would therefore be unable to support the sky as legend requires.

Must we then think of Meru as a third axis of the earth? It would seem so. Guénon calls it the world's omphalos, the hub around which everything turns, the fixed point and unmoving mover at the center of things, the "spiritual pole" and the Invariable Middle, and states that it implies rotational and dipolar magnetic properties that are reflected in the geophysical functions of the two better-known axes, which act as its auxiliaries. He draws attention too to Meru's unique *spiritual* function as an outlet of terrestrial shakti that opens the earth up to higher dimensions, in the same way that kundalini, when it passes through the *brahma-randhra* or fontanelle in the crown of the head, unites with the descending "solar ray," thus raising the consciousness of the yogi to spiritual dimensions beyond the mind and opening him to their down-pouring energies. So too does Meru, escaping earth's gravitational and electro-magnetic fields, connect our planet in a two-way exchange to the spiritual universe.

Guénon therefore does seem to be inviting us to envisage a tri-axial planetary system in which the major axis, emerging in the northern hemi-sphere somewhere in Central Asia, possibly in the Pamirs or the Tien Shan mountains, and in the southern hemisphere somewhere in the vicinity of Eas-ter Island, is a psychospiritual energy current distinguishable from either the spin axis or the magnetic axis; that contributes dynamic balance to the whole; that is free of the earth's pull; and that consequently extends like a giant an-tenna beyond its gravitational and magnetic fields to resonate with enormously high frequencies from star systems in the depths of space.

Let us note here that the concept of a third axis should not be dis-missed out of hand because of being a mere abstraction without the slightest visible or self-evident reality, since the two known axes are equally invisible to the senses. As we know, both the North Pole and magnetic pole are geophys-ical abstractions arrived at only inferentially from observed data and have in themselves no self-evident physical reality: a traveler could learn nothing about them merely from traveling without a compass in Spitzbergen or the extreme north of the Arctic zone. Moreover, they were discovered only when the cli-mate of scientific enquiry, of philosophical motivation, was ripe for it, when the older and more naive worldview had failed to satisfy. We may expect that if the earth sciences ever confirm Meru as a third axis of the earth it will be under similar conditions of psychological preparedness and the practical need to understand more fully the mysterious processes of Mother Earth.

Guénon's work shows us that the belief in a tri-axial cosmography has been hidden by means of various codes and ciphers in the world's sacred texts, for he traces its articulations in his syncretic studies of Taoism, Vedanta and the Cabala, and particularly in the tantric material concealed in passages of the Pentateuch. One of the very few Cabalists to draw attention to the layers of symbolism buried in the Old Testament texts, sometimes to a depth of two or three strata, he throws light on a number of seemingly simple folk legends in the Bible of an edifying or pseudohistorical nature whose true meaning is hidden in numerical codes and skillfully constructed metaphors that follow certain set rules of symbolism. The practice has made the Bible, and in particular its first five books, into a mosaic of baffling and contradictory passages which, left undeciphered, degrade and confuse the general textual sense. Yet given the kind of key Guénon provides, it is a fountainhead of secret cosmological wisdom, as well as containing a record of early Hebrew religious history that is never brought into the public view and is rarely suspected.

Professor Joscelyn Godwin of the Colgate University of New York State, who has written a number of works on mysticism and magic, comments that "when Kabbalists analyse the Pentateuch, breaking down the words into their numerical equivalents, they find metaphysical and cosmological doctrines concealed in the very letter of the Law. . . . This suggests that whoever wrote those earliest Hebrew Scriptures was already adept at understanding and concealing the most profound knowledge."[6] And in the *Essene Odyssey*, Dr. Hugh Schonfield, author of the best-selling *Passover Plot*, cites a number of secret codes used in the Bible, among which is one of an alphabetical nature known as the Atbash cipher, which is used in the Book of Jeremiah and the Dead Sea Scrolls.[7]

In illustration of his axial thesis, Guénon discloses another type of code in the Genesis story of Jacob's Ladder, which he shows to be a tantric metaphor whose meaning goes far beyond the overt Hebraic tribal motifs of the period. Obtaining some of his material from the *Jewish Encyclopedia* and the rest from Cabalistic tradition, he interprets on two different levels the folktale about Jacob's famous dream (Gen. 28:11–16); first, as the veiled account of a yogic initiation that gave the Hebrew patriarch a spiritual mandate to found the nation of Israel; and second, at a deeper cosmological level, as a metaphorical description of Meru. The story was inserted into the original text at a late date, probably after the Babylonian exile when most of the Jewish scriptures were compiled, and reflects the mystical Solar doctrines of Zoroaster then influencing Judaism as well as the other religions of the Near East.

On the face of it, the story is simple. It tells how Jacob came in the course of his travels through Canaan to a town called Luz, where he lay down to sleep, his head on a stone, and dreamed of a ladder reaching from earth to heaven. Upon this ladder angels ascended and descended, while at the top was God Most High. "Surely God is in this place and I knew it not!" Jacob cried out in awe on awakening. "This is none other than the house of God, and this is the gate of heaven." And after the event he renamed Luz Beit-el, the House of God, and erected a standing-stone there which he anointed with oil to commemorate the laying of a sacred navel-stone at the absolute center of the new land of Israel. In accordance with initiatic convention, Jacob's name was later changed to Israel, meaning "elevated, princely," even as his grandfather Abram's name had been changed to Abraham.

Abraham, it will be remembered, was the merchant patriarch who traveled with his flocks and his many clan members from Babylonia into Canaan, where he was initiated by Melchizedek, the priest-king of Salem, into the worship of El or Elyon, God Most High.[8] Guénon refers to this mysterious hierophant as the type of a Son of the Sun from Central Asia and a prophet of the highest rank.[9] The time was probably around the early part of the second millenium B.C., when new prophetic teachings were spreading into the Near East, bringing with them high Solar doctrines and practices from beyond the Caucasus mountains. It was a religious innovation whose limited form of monotheism was to raise the simple tribal faith of the Hebraic pastoralists into a great prophetic tradition.[10] The same Indo-Aryan influence brought to Egypt and Lebanon new yogic techniques, a new science of the spirit and a new impetus to civilization that further influenced Israel.

According to esoteric tradition, it was through his meeting with Melchizedek that Abraham received the Cabala and founded a new spiritual lineage, and the story of his grandson Jacob therefore continues the same theme of dynastic and religious empowerment whereby his people were to be unified into a nation. But since in those days no king could be crowned, no town built, no nation founded without a mandate from heaven accompanied by the necessary initiatic rituals, Jacob's dream may be interpreted as a symbolic account of just such an auspicious and holy event.

But occult symbology suggests it was more, much more; that it was also a cryptogram written in the secret language of the brotherhoods enshrining the mystical cosmology of practical Cabala. Encapsulating the spiritual knowledge poured out upon Jacob during his night of initiation, even as it had been poured out upon Abraham, the story was, Guénon suggests, a record in code of the highest metaphysical teachings of the Jewish race.

The name of the town Luz provides the key. Traditionally, this town of Luz that became Beit-el (i.e., Bethel), the site of a very ancient Israelite shrine, had a number of very enigmatic features. Some legends have said that, like Agarttha, it was an underground city near a sacred mountain called the "abode of immortality"; that, again like Agarttha, the Angel of Death could not enter it and had no power over it; that an almond tree, named *luz* in Hebrew, grew near it, a hollow in its roots leading down to the underground center; and that it was sometimes called the Blue City, blue being the celestial color associated with the meridional face of Meru. Guénon implies that here, embodied in an ancient mythology, we are glimpsing in yet another guise the archetypal mountain/tree/cave complex symbolizing Shambhala.[11]

The real significance of the town of Luz, he said, is that it corresponds in planetary terms to the lowest of the seven chakras in the human nervous system, the muladhara chakra, whose Cabalistic name in Hebrew is *luz*. The name derives, like the name Agarttha, from a root word denoting everything covered, enveloped, concealed, secret and silent, and has acquired its esoteric connotation from the fact that in the ordinary way luz means an almond or almond tree, and also a kernel, which is the inmost, most hidden and enclosed part of the almond, even as the seat of kundalini is the most hidden and enclosed part of the muladhara chakra. The esoteric meaning of *luz* is therefore that of a kind of egg or embryo or kernel of the immortal nourished in darkness. And the kernel, says Guénon, "also gives rise to the idea of inviolability that is found in the name Agarttha."[12]

More specifically, luz is the Hebrew name given to an indestructible organ in the subtle body symbolized by a very hard bone (here Guénon probably means the sacral bone), which lies at the base of the spine and which holds the germ of life containing all the elements necessary for human existence. After death the subtle body remains attached to the luz and so provides the channel whereby the individual can be reconstituted. This restoration will "operate under the influence of a 'celestial dew' [the shakti] to revivify the dry bones";[13] for as the kernel contains the germ and the bone the marrow, so the *luz* contains the renewing, reincarnating principle that is immune to death. And everything that is said about the luz can be said of Shambhala-Agarttha. The imperishable luz is the "kernel of immortality," even as Meru is the "abode of immortality"; "there stops in both cases," says Guénon, "the power of the Angel of Death."[14]

According to his interpretation, the stone on which Jacob rested his head symbolized the lowest chakra, the "earth-center," which is opened by initiation into Kundalini yoga, and the ladder symbolized the sushumna, the subtle conduit up which the awakened kundalini ascends, passing from the physical pole at the root of the body to the divine pole at its crown, where deity dwells; and the angels symbolized the movements of higher consciousness whereby the new man was divinized. "What seems to come out of this," Guénon concludes, "is that the given position of the *luz* in the lower part of the body . . . compares to the location of the supreme spiritual center in the underground world."[15]

He is saying that as the microcosm is, so is the macrocosm. As the sushumna is in the human body so Meru is in the earth's; its *merudanda* or axial-staff, its central path of shakti. Jacob's Ladder is in effect an archetype that applies equally to the human being, to the planet, to the solar system and the galaxy, and quite probably the universe. And so the story, couched in biblical shorthand, is about an initiation; it recounts how Jacob received his vision in an underground place, as was customary in the Mystery schools of the time, how his level of attainment was the divine world, indicating a high grade of adepthood, and how his ascension of consciousness was up the world's sushumna, the trafficway of angels and devas and the divinities who belong to the kingdom above our own. The story is telling us too that the World Axis is closely associated with the religious function in human beings, and that it is accessible anywhere in the world to those in a receptive state of consciousness.

But Jacob's model of the world was not ours. The great Ladder of Being he saw ascending to the stars revealed its presence to eyes that were subject to a collective cosmography still fluid and ensouled. Like the unknown Exilic prophet who inserted the story so deftly into the old Hebrew records, Jacob subscribed to a geography of the world not yet immovably fixed in a three-dimensional frame; it was still transparent to its spiritual matrix; it was still alive.

THE EARTH'S CHAKRIC SYSTEM

"Viewed from the distance of the moon," writes Lewis Thomas in *The Lives of a Cell,* "The astounding thing about the earth, catching the breath, is that it is alive. . . Aloft, floating free beneath the moist gleaming membrane of bright blue sky, it is the only exuberant thing in this part of the cosmos. . . . It has the organized, self-contained look of a live creature, full of information, marvellously skilled in handling the sun."[16]

This view of the earth as a beautiful living being is one that ethnic races have intuitively always held and that they are now finding ways of communicating to the dominant Western race. As they become more keenly aware of the vitality and value of their own spiritual traditions that elevate Mother Earth to divine status, and are increasingly articulate about them, they are bringing into ever-clearer focus the poverty of the western concept of the planet as a dead and inorganic thing hurtling blindly round the sun without purpose, without soul, surrounded only by a thin film of equally purposeless life-forms ruled by chance. Moreover, the stability of native traditions, which have survived and successfully served the earth's ecology for countless thousands of years, is increasingly reminding Western science of its mortality; is increasingly stressing that by comparison its clockwork conception of Mother Earth is only two hundred years old and fragile and already threatened, and that it may well be no more than a momentary aberration in the vast span of human history.

Before the seventeenth century and even as late as the eighteenth century, the nature of the planet was universally assumed to be similar to the organic and spiritual nature of man himself, and this was especially the case in esoteric circles from Pythagoras onward. Gnostic-Hermetic initiates like Iamblicus, Porphyry, Paracelsus, Fludd and many others who spent their lives in pre-Renaissance and Renaissance times studying the hidden principles of Nature paid homage to the earth as a great being infused with spirit which consciously cradled and nurtured humanity in its epic journey to God. Vasilius Valentinus, an alchemist of the Middle Ages, said, "The earth is not a dead body, but is inhabited by a spirit that is its life and soul. This spirit is life, and it is nourished by the stars, and it gives nourishment to all the things that shelter in its womb."[17]

Similarly, John Michell says that in the eyes of the philosophers of the ancient world, "the earth was a living creature and its body, like that of every other creature, had a nervous system within and relating to its magnetic field."[18] This terrestrial nervous system with its flowing and spiralling electromagnetic lines of *yin-yang* force was once the subject of a universal geomancy, a science of spiritual engineering called *feng shui* by the Chinese, by means of which vast tracts of populous and cultivated land stretching from the Far East to Africa were surveyed and landscaped in harmony with the movements of the earth spirit. By this method regions now desolate and depopulated were once induced to yield rich harvests to a dense and thriving population of neolithic farmers.

"They grew corn on the sides of hills which we now never attempt to stir," said William Cobbett in his early nineteenth-century travels, as he observed the ramparts and terraces of neolithic cultivators all over the deserted downlands of southern England.[19]

Geomancy of this order was probably a lower branch of the science that produced the network of holy places reported by Michell. Whole countrysides were remodeled and transformed by the diviner's art into landscapes of great beauty and agricultural utility, as can be seen to this day in China, Britain and Africa: shrines, temples, farmhouses, churches, market-towns, pyramids, cities, palaces and avenues of communication were all sited according to geographical arrangements that followed the arteries of electrical and magnetic subterranean influence, and so were standing stones, burial mounds, defensive earthworks, wells and other works of prehistoric communities around the globe. And conversely, the pattern of these structures laid out on the earth's surface in some way no longer accessible to us modified the flow of subtle forces within the earth, so that a two-way exchange and transformation of energies was effected that benefited both humanity and the planet.[20]

In *The Rebirth of Nature*, the biologist Rupert Sheldrake points out that the profaning of the natural world was taken to its ultimate conclusion in the seventeenth century, when feng shui became obsolete, at least in the Western hemisphere:

> Through the mechanistic revolution, the old model of the living cosmos was replaced by the idea of the universe as a machine. According to this new theory of the world, nature no longer had a life of her own; she was soulless, devoid of all spontaneity, freedom and creativity. Mother Nature was not more than dead matter, moving in unfailing obedience to God-given mathematical laws.[21]

There are signs that the vitalist philosophy that became obsolete with the industrial revolution is now reviving. Nevertheless, the concept of a terrestrial life-force implicit in geomantic practice remains an amorphous and ill-defined idea at the outer bounds of scientific credibility, despite the green revolution and the valuable work done in the field by ecologists like James Lovelock. And this is because of our closed model of the world; because science has no workable theory about an ultimate causal energy emanating from an overarching Divine Presence in the universe. With its exclusion of a divine *dynamis* from the world, the central principle underlying feng shui has no meaning for science and with the best will in the world cannot be put to work.

The nature of the spirit that animates the earth, "subtle, omnipresent, yet ever indefinable in terms of the dimensions apparent to our senses," says Michell,

> forms the ultimate problem for modern physicists as it did for their predecessors, the magicians. . . . Yet we can be certain that this force, formerly identified with the holy spirit, provided the power and inspiration by which the ancient civilization was sustained. . . . It was held to be what some now call the life-essence, the pervading flow with which at death the spirit becomes merged, and from which arises the vital spark that stimulates new growth.

Its names are legion. It is the *prana* or *mana* of eastern metaphysics, the "vril," the universal plastic medium of occultists, the *anima mundi* of alchemy.[22]

Wilhelm Reich called it the orgone force, the Chinese call it *qi* or *chi* and understand its causal relation to all other forces.

"Chinese philosophy," says Paul Dong, an American-Chinese author writing on paranormal phenomena in mainland China, "holds that qi is the primal matrix of creation from which springs the *yin* and *yang* forces that give rise to substance and material forms . . . and thus a master of qi is one who controls the very forces of life. Such a person can perform feats that are truly paranormal."[23]

In Guénon's view, the vast network of terrestrial magnetic and electrical currents which the Chinese call respectively blue dragon and white tiger lines is analogous to the Indian system of *nadis* in the human body and is similarly fed by the main artery of terrestrial kundalini that runs like a great unifying spine through the planet. There are power centers other than Meru scattered about the globe: Mount Athos, Mount Shasta, Mount Kailas, Arunachala and others; but these Guénon regards as auxiliaries of the main power center in Shambhala, even as the large nerve centers in various limbic parts of the human body are auxiliaries of the central nervous system.

The idea of an energetic correspondence between the human and planetary systems has also been voiced by Lyall Watson, a naturalist, anthropologist and archaeologist, who discusses the harmony between the two systems in terms that suggest their synchronization of activity. "Earth's magnetic field," he writes, "fluctuates between eight and sixteen times per second. The predominant rhythm of our brains lies in the same area."[24] Learning that at sunrise in many parts of the world there is a unique electromagnetic transmission, he notes: "We find that frequency associated with physiology. . . . Our systems, both planetary and personal, are governed by the same timekeeper."[25]

According to the ancient cosmology, that synchronization was rendered possible because one universal energy gave rise to the multiplicity of all known energies, all known phenomena, whether organic or inorganic, meaningfully relating every part of the universe to every other part. Guénon's worldview rests on the same unitive principle. He sees the universal energy as synergistic, as outside the entropic processes of the cosmos and knowable only indirectly by reference to its reflected properties in spacetime. Whether we call it Kundalini, Divine Light, Holy Spirit, Shekinah or Great Life-Force—and he uses all these names in turn from the roll call of religions—it is conceived of as superordinal to all else, a power inhering at the center of all phenomena in a zone of absolute reality, absolute being and transcendental radiance that lies beyond them, yet informs them all. That power, Guénon believes, not only radiates out from the center of Shambhala, inspiring and sustaining its communities, but also plays an unsuspected central role in the life of the planet as a whole, which cannot be understood without it.

GAIA: THE EARTH AS A LIVING ORGANISM

Guénon's conception is a grand one that dignifies the earth with life, consciousness and soul. In every essential it accords with James Lovelock's Gaia hypothesis, although it goes much further. As is well known, Lovelock, a British biologist, has graced the earth with the beautiful name of Gaia after the ancient Greek earth-goddess, on the grounds that she is intelligent and purposive, "a super-organism, a living being of planetary proportions"[26] who, like all organisms, is self-organizing and capable of maintaining her own life and well-being.

In *The Ages of Gaia*, published in 1988, he conceived of the planet as an integrated whole, a mothering web of life in which the organism and the environment interact and evolve symbiotically so as to form a single living entity, each part cooperating with every other part to promote a continuation and evolution of more life. All the planet's self-regulating mechanisms, he believed, point to this conclusion. The stability of the atmosphere over millions of years despite its unstable and reactive gases, the maintenance of an even temperature despite the sun's growing heat, and the earth's apparent ability to select, out of others equally possible, just the right climatic conditions and chemical constituents for the continuing health of its life-forms, points to the inherently living and purposive nature of our globe.[27]

Lovelock has come under a lot of criticism for his unorthodox views in scientific circles, and he has now modified his position. In 1990 his fellow-biologist, Rupert Sheldrake, referred to him as the leading proponent of the hypothesis that the Earth is a self-regulating living organism; but in a more recent essay (1996) by Don Michael in Jim Swan's *Dialogues With the Living Earth*, a footnote states that Lovelock now says Gaia *acts* like a living organism, not *is* one. Noting that the earth "has a tendency to produce stability, and to survive," he explains, "I needed to show that the stability emerges from the properties of the system, not from some purposeful guiding hand."[28]

No doubt there are many who regret Lovelock's reformulation, which seems to deny Mother Earth anything more than a robotic nature—if such a thing can be conceived without a guiding intelligence to motivate it. However, he has already done his work in sowing valuable seeds that can be further cultivated by others. Scientists, like Sheldrake, continue to search for a viable formula by which to express their vision of Gaia as a living, goal-directed organism. Especially since the physicists' formulation of the Unified Field Theory, the pressure to redefine the earth in holistic terms, as an animate and organismic biosphere, has steadily increased.

But as has been said, Guénon, faithful to the ancient Cabalistic-Hermetic tradition, goes further. The earth, he contends, is not only alive; it is a spiritual being, as man is. On the subtle plane it too has an inner body of light, a vajra body. It too is highly evolved, with something like the equivalent of our phylogenetic structure, the equivalent of a spinal cord, of a sympathetic nervous system and of a cortical governing center even as the human central nervous system has; and therefore Mother Earth operates under the same self-governing and self-maintaining evolutionary principles as are evident in human beings.

A Psycho-spiritual Model of the Natural World

Such a spiritual vision of the earth, implicit though it was in Lovelock's Gaia theory, brings into the open much more sharply the whole question of higher powers in the universe and the vitalist and purposive nature of evolution, issues that are already exercising the physical and biological sciences and bringing Darwinism, at least as originally propounded, under intense scrutiny. As Sheldrake says, what is at stake are fundamental models or paradigms of reality. Are we bonded to a living Nature and to her organic and regulatory goals? Are there self-determining, intelligent and cooperative soul-qualities at the heart of living things, or are we and all other life-forms the product of randomly directed physical and chemical interactions in the environment (as most scientists still believe), the denizens of a mechanical universe ruled by the blindly competitive will to survive at the expense of all others? Where does the truth lie?

The esoteric conception of a psychospiritual energy core to the earth—its soul or organizing principle—presents a serious challenge to all the contemporary theories of either Darwinism or Creationism, and completely overturns the mechanistic approach most biologists bring to bear on the development of the biosphere and its life-forms, including that of humanity itself. It tells us that determinism exists, but that creative freedom transcends it. Chance exists, but is not at the helm of evolution; a divine Presence exists in the universe, but is itself evolving through the medium of its created forms. There is room for natural selection, yet in the broad view evolution is driven by intelligence, conscious benevolence and the will to joy, to perfection, to harmony with the whole, even though these higher drives take forms that are beyond our limited range of experience. The whole of creation, in other words, may be seen as a spiritual undertaking involving many different subsidiary levels of organization, each one valid within its limited frame of reference. The physical world lies within that organizational spectrum, but on its lowest level; there it has reality, but reality of a kind increasingly limited by the levels above it.

The Unified Field: Is Dark Matter Kundalini?

To sum up, the Cabalistic-Hermetic tradition as interpreted by Guénon proposes that the earth's cortical governing center is situated in Shambhala and that the Hierarchy headquartered there is the monitor of both human and planetary evolution, since the two are inseparably joined. Moreover, the theory recognizes what has been clear for a long time to thoughtful people, that if a congruent relationship exists between organisms and the natural environment that supports them it must be because of a common factor, an implicit link-term. That factor is understood to be shakti, the fundamental formative energy of the universe that flows in its kinetic form equally through all its creations, organizing and vivifying the earth as it does the biosphere, yet remaining forever apart: a plenum inexhaustible, unknowable.

This is a very important concept in today's scientific climate, for it resonates to a remarkable degree with the physicist's discovery of dark matter. Dark matter, it is found, makes up ninety to ninety-nine percent of the whole universe, yet apart from its powerful gravitational effects its constitution is utterly unknown, being unlike any kind of matter with which physicists are familiar. The discovery of this massive shadowy presence beneath the visible universe is bringing some scientists to the brink of a new organic conception of the universe that may be more consonant with esoteric theory as propounded by metaphysicians like Guénon. Astronomers, a scientific writer reports, "have slowly, reluctantly recognized a darker, more passive presence beneath the pale film of the visible universe" which may one day, through the contractive pull of gravitation, bring the universe to an end "in fiery and terminal splendour."[29] It is obvious that this ocean of dark matter within which we all live bears a close resemblance to environmental kundalini; and indeed Sheldrake seems to say something of the sort.

Equating the traditional concept of the soul of the earth with its purposive organizing principle, he asserts that "in modern evolutionary physics, the old idea of the soul of the universe has been replaced by the idea of the primal unified field, from which the known fields of physics arose and of which they are aspects. Likewise the soul of the Earth may best be thought of as the unified field of Gaia."[30] Through this field, dark matter shapes the way in which everything develops. Sheldrake continues: "Since these dark particles scarcely interact with familiar material things, with our senses or with our instruments, they are by their very nature elusive. They are all around us without our knowing it. Their possible properties are still a matter of speculation."[31] Yet through the universal gravitational field dark matter has shaped the development of the universe, even as kundalini shakti gives birth to the worlds.

Discussing this invisible cosmic ocean, Sheldrake even invokes the name by which Hindus address the great causal womb of being: Maha-Kali, Mother of Space and Time. This dark matter, he says, "has the archetypal power of the dark destructive Mother; it is like Kali, whose very name means 'black.'"[32] It recalls the ocean of infinite creative power that Indian sages call *adhar shakti* or basic shakti, "on whom," says Gopi Krishna, a modern Indian mystic and yogi, "depends the existence of the body and the universe, the microcosm and the macrocosm";[33] and it recalls too the Hindu belief that at the end of every great aeon Brahma destroys the universe by recalling it into his undifferentiated substance, there to rest until the next act of creation.

Clearly modern physics and Yoga Tantra are converging on an elucidation of the great mystery that preoccupies contemporary thought; that is, the source of the universe and the natural order. But whether the physical sciences can succeed in the enterprise without recognizing, as Yoga Tantra does, a hierarchy of planes of existence beyond this one and one universal energy that informs them all is highly problematic.

THE PERFECTION
OF THE SHORTEST PATH

The soul's gradual progress to God in terms of a spiralling pathway up the side of the cosmic mountain, from one spiritual station to the next, is an image common to almost all of the world's mystical systems; but few mention the direct path from the base of the mountain straight up to the summit. Even the Bardo Thodol mentions the direct path only once, and then glancingly, confining itself solely to a description of the soul's circuitous afterlife journey through the heaven-worlds. The shortcut for heroes that bypasses the heaven-worlds or bardos and takes them straight to the divine world—in one lifetime, so it is said—is so well guarded in religious literature that the relevant Tibetan Buddhist texts are written in the "twilight language," a cipher that can be understood only with the help of revelation. It is a subject closely related to that other area of esoteric knowledge concealed until very recently; that is, the World Axis and its current of terrestrial shakti. For that is the course of the direct path.

Our understanding of universal shakti is very young indeed, barely a few decades old and rudimentary in the extreme, and very little material exists to help us. For hundreds of years Kundalini yoga had fallen into disrepute in India and had languished as a discipline, its initiation seemingly lost to the world. It became merely a theoretical abstraction expounded by pundits who had no firsthand comprehension of its workings and who were, therefore, responsible for circulating many erroneous ideas about the kundalini energy.

But during the sixties the ancient Vedantic systems of Siddha yoga and Sahaja yoga came out of retirement to become the first genuinely tantric yogas to offer kundalini-awakening to all in both East and West, and to open up some of the practical secrets of Tantra. The work of these and others of the new Shakti schools, such as the Shinto-Buddhist Mahikari sect, the Indonesian schools of Subud and Sumarah, and the Tibetan Buddhist Vajrayana and Dzog Chen schools, all of which are introducing in their initiations gentler and safer methods of awakening kundalini than were utilized in the past, has led to the opening of new avenues of psychological research into the kundalini phenomenon.[1] As a consequence, we are now learning a great deal more about the evolutionary energy as it applies to human beings. But very rarely is the kundalini concept extended to apply to Mother Earth, as it should be and as was done by early races. Accordingly there is a dearth of information about its wider applications.

Furthermore, it must be said that because kundalini is a proto-psychic, proto-conscious, proto-purposive force that is closer to us than the jugular vein and yet outside our visible continuum, and because its interaction with the would-be observer is unpredictable and peculiarly elusive in its effects, it has remained very difficult to get objective information about it from first-hand experience, and almost impossible in a geophysical context. Terrestrial kundalini, though not unknown, has as a consequence been all too rarely subject to observation. Even in those few cases where scientific observation has been attempted the results have not been notably successful or well understood.

Cosmic Kundalini in Concentration

Someone who explored the possibility of inducing a concentration of the universal energy from the natural environment was Wilhelm Reich. Reich was a Viennese psychoanalyst with a visionary bent who, almost accidentally and in defiance of his scientific and cultural conditioning, arrived at the concept of a universal energy common to both man and the planet via his research into sexual energy in human beings. He called it orgone force and believed this primary creative energy could be accumulated and condensed in such a way that it could be used for the benefit of humanity.

It is a theory not without backing from spiritual sources. Ramakrishna, when explaining the Hindu conception of an avatar, said: "Take the case of an ocean. It is a wide and almost infinite expanse of water. But owing to special causes, in special parts of this wide sea the water becomes congealed into ice. Even reduced to ice it can easily be manipulated and put to special uses."[2] The saint applied his example to the case of a divine Incarnation, but could have applied the principle just as easily in other directions. Likewise the young Indian Avatara Mother Meera, speaking of the Paramatman Light which she brings down for our benefit, says that it has never been *used* before. "Like electricity, it is everywhere, but one must know how to activate it."[3] Like any of the lower energies, it too can be channelled and controlled in a concentrated form by an adept advanced enough to resonate to it. It is what Reich himself believed.

Migrating to America, where he was assisted by an enthusiastic American coterie of well-qualified young medical and scientific researchers, he conducted exhaustive experiments with orgone energy. They revealed, says John Michell, that this energy "is present throughout the universe in every particle of matter, in every area of space. It is in constant flow, ever initiating new cycles of creation, growth and death. Though mass-free and therefore hard to isolate, it provides the medium through which magnetic and gravitational forces manifest their influence."[4]

Believing that the vital energies in people and nature could be stimulated by an increased flow of orgone energy, Reich built a special cabinet called an accumulator. This cabinet, he explained, could accumulate the orgone energy within it by the device of lining the chamber with some inorganic material and then covering it on the outside with alternate layers of organic and inorganic matter—a constructional principle, Michell points out, used by ancient peoples in their building of the mysterious mounds found in Britain and elsewhere. Their use is usually assumed to be for the burial of chieftains, but archaeologists admit their purpose is not really known. Reich declared that his accumulator condensed universal orgone energy out of the environment.

Under special conditions the cabinet was observed to emit a faint blue glow and to grow slightly warmer than the temperature outside. Thus concentrated, the orgone energy was, according to its promoters, shown to be able to help in the healing of cancer and psychological disorders, to change weather patterns, make rain and demonstrate in general that the process of matter-formation apparently continues uninterruptedly in the cosmos. [5]

Here Reich was echoing contemporary scientific theories, for Sir James Jeans, the British astronomer and mathematician, voiced something similar in the early part of the century when he stated in the context of the spiral nebulae that there exist in the universe singular points or centers of creation at which energy from a higher sphere streams into our world from some other spatial dimension, so that to an inhabitant of our universe they appear as points at which matter is continually being created, rather as it appears in the organic world of plants. Jeans' notion has been rather eclipsed by the Big Bang theory, but all occult theory supports it, as do recent astronomical sightings in which about twenty new suns are to be seen coming into existence in the center of the universe. Reich passionately believed in his astrophysical conclusions, and it would seem they have not yet been disproved.

However, his eccentric behaviour and unorthodox experiments, particularly with cancer patients, brought him into a fatal conflict with U.S. authorities. He ended his life in prison, his theories discredited. Yet Colin Wilson, one of his many biographers, regards his extravagant claims for orgone energy as justified in view of the impressive positive evidence the inventor was able to assemble, and that even his most hostile critics—and they were legion—were unable to break down. Wilson believes his claims were so well-substantiated that the charge of self-deception was untenable. Certainly Reich's concept of a universal orgone energy does bear a striking resemblance to terrestrial kundalini, and his experiments suggest that he had unwittingly rediscovered a knowledge of which ancient peoples were once well aware.

Another case, initially more successful and even more interesting, was that of the Czech inventor Robert Pavlita who became well known in the Soviet Union for his unmechanized "psychotronic generators" that concentrated bionic energy from the cosmos and the environment as well as from the force field of human beings. According to observers, so effective were these gadgets that they simulated with one hundred percent reliability every kind of paranormal phenomenon, from psychokinesis to thought reading, as well as producing miraculous physical effects. Sheila Ostrander and Lynn Schroeder, two American journalists with scientific training, attended the Moscow Para-physical Congress of 1968 in which Pavlita demonstrated his inventions, and after observing their performance closely under strictly controlled conditions, the two became convinced that they were witnessing something new and re-markable that upset the known laws of nature; that is to say, they were wit-nessing the operations of an energy as yet unknown to science.

In their book *PSI: Psychic Discoveries Behind the Iron Curtain,* Ostrand-er and Schroeder explained that the conception behind Pavlita's remarkable generators was that there is an energy in human bodies, an electronic bioplas-ma, that can be transferred to nonliving matter. The Chinese call it chi, the Hindus *prana*, the Polynesians *huna* or *mana*, and current medicine calls it psychosomatic energy, but it is the same bio-energy in all cases. The two jour-nalists reported: "Human beings and all living things, say Czech scientists, are filled with a kind of energy that until recently hasn't been known to Western science. This bio-energy . . . seems to be behind psychokinesis; it may be the basis of dowsing. It may prove to be involved in all psychic happenings."[6]

In the experiments Ostrander and Schroeder witnessed at the Con-gress, Pavlita and his daughter stood by the generators and silently charged them with mental energy for several minutes, having explained that the gener-ators' secret lay in their shape. It was the shape that allowed their accumula-tion of bio-energy, which could then be turned to whatever purposes were required. "According to Czech scientists," said the journalists, referring to the Pavlita manifesto, "the psychotronic generators draw this bio-energy from a person, accumulate and use it. Once charged with your energy, the generators can do some of the things a psychic can do."[7]

The generators were observed performing many different tasks accord-ing to their shape and material. One could turn a metal flywheel, another purified polluted water, another accelerated the germination and growth of seeds, while others did the work of psychics. The two authors wrote that this strange energy "could create effects similar to magnetism, electricity, heat and luminous radiation, but was itself none of these. . . . It conducts slower than electricity, but can build up something similar to an electro-static charge . . . and can be conducted by paper, wood, wool, silk and many substances that are electrical insulators."[8]

Since 1968 Western quantum physics has greatly expanded its understanding of the subatomic energy claimed to have been tapped in the Pavlita experiments, exploring its potential in the theory of "zero-point" energy, cosmic vortex theory and David Bohm's theory of multidimensional implicate and explicate orders. But the 1968 Moscow Congress remains an important benchmark in the field because of its psychic orientation. The Czech manifesto presented at the time of the congress called the unknown energy the Third Energy—the bridge between animate and inanimate systems—and emphasized that under scientific investigation it showed itself to be superior to all other forms of energy. In conformity with the laws of transformation, it could apparently reduce to lower forms—electromagnetic, gravitational and other—"in the same way as electromagnetic energy is transformed into corpuscular energy when a gamma ray is traversing a strong nuclear field."[9] This would explain why it is masked behind the grosser energy manifestations derived from it and so escape detection. But most cogently, Moscow scientists admitted that "the mind seems to control this energy," having the ability to concentrate and direct it at will.

In an addendum to their book, Ostrander and Schroeder say that soon after the Moscow Congress, when Czechoslovakia was annexed to the Soviet Union, the Russian military was believed to have taken over the invention and withdrawn it from public notice. Certainly no mention of the Pavlita generators now exists in current scientific or parapsychological literature, so their authenticity cannot be checked. However unsatisfactory the outcome, Pavlita's work, like Reich's, bears out the idea that one universal creative energy underlies human, planetary and stellar life alike, permeating all space and connecting all things to each other, and that it is psychospiritual in nature.

THE UNIVERSAL ENERGY FIELD

More recently, the clairvoyant observations of the physicist and healer Barbara Ann Brennan have made a further contribution to the subject. She frankly equates the universal creative energy—Reich's orgone energy—with the Universal Energy Field discovered by science, stating that it "is always associated with some form of consciousness, ranging from highly developed to very primitive."[10] Composed of energy previously undefined by Western science, it has been known and studied throughout the ages, although each culture has had a different name for it.

According to Brennan:

> Visual [clairvoyant] observations reveal the field to be highly orga-
> nized in a series of geometric points, isolated pulsating points of
> light, spirals, webs of lines, sparks and clouds. It pulsates and can
> be sensed by touch, taste, smell and with sound and luminosity
> perceivable to the higher senses. . . Investigators state that the UEF
> is basically synergistic. . . . the opposite of entropy, a term used to
> describe the phenomenon of the slow decay . . . and breaking-
> down of form and order. The UEF has an organizing effect on
> matter and builds forms. It appears to exist in more than three
> dimensions. Any changes in the material world are preceded by a
> change in this field . . . Some scientists refer to the phenomenon
> of the UEF as bio-plasma.[11]

And she makes mention of its pleromic character as an inexhaustible potentiality, a cornucopia that never diminishes in content however much is poured
out.

All the properties cited by Brennan as belonging to the Universal Energy Field of modern science traditionally belong to terrestrial/cosmic kundalini
and, as she says, have been known to mystics from antiquity. Thus the Upanishads, written about 400 B.C., make many allusions to the divine Shakti in
terms we can readily interpret as describing the dark matter of the Universal
Energy Field.

"Shakti is the root of all that exists," says the Tantra-tattva. "It is out of
Her that the universes are manifested, it is She who sustains them and, at the
end of time, it is in Her that the worlds will be re-absorbed."[12] And again the
Devi-Bhagavata, the hymn to Shakti, declares:

> It is thanks to thy power alone that Brahma creates, Vishnu pre-
> serves, and that Shiva, at the end of time, will destroy the universe.

Without thee they are powerless to fulfill their missions, therefore it is thou who, truth to tell, art the creator, preserver and destroyer of the world.[13]

How long ago the secrets of terrestrial kundalini were discovered we do not know: the Upanishads were themselves compiled from oral traditions incomparably older and dating from a time when human consciousness was far more deeply bonded to the natural world and its subtle energic substructure than it is possible for us easily to imagine today. In the past five thousand years or so our perceptual boundaries have shrunk, effectively excluding any direct awareness of the subtle streaming of creative forces in our environment or of their complex underlying structure; we are imprisoned in three dimensions. We see only the decay of things, the running down of the cosmos and nothing of its underlying causes.

Hindu-Buddhist cosmographies are not so limited. They do not correlate with our own world geography because they were originally mapped by adept-magicians of an earlier age, mystics who perceived shakti directly and included its world-building operations in their conception of the cosmos. And in those cosmographies terrestrial kundalini is concentrated in a great central path through the planet and called Meru.

Meru: A Hindu-Buddhist Mystical Geography

In an ancient Hindu mystical geography closely related to the Tibetan (Figure 5), Meru is identified with the Altai mountains and is presented as a world axis that runs through the core not only of the earth but of the heavens and Pure Lands that lie above and surrounding the earth, though they are not shown on the map.[14] The same world axis, with its jewelled palace of Indra on top, is intended to signify the current of universal Kundalini Shakti streaming through the center of Shambhala and through the successive centers of the heavens above, uniting them all in a single cosmic system.

In his introduction to the Bardo Thodol, the Tibetan Book of the Dead, the Buddhist scholar Dr. W. Y. Evans-Wentz says that the Kalachakric commentaries elucidating this cosmography "suggest far-reaching knowledge, handed down from very ancient times, of astronomy, of the shape and motion of planetary bodies, and of the interpenetration of worlds and systems of worlds, some solid and visible. . . and some ethereal and invisible existing in what we may perhaps call a fourth dimension of space."[15] It is in these invisible higher-dimensional worlds that surround the earth like the layers of an onion about its core that he locates the after-death astral worlds that Tibetans call bardos.

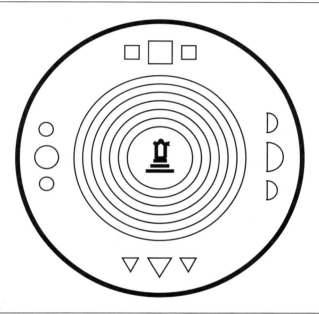

Figure 5. *A Hindu-Buddhist System of Mystical Geography. Mount Meru is in the center, the palace of Indra on its summit. The heaven-worlds are above, though these are not shown on the diagram. Mount Meru is surrounded by seven rings of golden mountains, and in Hindu mythology the southern continent, marked by a triangle, is generally thought to be India. It is flanked by two satellite continents, as are the western, northern and eastern continents.*

He portrays the sacred mountain as an axis through the earth that pierces the highest and subtlest of these heaven-worlds before escaping into cosmic space like a giant antenna. "We may regard the central mountain," he says, "as the universal hub, the support of all the worlds . . . and as the gravitational center of the universe."[16] It is the gateway to the various bardos of the afterworld and is often described in after-death experiences as the tunnel of light each soul must pass through on its journey towards new life.

This geography, so like and yet so unlike our own, has many features we find mysterious and baffling. It has been traced back by prehistorians to the most remote times, and most attribute the naivete they see in the system to its ignorance of true geophysical principles. But the truth is rather that different realities are involved. The cosmography of early man cannot equate with ours because the picture his shamans formed of the world included what they saw clairvoyantly as well as what they based on data acquired in the usual sensory-intellectual way, though it may not in the least have precluded a sophisticated understanding of geophysical principles. Looking up with the inner eye, they saw a spectrum of worlds of progressively finer matter enclosing our earth, and, threaded through them, the mighty path of terrestrial kundalini.

Consequently, the diagram based on a Hindu-Buddhist worldview invites us to look down from interstellar space onto an unfamiliar earth-system that combines our dense physical world with surrounding ones that are composed of increasingly fine astral matter, as well as some that lie within the earth itself and are presumably composed of even denser matter than that with which we are familiar. These are the nether worlds, the hells. All of them—heavens, earth and hells—are held in manifestation by the power of Kundala Shakti.

The system is represented by a Hindu-Buddhist cosmic mandala in which different frequencies of light define by color the various spheres.[17] The three nether bardos beneath the earth are deep red shading into orange, while above them is the golden ring of the earth bardo of human embodiment modulating into the astral realm, the highest level of which shades into silver. These lower planes are ghostly and illusory realms peopled by souls who live in a dream-state, believing it to be reality. For even our apparently solid and real earth-world, including the heaven our religions promise us in the after life, is known to Sufis as *alam-i arwah*, meaning the world of spirits or ghosts. Such astral worlds are unreal in the sense that they are built up of emotional energies or passions which cast a glamour of illusion over the souls that live in them, even as our night-dreams give the illusion of reality, yet are not true.[18] Above the passional worlds are the ascending rings of the subtle mental worlds, the higher heavens or paradises that shade from deep blue to palest blue-white; and even these, glorious though they may be, lie still within the parameters of sleep and illusion to some extent, for the souls that inhabit them have not yet awakened to the World of Truth.

The Sufi metaphysic underlying these ideas will be explored more fully in a later chapter. Suffice it to say here that they involve a closed system insofar as the soul, however far it ascends the spectrum of planes after death, even to the highest paradise, and however long it remains there, must eventually return to the bardo of rebirth on the fourth level and once again suffer the earth's life-death cycle. This is because its only hope of liberation from a field of existence which is not its true home lies in Meru; only if it bypasses the heavens and enters the direct stream of the World Axis can it reach the spiritual universe beyond, where its true destiny lies. Only then can the soul say: "Rebirth is no more. There is no return. Consequently, knowing Meru as the direct path, a lama told Nicholas Roerich: "Verily, only through Shambhala, only through the teaching of the Kalachakra can you attain the perfection of the shortest path."[19]

The commentaries from which Evans-Wentz quotes have been interpreted by Tibetan scholars with varying degrees of accuracy over the centuries, leading to considerable confusion. This was inevitable. For as Evans-Wentz is at pains to convey, the Hindu-Buddhist mystical geography not only combines different orders of worlds, it is also a two-dimensional representation of an earth-centered but multi-dimensional system, and as such can only be a very imperfect approximation of the reality. The fact that shamans, mystics, and some clairvoyants can sometimes gain access to that reality at supersensory levels not possible to normal waking consciousness tends to increase rather than diminish the confusion that is characteristic of everything connected with Shambhala, since there is always a subjective element that affects the geographical coordinates.

All we learn from Khamtul Rinpoche's vision is that he left India behind to the south and flew north for an indeterminate distance towards Shambhala, presumably beyond Tibet. But this information is not enough to answer the many questions that arise from an examination of Figure 5. Is the orientation of the observer north or south? What and where are the four continents said to be floating in an outer ocean? Are they earthly lands or, as some lamas think, separate worlds? What is the significance of the geometrical figures associated with them, and what of the auxiliary figures that flank each one?[20] And is the sacred mountain really in the Altai mountains—or at the North Pole, as Bernbaum suggests? Or in outer space? The lamas give different answers to all these questions, and Bernbaum's own tentative interpretation of the diagram is, he agrees, only one of many.

An Australian Woman's Journey to Shambhala

Perhaps more can be learned about Figure 5 from the unusual psychic experiences a young Western woman had in the early sixties, when the collective consciousness of the West was in general in a spiritually heightened state. In the archives of Dr. Raynor Johnson, an English academic who gathered from all over the world hundreds of firsthand accounts of mystical and paranormal experiences, many of which he included in his book *The Imprisoned Splendour*, there is one, unpublished, from a psychic who called herself simply L. C. W. (Most of Dr. Johnson's correspondents were known only by their initials.) L. C. W. claimed to have had several quite detailed visions of Shambhala and its central noumenon over a period of years.

She wrote:

At the age of 21 I began my attendance at what I came to know simply as Night-School, though I had at that time no idea of its location. After falling asleep I would fly at great speed across the earth to a place in which I joined a throng of other people, all like myself students at Night-School. In a large bare hall with a wooden floor we arranged ourselves in orderly formation and were taken through dance-exercises which later on I recognized as similar to the sacred dervish exercises taught by George Gurdjieff. Our teachers sat on a dais at the end of the hall. After several years of group exercises I was transferred to another grade, where I was taught on my own by a woman who set before me a great book of wisdom. As she turned the pages she explained the spiritual knowledge contained in them. At the end of about twelve years I passed an examination and someone said "Now you have been touched by the sun." To my knowledge I have not returned to Night-School since.

My background was Protestant and very limited, so that at that time I knew nothing about the Masters or eastern religions. But later I began to meditate and read mystical literature. More recently I have had a number of visions as though from outer space in which I have been shown the location of Night-School, somewhat north of western Tibet, and have realized that this must be the place they call Shambhala. I must have attended a Sufi school there and undergone some kind of initiation.

In parenthesis, it may be noted that L. C. W.'s Night-School bears a close resemblance to the astral Halls of Learning mentioned by Alice Bailey's close disciple, Vera Stanley Alder, and which she purports to have visited in an out-of-the-body experience in the company of a guide. "I was astonished to see," she writes,

> many other people journeying in the same way in their astral bodies, their shining life-lines stretching down behind them. . . . We had now passed into a great hall where many of the dreamers were already assembled. They were all earnestly occupied, studying from volumes which they took down from many bookshelves, or being instructed by companions who accompanied them.[21]

In the visions she had during the sixties, L. C. W. reported seeing, somewhere in the Pamirs or the Tien Shan mountains, an immaterial phenomenon associated with Shambhala that looked like a great mast or antenna, or a tree with cross-branches, soaring out of the earth into interstellar space.

I flew towards it and was taken up it into space by an invisible guide. Up close it was a great pillar of pure energy streaming and scintillating with light. Each junction with one of its branches had an opening or gateway into another world. There was a series of such inner worlds, one above the other, and each gateway was marked by a different geometrical figure: a circle, a triangle, a square, a Star of David and so on, written in light and apparently providing numerical keys to the various levels. Far below me to the south was India, to the east China on my right, to the west Turkestan and Russia and to the north Siberia; and each of these countries also had one of the geometrical symbols written above it. I remember that a circle stood over China.

Two sketches are reproduced below to help the reader visualize L. C. W.'s visions: Figure 6 is an elevation of the World Tree as she saw it, and Figure 7 is a plan of the same vision looking down from outer space. It will be observed that the second sketch is simply a modification of the Hindu-Buddhist system of mystical geography, the rings of golden mountains encircling Meru being here shown as Inner Asia, not the North Pole, the four continents being shown as the four lands grouped around Meru at the four cardinal points of the compass, and the geometrical symbols being reallocated according to L. C. W.'s recognition of a circular symbol over China. This alternative arrangement of symbols is in accord with esoteric tradition, which always associates the triangle (the Initiatic Triangle, the Spiritual Trinity) with the north and the pole star rather than with India, as Bernbaum proposes.[22]

Furthermore, the absence from the modern version of the two smaller islands flanking each of the "continents" may detract little from the essential meaning of the symbolism, since it is possible they represent an archaic geographical convention now outmoded. In antiquity, islands and continents did not have the clearly defined meaning they have today. It was customary for any foreign land, landlocked or not, to be called an island, and larger lands were called continents according to the same principle. The geoarchaeologist Eberhard Zanggar gives Egyptian, Greek and Hittite examples to this effect, and it may well be, therefore, that the early Hindus followed the same prac-

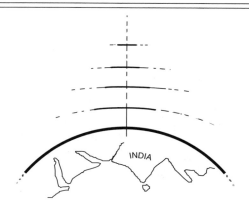

Figure 6. *A clairvoyant view of the World Tree in elevation. Gates to the various heaven-worlds are at the intersections of the axis and its branches.*

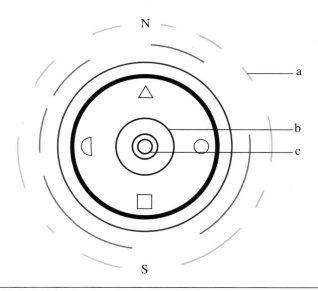

Figure 7. *Another clairvoyant view of the World Tree looking down on the earth from outer space. The diagram shows: a) Heavens b) Mountains of Inner Asia c) World Tree.* △ *Siberia* ○ *China* □ *India* ◖ *Turkestan.*

tice.[23] In that case the islands flanking the four continents in Figure 5 may simply signify that in each case the symbol standing over the premier country applies also to its smaller neighbors on either side.

In any case, in her report L. C. W.'s primary concern was with the nature of the column of spectral energy into which she had been drawn and which she had difficulty describing intelligibly. She said that in that central place inner and outer dimensions converged and became one, so that in the usual sense it was not a place at all. There were no coordinates. Nothing was visible or knowable there except the radiance, from which time and space unfolded as undivided potentialities, as though from seed. A person aligned to it could, she said, go anywhere; into the future or the past, instantly to any spot on the earth or to other dimensions, or out of the solar system altogether. Conversely, she believed souls from other systems in space could enter the earth sphere by the same route, carrying their own spiritual influences with them.

Illustrating the nature of this supernatural zone within the body of the earth, she described how in her vision, in response either to her own thought or her guide's, the central trunk suddenly put out something like a branch or a kind of pseudopod that became a trajectory of light along which she was rapidly carried downward and eastward across the earth, fetching up over China and simultaneously thirty years in the future. From the vantage point above China she was able to view the whole globe and all its continents and receive impressions of the enormous transformation in world conditions that was going to come about by the end of the century and over several centuries to come, ushering in a new evolutionary cycle. Her guide informed her that the earth was presently undergoing a period of major purification in preparation for the great rebirth to come.

In a vision she had about a year later in which a huge cross hung over the tree, L. C. W. saw that, while the gateways to the inner heavens were normally closed to the earth and invisible, they were now open. "The skies were opened one above the other as far up as one could see. The earth was receiving a divine influx from above. It seemed to me a kind of collective initiation," she wrote. And the falling of a cluster of stars from the height of the cross down to earth meant, she was told, that high souls were now coming down to help in the special event.

What was this place that is not a place to which L. C. W. was taken, this time that is before time? It seems to have affinities with the Dreamtime of the Australian aborigines, perhaps with the Hindu's incorruptible realm of pure spirit, the *Parabrahman*; and one recalls the Cabalistic *Ain Soph*, infinite and eternal Being without form, the pleromic region of which the Gnostic Stephan Hoeller says: "It is the ultimate context of transcendence, that which was and is and always will be; timeless, limitless, yet filled with the potential of all time, all space, all life, all consciousness."[24]

L. C. W. said that she herself came to be convinced that somehow it is possible to move into this pleromic state of potentiality that precedes creation; to enter proto-time, and from a matrix of temporal possibilities arrive instantaneously at any point in the past, present or future; or by the same token, to enter proto-space and from thence move instantaneously to the center of the universe or any other point in space. Likewise, at the intersection of all dimensions, where all points in space and time coincide, it is possible for all the planes to be instantaneously traversed, so that there the soul can bypass all the different planes of being and fly directly to God.

The Shaman's Astral Flight

The knowledge of the direct path to God along the World Axis may have been more readily available to the spirit-possessed Siberian shamans of long ago than it now is to us, for according to Ivar Lissner they had a direct religious awareness we have lost. His researches among the Tungus shamans of Siberia, who belong to one of the oldest living races extant, convinced him that they brought with them from primeval times a lively consciousness of a Supreme Being, and that present-day shamanism is no more than the degenerate remnant of a once-mighty religious tradition which for long ages dominated human culture around the globe. Centered on the World Tree, it was, he believes, of a spiritual purity and spontaneity unimaginable to modern man, for at that time nothing of a lower nature interposed itself between humanity and God.

The men who stood on the threshold between Aurignacian and Magdalenian (30,000 B.C.) had already reached the highest stage in mankind's intellectual development," Lissner declares. "In fact, in the religious sphere they were already on the downward path and had abandoned their intimate relationship with the high God in favour of magic. . . . Once they were closer to him, but then something new interposed itself between them and their god: art, the religious cult and magic.[25]

This claim, so curiously evocative of the biblical Fall, is made of a race, Cro-Magnon in type, that must have inhabited Middle Asia for countless millennia and developed there throughout the Ice Ages. For the major part of his evolution, says Lissner, *Homo sapiens* spent vastly longer periods in Middle Asia than in either Europe or the arctic north; and it was the Asiatic steppe, at that time clement, fertile and hospitable to human needs, being free of the ice sheet that intermittently covered much of the northern hemisphere, that provided long-term stable conditions for a maximum flowering of human culture.

And it was there that Ural-Altaic shamans roaming between Mongolia and Russia must have gazed with awe on the same phenomenon that L. C. W. saw, the same ghostly mast ascending to the stars, dark from a distance but glowing radiantly close up; the same impression of a shining phantasmal tree towering night and day above the highest mountains and reaching to heaven; and must have been drawn to it as she was, and intuited the same profound truths. They too must have recognized it as holy, as a spiritual emanation of the earth and the path of the terrestrial soul. To them too it must have been revealed as the shortest route to the divine, as the great mother of life, of knowledge and powers, who drew them irresistibly into her ambience to become the first exponents of the direct path. For we know, not only from Lissner but from the researches of a number of anthropologists among Siberian medicine men of the present day, that shamans have an immemorial tradition to this effect and that it has survived to some extent in their practices.

The true shaman, it has been found, is an ecstatic and clairvoyant who has been initiated, not by a living master, but by the spirits of his ancestors and has mastered the secrets of astral flight. He knows Meru as the World Tree at the center of the earth and claims to be able to fly up to encounter the Lord of Life at its summit (or the Lord of Death beneath it) even as Jacob encountered God Most High at the top of the angelic ladder. Eliade reports that it is from one of the branches of the tree that the sage of the Siberian steppe fashions the frame of his magical drum, whose beating accompanies his rapturous trance states and his out-of-the-body flights. He represents the pillar of the sky by a young birch tree erected in the center of his tent, on the trunk of which he makes seven, nine or twelve notches symbolizing the celestial planes up which he must pass on his way to the High God; and it is in this symbolic fashion that he recounts to the assembled tribe the steps of his mystical journey to heaven.

But he is more than a clever mime. By means of the law of correspondences, he is at the same time taking flight to the real World Tree, on which he says his soul was born. "The frame of his drum," says Eliade, "being made of the actual wood of the Cosmic Tree, the shaman's drumming transports him magically near to the Tree; that is, to the center of the world, the place where there is a possibility of passing from one cosmic level to another."[26] Thus whether he is journeying upward to the Lord of the World or down into the nether worlds of the Lord of Death, the shaman is in actual astral flight around the World Axis; and that flight, moreover, takes place frequently in a state of ecstasy as he discharges the age-old function of healer, oracle, bard and exorcist that the tree itself bestows on him.

In postglacial times Vedic priests extolled Maha-Kali as the Mother of the world and the gods as they wandered southward through Central Asia; and so also, even earlier, did Palaeolithic shamans revere the spirits of the earth and sky that came together in the Tree of Life that soared above their heads. The tree was the mother of wisdom; it gave them the alphabet and number and their first intimation of an ordered cosmos; it taught them how to interpret the turning wheel of time and yielded the secrets of the stars. Above all, long before yogas or theologies arose, it was the primordial mother of religion, the direct path to the Great Spirit in the sky. Only much later, as Lissner says, came the sacred symbols and sacraments of cult and magic that mediate divinity, and with them many of the sorrows we know today.

THE KALACHAKRA:
PROPHECIES OF SHAMBHALA

$\mathbb{L}$amas say that the Kalachakra, the doctrine of the Wheel of Time, is a science that will lead one directly to the hidden country of the Bodhisattvas, for the Kalachakra is their own body of teachings. A compendium of scientific, prophetic and mystical tantric writings, it is generally regarded as one of the most abstruse and little-known spiritual systems in the world. One tradition of Tibetan Buddhist lore claims that every Buddha is initiated in Shambhala, and that on each occasion he enunciates the principles of the Kalachakric teachings, some of whose deeper doctrines have remained an oral tradition and have never been committed to writing or to profane scrutiny.

Before the Chinese invasion of Tibet, the system was taught mainly in Kalachakric colleges attached to the Tashi-lhun-po monastery in Shigatse and the Kumbum Lamasery in northeastern Tibet. Only the most intellectually and morally gifted of the lamas were able to enroll in them, the ultimate aim of all Kalachakric initiates being to advance sufficiently to enter Shambhala or to achieve telepathic communion with its great Ruler.

The Tashi-lhun-po monastery was once the home of the Tashi or Panchen Lama, who was second only to the Dalai Lama in spiritual authority in Tibet. But the Sixth Panchen Lama, famed for his mastery of the science, fled to China in 1923, as a result of an internal political dispute. He died in 1936. His spiritual successor, the Seventh Panchen Lama, came to Shigatse in the 1950s. He died in 1988. Some Tibetans believe the Tashi Lama will be the next King of Shambhala and that when the Sixth of that lineage left Tibet, he weakened the spiritual strength of the nation, opening the way to the Chinese armies of occupation. These invaders, it is firmly held, will not depart until the Tashi Lama returns to Shigatse.[1] The present Dalai Lama recognized a new incarnation of the Panchen Lama in 1995; however, the young lama was immediately arrested by the Chinese. In recent years, the Dalai Lama has also given the Kalachakra initiation to thousands of lay people, Westerners and Tibetans alike, continuing a tradition of other historical holders of his office.

Some Kalachakric masters have become legendary figures in Tibetan history because of their miraculous powers. The biography of one such adept, Vanaratna, relates how extraordinary supernatural phenomena such as showers of flowers and rainbows were witnessed inside his dwelling where he died in 1468 of his own free will, sitting erect in the yogic position. At his cremation a canopy of rainbows covered the country of Nepal. And in the twelfth century another Kalachakric adept called Bon-don Rinpoche performed a consecration ceremony at which flames from the candles grew into fiery diagrams and symbols. At the age of fifty-one, says his biographer, he proceeded to Shambhala.[3]

Countless such sensational tales of magic and sorcery are linked with Kalachakric practice, to the extent that many Tibetans regard psychic phenomena of a miraculous kind as the outstanding achievement of practitioners of the art. However, the Kalachakra is associated by its exponents with the birth of all forms of spiritual knowledge, not just magic; with an understanding of the Namig or Heavenly Letters, as the primordial alphabet is known; with number, astronomy, geometry and the attainment of the Great Time, by which prophecies are made and the secrets of cyclic time uncovered; and also with the conquest of all natural forces. "Who can exist without food? Who can exist without sleep? Who is immune to heat and cold? Who can heal wounds? Verily, only he who studies the Kalachakra," an old lama told Roerich. "How shall we develop our great understanding? Verily, we are wise in spirit and know everything—but how shall we evoke this knowledge from the depths of our consciousness and transmit it to our minds?"[4] Only, he said, through the practice of the Kalachakra.

There is considerable disagreement on the age and provenance of this great system of wisdom and magic. Some scholars trace its origin to tenth-century India, others to the early Buddhist period in Central Asia; but Kalachakric initiates believe its ring symbols, found in petroglyphs around the globe dating back to the Magdalenian culture, c. 15,000 B.C., prove its immense antiquity and worldwide distribution. Probably embodying the esoteric dimension of the postglacial Sun religion of the Vedic peoples, it was spread, so Roerich believes, by successive migrations into every quarter of the globe. But in the intervening ages it has absorbed elements from many different traditions and under the aegis of Buddhism has become an incomparably richer and more complex corpus of teachings. Its colleges now exist only in Far Eastern countries, but there is evidence that long before the advent of Buddhism more archaic versions of the system were practiced elsewhere. Some initiates believe the Druids of Britain, themselves heirs to a far older tradition, possessed the Kalachakra. But all agree that originally it came from Shambhala, appearing in Kashmir and Bengal in the tenth century C.E. and in Tibet in the eleventh.

THE THREE LEVELS OF THE KALACHAKRA

The Kalachakra Tantra belongs to the highest class of tantric teachings and is known as the Anuttara Yoga. Its method rests on a practical knowledge of Kundalini yoga and the secrets of kundalini shakti. The tenth book of the Blue Annals, composed by Gos Otsaba Gzonnu-dpal around the fifteenth century, gives hints as to the nature of the practice. It refers to the correspondence that exists between the sun, moon and stars and the chakras of the human body, and says that "wisdom comes to one who is able to control the breath"; alluding further to the "House of Kundala aflame with inner heat" and to kundalini at the base of the spine. "Then my illusory [physical] body," it says, "consumed by shining flames, I threw away as a snake its skin."[5]

The lama who gave Roerich his information about Shambhala said that the Kalachakric teachings of the Bodhisattvas are unknowingly used in the sciences of both East and West, but that they would bear greater fruit if scientists were consciously aware of kundalini, "this eternal energy, this fine imponderable matter which is scattered everywhere and which is within our use at any moment. This teaching of the Kalachakra," the lama added, "this utilization of the primary energy, has been called the teachings of Fire, of Agni . . . the new teaching for the New Era."[6]

The early architects of the Kalachakric Tantra appreciated that an understanding of both the intrinsic and extrinsic aspects of reality is essential to the spiritual aspirant; that both inner and outer, self and universe, are aspects of the one transcendental reality, and that it is only when the initiate can say "I am that Reality" that he has reached the end of his quest.

Consequently, the modern assumption that a knowledge of the true structure and natural laws of the universe are irrelevant to religious belief—that the religious man can believe anything he likes about the physical world—would have been entirely alien to the Hindu Vedantists who finally framed the version of the Kalachakra that we know today. For them science and religion were different aspects of the one overarching field of study: the study of Reality. And for that reason they sought to frame a metaphysic that would "embrace all phenomena, from the workings of the mind to the layout of the universe, in one all-inclusive system of knowledge and practice."[7]

This they did by dividing the study into three distinct parts according to their degrees of inwardness and secrecy. These parts are known as the "outer" Kalachakra, the "inner" Kalachakra and the "other" Kalachakra, of which the first part deals with the natural universe and its history and is relatively exoteric and openly discussed by the lamas, while the second and third are in general kept secret and revealed only to initiates. The "inner" Kalachakra is concerned with kundalini yoga and its teachings on the physiology and psychology of the individual, and explains the operation of the psychic nervous system in general and its relation to sensory function and modes of consciousness. It also explains various illnesses, both physical and mental, due to imbalances in the flow of energy through the body, and prescribes cures for various ailments.[8]

The practice of the "inner" Kalachakra is essential, at least to some degree, for the comprehension of the other two parts; while the last and most deeply esoteric of the three is concerned with the divine hierarchies: that is, the invisible nonhuman kingdoms that share our world with us and the great extraterrestrial beings who govern it. This latter system is called the "other" Kalachakra and is a category that can rightly be called neither inner nor outer, but one that transcends and includes both.

The Tibetan calendar and astrological systems are drawn from the "outer" Kalachakra, which deals with all aspects of the external world. It was Somanatha, a Kashmiri Brahman of the eleventh century, who, with the Kalachakra, brought to Tibet the sexagenary calendrical system based on the twelve-year revolution of the planet Jupiter around the sun in 11.86 years.[9] The "outer" Kalachakra is also the part of the system concerned with Shambhala's prophecies, which cover thousands of years. Ossendowski cited a Mongolian legend according to which the priest-kings of Mongolia, most of whom were Tibetans, were able to predict the future by the use of a fragment of the Chintamani stone from Shambhala. The high lamas were able to read the signs and letters that appeared on its surface, giving prophecies for whole nations in conjunction with the Kalachakric texts.

Closely related to the prophetic art is the study of astronomy, geography and mathematics, and above all, an understanding of cyclic time. The main emphasis is on the Time Wheel, a system centered on a cosmic clock in the form of a mandala. The famous prophecies of the Lhasa Oracle, made before the Chinese takeover of Tibet, attest to the extraordinary efficacy of this system as an instrument of prediction.

In the nineteenth century the Oracle circulated a prophesy that in 1904 Lhasa would be occupied by a foreign power, thus accurately forecasting the attack on the city by the British Military Expedition against Tibet launched in 1903. In the same century it also predicted the downfall of Germany, which occurred at the end of the First World War; and several years before it happened, it circulated throughout Tibet a printed forecast of the Chinese Revolution of 1911 and the collapse of the Celestial Dynasty. In 1920 the Tenjyeling Monastery circulated a prediction that the thirteenth Dalai Lama, then reigning, would be the last; and in 1933 the Dalai Lama himself confirmed the prophecy from Lhasa and announced the forthcoming end of Lamaism in Tibet. Within three decades his prophecies came true. The fourteenth Dalai Lama fled to India and the Chinese began their ruthless dismantling of monastic Buddhism in Tibet.[10]

SHAMBHALA AND THE COSMIC CLOCK

Short-term predictions like the above are not the chief preoccupation of Kalachakric initiates seeking a glimpse into the future. They are even more concerned with long-range prophecies centering on Shambhala itself, from which all spiritual benefits are conceived to flow. Among the lamas, therefore, Shambhala's life expectancy is a matter of considerable importance on which opinions greatly differ. According to one prophecy, after Rudra Cakrin's introduction of a golden age on the earth, eight more kings of Shambhala will follow him, making forty in all. During their reign the golden age will fade, the Buddha's teachings will continue to degenerate and evil conditions will once again prevail. Many of the lamas believe that at that time, about five thousand years after the birth of the Buddha, Buddhism will die out, and when it does so Shambhala too will come to an end.

But the oldest and most authoritative of the Kalachakra texts do not mention Buddhism at all, nor give any indication that Shambhala will ever pass away. Consequently, other lamas who follow these texts assert that before Buddhism arose other religions were taught in Shambhala, and that even if the golden age declines in time and even if Buddhism dies, as all religions must, Shambhala will live on as it does today, sending forth new religious impulses into the world, for its function is eternal.

This is the general view. Shambhala's function is not dependent on any particular religion; it transcends them all and is everlasting. It is the earth's heart and will beat as long as the earth lives. Therefore Helena Blavatsky's statement that the heart of Mother Earth "beats under the foot of the sacred Shambhalah" is not a picturesque figure of speech; it accurately reflects occult tradition. According to that source, Shambhala's activity depends on the current of Meru, which waxes and wanes with the slow breathing of the cosmos and endows the life of the earth with pulse. By the same rhythmic action it creates evolutionary cycles that Shambhala must follow. This is why some Sufi initiates say that the flow of wisdom transmissions from Shambhala out into the world keeps pace with the breathing of the cosmos and is therefore periodic rather than continuous, manifesting in alternating cycles of conservation and distribution, and again conservation and distribution *ad infinitum*.[11] The study of the Wheel of Time is overwhelmingly concerned with the wave form of this initiatic work and with the need to determine its periodicity and, if necessary, to plot its course over vast spans of time in order to prepare for long-term changes in human affairs.

To that end, initiates evolved at an early stage of history a science of cyclic time or Great Time that was partly based on astronomy and partly on revelation. It received its astronomical component from an awareness of the phenomenon of stellar precession, in which a very slow motion of the earth, a kind of wobble of the celestial pole, causes an apparent shifting of the position of the stars in the heavens that takes about twenty-six thousand years to complete. During that time the constellations appear to rise gradually to the zenith, cross the sky and descend again.

This apparent precessional change in star patterns over thousands of years is now believed by some scholars to have been observed and monitored at a very early period of human history and to have been imbued by initiate-stargazers with deep religious significance. Joseph Campbell points to the possibility that as far back as the fourth millenium B.C. the Sumerians may have known that at the moment of the spring equinox (March 21) the heavens are never in quite the same position they were in the year before and that in 2,160 years they lag by thirty degrees, which is one sign of the zodiac; while in 25,920 years they precess through a complete cycle of the zodiac, called the "Great" or "Platonic Year."[12] And Jane B. Sellars, an American Egyptologist who has closely studied the Pyramid texts, considers the ancient Egyptians may even have assembled these stellar facts as far back as the fifth millennium B.C., and that they explain the development of the religious ideas of predynastic Egypt.[13]

However, the whole tenor of our investigation into the legend of Shambhala points to a far earlier seedbed of civilization than any our historians have so far envisaged, in which astronomical knowledge was already advanced. We must consider the possibility that a forgotten root-civilization with its capital in Central Asia preceded all those we know; that it had a different power-source than our own, one that probably drew on the magnetic field around the earth, but that it studied the same starry heavens as we do and the same relative motions of the earth, and by establishing initiatic centers around the world, passed on its knowledge to the infant civilizations of a later age. We must also encompass the unfamiliar idea that its goals were spiritual rather than technological, and that out of its vast fund of knowledge acquired over many thousands of years it evolved the mighty foundations of the Kalachakric system and its celestial clock as its chief glory.

The adepts of antiquity believed that the stars were great divine beings who obeyed the laws of the universe and whose movements could therefore throw light on our life on earth. They were led by their stellar observations to evolve a sacred clock of the universe whose moving hands could be read with far more exactitude than is possible today, when knowledge of the astrological science has been almost lost. This clock was the Wheel of Time, incorporating certain esoteric Taoist principles little understood today. Its long-range predictions of relevance to the community aimed at keeping human affairs in harmony with the cosmos and affected many decisions relating to such things as migrations, religious reforms and averting natural disasters.

The Japanese mystic and Shinto-Buddhist initiate, Sukuinushisama, founder of the modern Mahikari sect, gives an illuminating description of the Kalachakric cosmic clock in a similar Shinto-Buddhist one he received by divine guidance and on which his own famous prophecies are based. Its dial shows three concentric circles: one in the center, where Su God presides, a further one denoting the astral world, and an outer one representing the physical world. The dial is divided into sixteen segments, and on its face the moving hands are the blue yin and red yang forces, and the hours are ages of twelve thousand years each. The dial is further divided into four by the arms of a cross, one of which is the vertical-spiritual axis of the universe, the other the horizontal-material axis. The four segments thus marked out on the clock's face represent the four entropic ages through which the cycle as a whole must run. Of these the first is known in the Indian Kalachakric system as a golden or Sattvic Age, the last as a black or Kali Age. Sukuinushisama teaches that in the hands of an illumined adept this clock of cosmic time opens the way to many long-range insights into future events.[14]

But the primary purpose of these time-mandalas has always been hieratic, for they provide, above all, information about the most auspicious times for initiation, since only the beginning of cosmic cycles, when transmission from the divine powers above is at its height, is believed to be propitious for the purpose; whereas in their final stages, transmission ceases altogether and the path of high initiation for most people is completely closed—as has been the case in modern times until very recently. And the same principle applies to the smaller subcycles as regards the lower initiations. In prehistoric times, therefore, stargazing was brought to a fine art. According to Tomas, it began in Shambhala, where it laid the foundations for the calendrical knowledge and mathematically complex astrologies of the later Mystery schools, all of which are based on an understanding of cyclic time.

LINEAR TIME OR CYCLIC TIME?

The question arises here as to whether cyclic time, with its inherently mystical and soteriological overtones, has any genuine validity in the late twentieth century. Is the concept merely a reflection of the naive and ignorant view the ancients had of the universe, or is it a viable way of ordering history? Until the seventeenth century a long line of luminaries of the classical world from Empedocles to Nostradamus believed it was the latter. But since then the cyclic theory has suffered a severe loss of credibility and has been relegated to the category of myth. Academia has discarded it along with the flat-earth theory and angelology, and historians like Oswald Spengler and Arnold Toynbee, who invoked cyclical theories in their explanations of history, have to that extent forfeited respectability in mainstream academic circles. Linear time, with its infinite progression into the future, uncaused and purposeless, has been proclaimed not only an adequate method for ordering history, but the only legitimate one.

But is it? About fifty years ago a counter-current set in, a new thrust springing from an awakened psychological awareness in the West that questioned the old assumptions on which our secular culture has been built. It asked, is there really only one way of perceiving reality? Can it be that the living drama of history with its sense of meaning and purpose, of a grand moral design, is perceived in a different time-mode from that normally registered by the senses? In other words, can there be two different modes of perception, one of a higher and more abstract order than the other, which determine how we experience the unfolding of our world in time?

We know that in traditional societies an ordinary linear system was employed in their calendars for the measurement of relatively short periods of time, but that their priesthoods also used a more esoteric cyclical system incorporating Great Time for the measurement and meaningful evaluation of larger intervals, those well beyond the cognizance of the senses; and that in the temples and ashrams Great Time was understood to belong to a higher cognitive order attainable only by initiates. Should we return to this traditional recognition of a multivalued temporal reality?

A growing new school of transpersonal psychology believes so. What we see depends on how we look, says the physicist-author Fritjof Capra. Patterns of matter reflect the patterns of our mind.[15] Capra traces massive cultural changes already being wrought by the transcending of the narrow and inadequate habits of reality perception engendered by the Cartesian philosophy. "What we need, then, is a new 'paradigm'. . . a fundamental change in our thoughts, perceptions and values. The beginnings of this change, of the shift from the mechanistic to the holistic conception of reality, are already visible in all fields."[16]

The shift has a close bearing on our interpretation of history, for Capra shows that it corresponds to what some leading psychologists call the absolute differential between two distinct but complementary modes of human consciousness, the particular and the holistic. The first pertains to our ordinary "daylight" state of consciousness, which is appropriate for small spans of attention; the second to those mystical, paranormal or highly intuitive states appropriate to the more spacious perceptual vistas that encompass "wholes." And while both modes are necessary for a complete overview of reality, each of the two ideally requires its own language, theoretical framework and worldview for adequate self-expression. Capra stresses that it is only in the latter mode that we can express and meaningfully evaluate our aesthetic, moral and religious experiences.

"In the Cartesian-Newtonian mode," says the American psychologist Stanislav Grof, "we perceive everyday reality in terms of separate objects, three-dimensional space and linear time. In the transpersonal mode, the usual limitations of sensory perception and of logical reasoning are transcended and our perception shifts from solid objects to fluid energy patterns."[17] Three-dimensional space then becomes multidimensional, linear time becomes cyclical, and the pragmatic and concrete, the merely factual, modulates under the influence of a spiritualized intellect into the metaphysical. The former category is purely utilitarian and for everyday use, while the latter mode, with its capacity for an intuitive grasp of abstract processes and values, can work most creatively with the spiralling movements of historical forces in the large. This was the dual way in which the adepts of the ancient world approached the flux of time, and there is no reason to suppose it does not remain a viable possibility today.

The Wheel of Time: Its Prophecies

All ancient civilizations came to believe that the universe gradually runs down in four well-defined temporal stages to an apocalyptic end and then renews itself, creating entropic cycles of regular periodicity that repeat themselves forever along a gradually ascending evolutionary spiral. This apocalyptic worldview had its Chaldean, Iranian, Germanic and Greek versions, all of which varied somewhat from each other and from the Indian version. But the latter has best survived the passage of time, not only because of its bolder organization but also because of its profounder philosophical base, which attaches paramount importance to consciousness and its states as the fundamental nature of the universe. "It is these states," says Sir John Woodroffe (Arthur Avalon), the great Western authority on Indian tantra, "that create, sustain and destroy the worlds. Brahma, Vishnu and Shiva are the names for functions of the one Universal Consciousness operating in ourselves."[18] The destruction and rebirth of worlds throughout time therefore takes place against a background of eternal and unchanging Being, that of universal consciousness such as we find in ourselves. This comprehensive metaphysic has given Indian thought enormous power.

The length of the entropic cycle varies quite widely according to different racial traditions, but in the earliest Indian system the *yuga* is the smallest unit of cosmic time, and four yugas make up a *mahayuga,* which is twelve thousand years in length (Manu I, ff; Mahabharata III, 12, 826). Each mahayuga modulates through a cycle of creation, wear and dissolution that ends in a reversal of energies and the birth of a new cycle, while two such mahayugas correspond to the ascending and descending phases of the zodiac and make up one Sidereal Year. Later speculation, says Mircea Eliade, "only amplified and reproduced ad infinitum the primordial rhythm of creation-destruction-creation, by projecting the unit of measure, the yuga, into more and more extensive cycles."[19] The resultant system of overlapping ages, rounds and aeons, some of unthinkably long duration, is a well-known feature of Theosophical teachings that sometimes obscures by its complexity the basically simple formula from which it is derived.

Hinduism has woven into this formula its prophecies of Shambhala, in which the next king will be Sri Kalki, the last of the ten incarnations of Vishnu to appear in the course of a great cycle. According to the Mahabharata texts, each cycle starts in a Sattva Yuga (sometimes called a Krita Yuga), a long golden age of high creative energies that gradually run down through two further ages to a final nadir, a short and catastrophic "black age" governed by Kali, the goddess of death, and therefore called a Kali Yuga. The latter is a period of intense purification of the world, after which the tenth incarnation of Vishnu appears in the guise of a savior on a white horse to usher in the next dispensation. He is now being eagerly awaited by millions of Hindus, for according to most occult computations we are currently in the closing phase of just such a period.

In the Kali Yuga the running down of cosmic forces plunges humanity and its civilizations into a final stage of devolution, of brutal materialism, ignorance and desuetude, of which the Vishnu Purana says:

Wealth and piety will decrease day by day, until the world is wholly depraved. Then property alone will confer rank; wealth will be the only source of devotion; passion will be the sole bond of union between the sexes; falsehood will be the only means of success in litigation; and women will be objects merely of sensual gratification. Earth will be venerated only for its mineral resources. . .[20]

Humanity's longevity, morality and intelligence will decline until finally barbarians without spiritual insight will take over the world and will even discover and overrun Shambhala.

Then will Vishnu, the Lord of Civilization (so the Hindu prophecies continue), take birth in Shambhala in his saving aspect: as Sri Kalki Avatara he will gather together a great army of faithful souls and will ride forth from his palace on a supernatural white charger that has the power of flight,[21] and will conquer the barbarians and renew the world, returning it to the golden age in which all began. "He will then reestablish righteousness upon earth," the Vishnu Purana continues,

> and the minds of those who live at the end of the age of strife shall be awakened, and shall be as pellucid as crystal. The men who are thus changed by virtue of that peculiar time shall be as seeds of human beings, and shall give birth to a race who shall follow the laws of the golden age of purity.[22]

Buddhist lore contains a very similar theme. To Buddhists the next King of Shambhala will be Rudra Cakrin, an incarnation of Manjushri, the Bodhisattva of Wisdom; but at least one Sanskrit version of the main Kalachakric text refers to him as Kalki. He too will ride forth from his palace on a flying white or blue horse, followed by a great army, in order to vanquish the forces of evil that will mass at the very gates of Shambhala and to preside at the birth of the new age. And similarly the Mongolians believe that their great hero, Gesar-Khan, lives on in an underground kingdom with his horde of warriors waiting to be reborn in Shambhala, from whence he will ride forth at the end of the age, again on a flying white steed, to deliver the world from the demonic power of the barbarians.

In 1921 a high Mongolian lama told Ossendowski that the King of the World had appeared before the lamas of his monastery in 1890 and had made specific prophecies for the coming half century. According to the King of the World's prediction:

> "More and more the people will forget their souls and care only about their bodies," the King of the World predicted. "The great-

est sin and corruption will reign on the earth. . . . The 'Crescent' will grow dim and its followers will descend into beggary and ceaseless war. People will become as ferocious animals, thirsting for the blood and death of their brothers. . . . The crowns of kings, great and small, will fall . . . one, two, three, four, five, six, seven, eight . . . There will be a terrible battle among all the peoples. Kingdoms will be scattered . . . whole peoples will die . . . hunger, disease, crimes unknown to the law, never before seen in the world. The enemies of God and of the Divine Spirit in man will come. Those who take the hand of another shall also perish. The forgotten and the pursued shall rise and hold the attention of the whole world. There will be fogs and storms; earthquakes will come . . . Millions will change the fetters of slavery and humiliation for hunger, disease and death. The ancient roads will be covered with crowds wandering from one place to another. The greatest and most beautiful cities shall perish in fire . . . one, two, three . . . Families shall be scattered . . . Truth and love shall disappear . . .

Then I shall send a people, now unknown, which shall tear out the weeds of madness and vice with a strong hand and will lead those who still remain faithful to the spirit of man in the fight against Evil. They will found a new life on earth purified by the death of nations. In the fiftieth year only three great kingdoms will appear, which will exist happily seventy-one years. Afterwards there will be eighteen years of war and destruction. Then the peoples of Agharti will come up from their subterranean caverns to the surface of the earth.[23]

The likeness this ominous picture presents to our own civilization is unmistakable, and if the prophecies are to be believed, bodes ill for our immediate future. But we must be very careful in our interpretations of these prophecies from Shambhala that speak, like all true prophecy, in the language of poetry rather than prose. The "Crescent," of course, would appear to mean Islam. Whether the King of the World was alluding to the three great "kingdoms" that survived the second World War—that is, Britain, America and Russia—we cannot be sure; but it is probable. That they have existed "happily" since 1945 without global warfare in a virtual state of peace, however uneasy, is certainly the case; and that they may do so until 2011 is also probable. Also that eighteen years of war and destruction are to follow is a further possibility that must surprise no one living through these catastrophic times of ours. But who is the unknown race that will "tear out the weeds of madness and vice"?

In prophecy, time is not as sequential nor facts as well defined as in the prose language by which we habitually attune ourselves to reality; and so when the prophet overviews the future as an instantaneously present picture (as he always does) he sees it surrounded by a penumbra of temporal possibilities only loosely and poetically linked. Everything he says may be true—but not quite literally.

Thus in the above prophecy, "the race now unknown" who appears before the fiftieth year of the twentieth century is most probably not a militant nation as we might suppose, but a foreshadowing of the theme announced at the end of the prophecy concerning the people of Agharti-Shambhala. It is they who will tear out the weeds of madness and vice with a strong hand after eighteen years of war in the new millennium. But they are mentioned as appearing much earlier because the King of the World is predicting that they will *begin* to emerge before the second World War, and will *begin* to "found a new life on earth purified by the death of nations." Their work will continue and accelerate until the final salvific victory over the forces of evil, when their presence *will become known to all.*

And in fact by the middle of the century a galaxy of new spiritual leaders had begun to appear among us, bringing with them not so much new teachings as revolutionary new energies—new transmissions powerful enough to stem the disintegration of human culture—as they will assuredly continue to do. Overall, therefore, there is a sense in which the prophecies of the Lord of the World are manifestly coming true and must be taken seriously. According to them, we are already in the path of mighty spiritual forces that have been set in motion at the highest Shambhalic levels.

WORLD INITIATION

Prophecies like the above, embedded in the great corpus of Kalachakric teachings, are echoed in the world's various myths of cyclic time and apocalypse; for most religious schools, whatever their provenance, enshrine in their teachings the act of salvific regeneration of the world which will rhythmically recur at the end of every major temporal cycle for as long as the universe continues. Even in the case of the Semitic religions, their doctrine of a messianic Judgment Day for humanity, which originated in Zoroastrian Solar philosophies as well as being strongly influenced by the Hindu-Buddhist eschatology emanating from Alexandria, is of the same religio-astrological stock, though it has suffered centuries of distortion at the hands of fundamentalist theologies.

Over the past fifty years numbers of psychics have received intimations of approaching apocalyptic events, and millennial prophecies are now being voiced on every side. If spiritually focussed, such experiences reveal their inner initiatic meaning and have tremendous transformative value. Esoterically, all such terms as the Day of Sri Kalki, the Christian Second Coming and the Muslim Day of the Lord refer to a collective initiation our world periodically undergoes in which man and planet alike are awakened to new potentialities, to new and higher energies it will be their task to materialize in the coming cycle. For so intertwined are the roots of human life and those of the planet, so interdependent are their Gaian destinies, that we must think of them as evolving together, being initiated together, as receiving the same cosmic transmissions in a manner analogous to the way in which the individual is initiated in Kundalini yoga. At that time the "solar ray," says Guénon, enters the sushumna or "coronal ray" in the orifice at the crown of the head in order to awaken kundalini; and so too do certain solar and interstellar radiations enter Meru at regular intervals in history in order to infuse our earth-system with new life and to fertilize the evolutionary seeds that lie dormant within it.

At such special times of soul development, the initiatic process begun on high activates the earth's subtle chakric system, leading to a cataclysmic passage of purification of the planet in which earthquakes, floods, possibly the extinction of many species not suitable for the new conditions, as well as upheavals in human societies, bring about world changes that have both spiritual and geological components. Thus Guénon speaks of the rise and fall of continents, of inundations and the shifting of the poles, and suggests that these events accompany changes in Shambhala's condition and in its relationship to the rest of the world.

At present Shambhala-Agarttha, as has been said, is occluded in the subterranean conditions appropriate to the Kali Yuga and is unknown and invisible to the majority of people. In fact, its most common iconographic depiction is similar to that of the four-spoked *muladhara* chakra, the subtle "earth-center" in the body that is similarly concealed from our sight and knowledge.[24] But, says Guénon, the hidden kingdom was not always concealed from view and will not always be so in the future. As the world evolves so will the sacred center rise into visibility, and in the more enlightened epoch to come, will become open and light-filled and will be laid out on different iconographic principles. It will then manifest those high energy states that lie beyond the domain of the *muladhara* in the spiritual ambience of the *anahata* chakra, the *ajna* chakra or the *sahasrara*, and will become the glorious paradise it now is only potentially, but once was in the earth's golden age, when all men were *hamsa*—beyond caste—and, through the direct path, could freely communicate with the gods.

Protected by geographical factors from the catastrophes that must overtake the planet in the End Times, Guénon believes the great mountain bastions of High Asia will be a sanctuary in the coming storm of world purification. He likens Shambhala to Noah's Ark, a vessel that is immune to natural disasters and to all the apocalyptic forces of destruction associated with the close of the Kali-yuga, and which, like the biblical ark, "contains all the elements destined for the restoration of the world, which are thus the seeds of its future state."[25]

And so he foresees that the sacred center, floating safely across the waters of universal dissolution, will enter into its active phase, as do the chakras in human beings after being awakened, and will disseminate in seed form all the possibilities to develop in the new cycle. From it spiritual teachers will emerge, and its creative energies will pour forth into the world to incubate new religions, new social and political systems and new modes of knowledge out of its inexhaustible plenum, and will ensure the safe passage of the initiatory tradition from the old cycle to the new.

Thus we can hope that at that time the physical brutalization of our planet will be reversed, and that with a new religion there will come a new science utilizing a source of terrestrial power that supports a less primitive and destructive technology than the one we have today. If so, the resultant golden age may last a long time, bringing humanity surcease from the sufferings of the End Time and the priceless opportunity of redressing the earth's present travail. But there will be many golden ages, we are told, followed by many gradual descents into dark ages, before human beings reach a level of enlightenment at which the conditions of a garden paradise can spread outward from Shambhala to cover the earth. A Bon prophecy predicts that about twelve thousand years hence, when religion has once again died out in the outside world, a great Bon teacher, the King of Olmolungring, will emerge from his hidden kingdom and bring a new and revitalized version of the primordial wisdom to the world,[26] and by such means enlightenment will be given again and again, throughout great cycles of time, until the earth becomes a Utopia.

THE HIDDEN DIRECTORATE

Are there superior godlike beings invisibly overseeing and influencing our life on earth? This is one of those controversial debates that seem to spring up afresh in every generation without ever being satisfactorily resolved. Although the myths of gods and goddesses have fallen out of fashion, today we have substituted for them the archangels and angels of medieval astrology or the even more up-to-date ones of astronauts from the stars or archetypal forces of the collective unconscious; so that in one way or another, the theme has never died. It is as popular as ever and has even gained currency in its original theistic sense, but with a humanistic twist. For since the late nineteenth century esoteric writers have joined with students of mythology in suggesting that the gods of antiquity were really spiritual adepts of unusually high stature.

The most important contribution of these writers has been to introduce into the modern world the concept of initiation and transformation, of personal transcendence, and the corollary of a graduated ascent to adepthood, leading on to the further idea of an initiate Hierarchy that guides human evolution. It is in this latter sense, they believe, that we must understand the secret meaning of our myths about deities and other supernatural beings. The divine epiphanies of history, the great religious Teachers and Messengers such as the Christ and the Buddha, can then be seen as they truly were, the visible members of a secretly organized and invisible fraternity of spiritual Masters.

It was a revolutionary idea in its day, causing a great deal of acrimony; and Edouard Schuré, whose seminal work, *The Great Initiates*, was published in 1887, said that at first it was greeted with icy hostility and disbelief, since it ranked Jesus Christ as an initiate like other great Messengers. But today, after a hundred years of increasingly open dissemination of sensitive esoteric material, there is a far readier acceptance of this kind of religious interpretation of ancient mythology.

Of all esoteric traditions, Sufism is the most informative about the initiatic lore that constellates around the legend of Shambhala. All Sufi schools believe in the existence of a spiritual Hierarchy countless thousands of years old whose uppermost echelons in Asia are shrouded in mystery. Those schools in particular who trace their origin to Central Asia, says John Bennett, "assert that there is a perpetual hierarchy headed by the *Kuth-i-Zaman* or Axis of the Age, who receives direct revelations of the Divine Purpose and transmits them to mankind through the Abdal or transformed ones and their followers."[1] This Hierarchy is the center for the production of energy of a very high level, according to George Gurdjieff, who believed that the destined role of man is to be an apparatus for the transformation of energy, and that underlying human development and human history, "there is an invisible action of the higher energies that makes the work of evolution possible."[2] This motif runs through all Sufic literature.

The picture that emerges from this and the theme of the preceding chapters is that of a spiritual energy source in the earth that correlates with humanity's own and is therefore highly magnetic to psychics, visionaries, saints and sages. These form a hierarchic adept fraternity that surrounds Meru and is maintained there by an influence infinitely wise and holy that loves humanity and has formed a symbiotic working relationship with it. Meru's location on the globe may shift, says René Guénon, and has done so many times in the past, but wherever it is located there is to be found the initiate Hierarchy, its chain of command at the highest echelons covering the solar system, its logo the sun, and at its summit a triumvirate of great interstellar Spirits concerned respectively with the "spirit," "soul" and "body" of our world.[3]

Under different names this creative governing trinity is revered in most of our religions. It receives from the supreme Source the divine will for this planet and passes it down to the initiate echelons in Shambhala that act as its regents on earth, and from thence its transmission flows outward in three major spiritual streams. These make themselves manifest in our particular cycle as the Vedantic, Taoist and Cabalistic traditions respectively.

Just as elements in the earth's structure transform universal Shakti into lower forms—such as the positively and negatively charged magnetic forces that circulate as yin and yang in the body of the earth—so Shambhalic adepts transform the high energies they receive from higher up the Hierarchy into lower energy states that are more compatible with the average human condition and transmit them to the rest of the world via esoteric fraternities, most often in the form of popular religious or metaphysical systems. This stepped-down transmission from Shambhala is essential to the health, evolution and very life of the race as a whole, since it is a direct emanation of the divine Source itself.

SHAMBHALA'S HIERARCHY

In his book *Mission de l'Inde*, the French esotericist Saint-Yves d'Alveydre describes this Hierarchy in Solar terms. "The highest circle, nearest to the mysterious center, is composed of twelve members who represent the supreme initiation and correspond, amongst other things, with the Zodiacal Zone."[4] This zone is the section of the heavens marked out by the circular motion of the celestial pole over 25,920 years. The twelve members are called the twelve Suns or the twelve rays of the Sun. Manu Vaiveswata, the Hindu Lawgiver commonly known as the Son of the Sun, and Moses, who received the Hebraic tablets of the Law from the summit of Mount Sinai, are, according to this occult tradition, both legendary members of this special band, at whose head Guénon places the Christ, linking him with the missionary Sons of the Sun from Central Asia.

For Guénon, the Christ with his twelve apostles represents the Lord of the World for this age who, during it, is the supreme Lawgiver for our earth. According to Guénon:

The title "Lord of the World" belongs properly to "Manu," the primordial and universal legislator. This is the name that in various forms is found amongst many ancient peoples: Mina or Menes of the Egyptians, the Celtic Menw, and Greek Minos. In reality the name describes not a figure that is more or less historical or legendary, but a principle, a cosmic Intelligence that reflects pure spiritual light and formulates the Law (*Dharma*) appropriate to the conditions of our world and of our cycle of existence. At the same time, it is the archetype of man in his uniqueness, that is to say, of man as a thinking being (in Sanskrit *manava*).[5]

Those on the human level of the Hierarchy who directly serve this principle mirror it from below and become themselves Lawgivers. They govern the ebb and flow of the culture tides emanating from Shambhala, according to which the spiritual brotherhoods move to and fro across the earth, obeying the obscure rhythms of history and civilization. These are the migrations that are rarely observed and never recorded in our history books, yet are the very mainspring of humanity's cultural evolution. The movements of the underground organizations that keep the religious spirit alive in society are monitored by Masters who inhabit Shambhala's inner zone.

Alice Bailey calls them Ascended Masters, Idries Shah calls them Guardians of the Tradition, John Bennett *psychoteleios* or "perfected ones," and they are also known as the Ancient Ones, the Watchers, the Immortals, the Monitors, the Hidden Directorate, the Children of Seth. All follow what is known as the Ancient Path. According to esoteric tradition, in remote times before the advent of the Mystery schools they lived in more open communication with us, but as the age advanced were compelled to withdraw into their present obscurity, so that now they are accessible to only the most highly purified souls and with rare exceptions are known to the rest of us only through the grace of mystical vision.

Those who live in Shambhala's transcendental inner zone are its engine, its powerhouse; their consciousness turns the wheel. They are the supreme authority for this planet, forming the governing core of Shambhala and, through the ashrams and monasteries of the outer region, of the world. The inner region no doubt has its hidden settlements and cultivated environs like the outer zone, and probably an even higher technology, but the inner Masters are no longer reliant on the physical state. Sometimes incarnate, but often discarnate, they are beyond religious and ethnic categories and work at energy levels that are entirely outside the frequencies with which ordinary humanity is familiar, in ways we are not yet able to comprehend.

Shambhala-Agarttha, says Guénon, is related to the zodiacal sign of Libra, which means "balance" or "scales," and is the quintessential point of balance for the planet; and in precisely the same sense the Directorate is a stabilizing and balancing force in the life of the race. No matter how eccentrically we deviate from the path of wisdom, no matter what descending cycle of destruction, what frightful chimeras we pursue in the course of our evolution, the Directorate negotiates a balance. It is the countervailing and normative influence in our midst, secretly conserving what we have lost, holding in our best interests what we carelessly throw away and safeguarding a future in whose reality we never really believe and are not capable of serving. In an age of superstition it promotes the sciences; when materialism prevails, it reforms religions. It waits when we rush forward, acts when we sleep, believes in life eternal when we do not, and the more we value the exoteric phantasms of the material world the more it withdraws into the invisible realms of soul, counterbalancing our periods of intense physical exploration with equally long periods of withdrawal.

THE SEVENTEENTH-CENTURY SPIRITUAL EXODUS FROM THE WEST

Guénon suggests that a cycle of initiatic withdrawal was completed in the seventeenth century, when the West embarked in earnest on its scientific exploration of the physical universe. In Europe, he said in 1928, initiatic activity had been steadily declining and was now virtually over, every consciously established link with the supreme center in Asia having been almost entirely broken—as it had been for several centuries.

For nearly six thousand years the psychic faculties of the race had been waning as its mental powers grew stronger, and by the seventeenth century "the last vestiges of the ancient clairvoyant vision had atrophied to close the gates of spiritual perception,"[6] in the words of Trevor Ravenscroft, even as they opened wide to the modern technological sciences. This was the point at which an exodus of spiritual luminaries from the Western centers of civilization reached its apogee; the point at which, as Guénon puts it, the rupture between the initiatic headquarters and its secondary Western centers became complete, leaving the way open for the rationalism of Descartes and the Encyclopedists. It was also the point at which the death-knell of traditional European civilization sounded, since it was then that orthodox forces in Christendom put to the sword the last major spiritual impulse to vivify the West by initiating a Thirty Years' War that forced the final withdrawal of its inner brotherhoods into Central Asia.

Much study has been devoted to this critical juncture in European history, but without giving sufficient attention to one of its most interesting features. The seventeenth century was the end of a major religio-cultural cycle that had begun in the centuries immediately preceding the Christian era, when a new wave of Solar religions from Central Asia poured into Rome and Alexandria, continuing the influx of esoteric teachings into the West that had begun with Zoroaster in the sixth century B.C. It was this rich new stream of Eastern wisdom, propagated by a wave of missionary initiates, that transformed Judaism from a tribal into a world religion, gave opulent new life to the learning of Egypt and Greece and brought Rome to its greatest flowering, shaping a high civilization there that would not be surpassed until the nineteenth century. Under the influence of such teachings as Persian Zirvanism, Indian Hindu-Buddhism and Chinese Taoism—all originally from Central Asia—the philosophers of Alexandria molded the foundations of the great Western scholastic tradition that would last for nearly two thousand years more and, through the Essenes, profoundly influenced the development of Christianity.

As we know, this marvellously fruitful seeding born of the Sun religions of Central Asia was the impulse that would bring European civilization into being. But by the sixth century C.E. the epoch of spiritual fertilization from the East was almost over, its high energies on the wane. Now barbarian peoples overran Europe, and at the same time Christianity became a powerful and intolerant state cult that persecuted any form of heterodoxy. Those movements belonging to the West's inner spiritual tradition started their drift back towards the East, from whence they had come. The inner fraternities that had served the West for so long did not die, as is frequently assumed, but unobtrusively migrated, regrouping in the high valleys and oases of Middle Asia.

Hugh Schonfield traces this massive spiritual exodus from the West which was to lead to our present secular society in his book *The Essene Odyssey*. The Essenes—both the Palestinian sect and those known as the Egyptian Therapeuts, who had absorbed the Egyptian Solomonic and Hermetic wisdom—amalgamated with other Occidental wisdom orders and, under the spur of Jewish persecution, migrated to Iraq and from thence to Turkestan and Afghanistan, where they found refuge. Equally persecuted Gnostics, Manicheans and Nestorian Christians left Christendom behind to found communities in the Tarim Basin and the Turfan Depression south of the Tien Shan mountains. The Zoroastrian magi, displaced from Persia by the rising power of Islam, settled in Afghan monasteries, and so too did many Mandeans, the ancient followers of John the Baptist. They were joined over the centuries, according to Schonfield, by Judeo-Christian Nazareans, the pre-Christian sect to which Jesus belonged and which was excommunicated by the Pauline Church, after which it formed centers in Afghanistan. There its members were known as the Nasar or the Nusairijah. There can be no doubt that this withdrawal of high-level initiates, the intellectual cream of their respective societies, contributed materially to Europe's subsequent cultural impoverishment and calamitous descent into a Dark Age.[7]

During the Middle Ages the eastward drift was halted and even turned back for a time as Sufis carried Islamic mysticism into the western countries, especially into Saracen Spain, bringing with them the new arts and sciences of Arabia that inspired the Cluniacs, the Chartres masters, the Knights Templar, the Cathars, the Illuminati and other medieval brotherhoods of Christendom. But the recovery was temporary only; as Christendom grew in political power so too did its intolerance and its bloodbaths, and the spiritual trend away from Europe and towards the Shambhalic region resumed. On a less conspicuous scale, the holy mountain men of China, the *hsien-jen*, were retreating during the same period into the Kunluns and the Tarim Basin to wait out the age of Confucian rationalism; the Siddhas, the Jains and other Indian yogic orders were likewise withdrawing to the Himalayas before the iconoclastic Muslim reign in India and the popular piety of Krishna worship, and tantric Buddhism was retreating even further north into Tibet.

Thus the seventeenth century is an historical benchmark, for it was the moment in modern history at which a revolution of the human spirit began. If we look back into the past, not until the end of the Bronze Age c. 1200 B.C., when the Greater Mysteries were at their height, do we find a comparably sudden decline in a long-established cultural order. Yet the seventeenth century had begun in Europe with high hopes. Manifestoes which had already been pseudonymously published in Germany by the Rosicrucian Brotherhood, thought by some to have been a Sufi organization, broadcast news of a coming Utopia in which the dignity and worth of every man would be recognized. They spoke of an invisible college dedicated to a commonwealth of man and initiated a great wave of interest in spiritual enlightenment and a general reformation in science, religion and social institutions. And although the brotherhood was never publicly identified despite widespread efforts to do so, there seems little doubt that large numbers of educated men of the day were secretly enrolled into its ranks and thereafter dedicated themselves to realizing its high aims.[8]

Frances A. Yates, a well-known British writer on Rosicrucianism and other occult movements of the Renaissance, believes the period of the sixteenth and seventeenth centuries can rightly be called the Rosicrucian Enlightenment and that it generated a great intellectual reforming movement[9] that could have regenerated Western culture after its terrible collapse during the Dark Age. But the movement was aborted by the Spanish Inquisition and the Thirty Years' War that ended in 1648, after which the Brothers of the Rose Cross are reputed to have left Europe and retreated into Asia.

It was the signal for a final global exodus. In the same century the company of the Sufi masters known as the Khwajagan, who taught in the foremost cities of Turkestan—in Samarkand and Balkh, Merv and Bokhara—and who had shed a brilliant light on Western culture for five hundred years, also withdrew into the hidden heart of Asia, to the foothills of the Hindu Kush; after which their beneficent influence on Christianity and Islam ceased to flow. While it lasted, the spiritual dynasty of the Khwajagan had been a bastion of religious freedom and direct mystical experience, teaching a doctrine of self-transformation through the power of divine love that was independent of any particular tradition, but which respected all religions and all spiritual ways. It was associated with the lamas of Tibet and Xinjiang and shared many of their secret tantric techniques, its teachings and practices illuminating European culture as far west as Spain.[10]

And in the seventeenth century, while the Sufi center of spiritual enlightenment in Samarkand was ceasing to radiate its light into the West, the Panchen Lamas, at that time the dominant spiritual influence in Tibet, began to turn their backs on the West with its imperialistic and inquisitorial goals and to establish an eastern chain of Kalachakric colleges in India, Mongolia, Japan, China and Indonesia. Thereafter we find the higher intuitive faculties in the Western psyche beginning to die, and Europe, rejecting the mystical natural philosophies of the Renaissance, turning instead to a mechanistic clockwork interpretation of reality in its burgeoning new physical sciences.

"The desacralization of the natural world," says Rupert Sheldrake,

> was taken to its ultimate conclusion in the seventeenth century. Through the mechanistic revolution, the old model of the living cosmos was replaced by the idea of the universe as a machine. According to this new theory of the world, nature no longer had a life of her own; she was soulless, devoid of all spontaneity, freedom and creativity. Mother Nature was no more than dead matter, moving in unfailing obedience to God-given mathematical laws.[11]

The new death-dealing attitude to Nature raised man above her as lord and master of all he surveyed, and it was precisely this *hubris* that severed his religious institutions from their mother-center in Asia and therefore from their primary source of spiritual nourishment. Hence the seventeenth-century development in the West was not, as many then thought, the beginning of a grand new age based on humanism and the power of the rational intellect, but the death-throes of the old; death-throes that had actually begun more than a thousand years before, and whose withering effects are still with us.

Everywhere during the Christian era, but primarily in the West, the high initiatic spirit receded from the great centers of civilization and flowed back into Inner Asia, into the refuge of Shambhala, leaving behind barren autumnal cultures whose higher energies, even by the seventeenth century, were on the wane and are today almost exhausted, either by fundamentalist theologies or the tide of Western technology and Western materialism. The prophecies of Shambhala that foretell this dire event thus appear to be borne out. Western civilization does indeed seem to be dying at its roots in the heart of its great cities; Chinese armies and oil rigs are indeed invading the stronghold of Inner Asia, and time seems indeed to have formed a two-thousand-year loop, its epicenter Meru's evolutionary axis (without which cyclic time would be no more than endless, meaningless stagnant repetition); and lastly, the world's greatest saints and sages do indeed seem to have gathered in the hidden kingdom as predicted, there to await the next turn of the wheel.

Is There An Inner Circle of Humanity?

We may not understand the underlying purpose nor the laws governing the cyclic patterns of history, some of which involve vastly greater time loops than the above, but the impression they give of providence, of planned programming, is undeniable. Sufis believe that nothing in history is by chance; new truths are seeded, new energies implanted in society according to operations set in train at the highest spiritual levels. "History is not the equilibrant of chance and hazard," says Ernest Scott.

> It does not just happen. The script for the long human story was written by intelligences much greater than man's own. Certain gains and goals for mankind—and for the biosphere of earth—must be attained within certain intervals of Earth time. These gains are essential for the balance and growth of the solar system of which Earth is a part. The solar system may itself be subject to a similar pressure in the interests of the galaxy of which it is a part.[12]

Such a broad approach to history, though once universal, falls strangely on ears attuned only to the small-scale linear philosophy of modern historians, for whom the explanatory role of divine providence has become superfluous. But although it runs counter to contemporary thought, there are many who now believe that, for a genuinely comprehensive understanding of history, a nonlinear modality of thought on the plane of creative intuition, in which purpose and meaning are integral factors and that takes account of earth's relationship to the greater cosmos, is both necessary and feasible.

In such a view the advancing and retreating waves of acculturation that help to define the historical flux are monitored by an invisible central agency which sends forth out of Asia and recalls in due season its bands of enlightened culture-bearers—missionaries, prophets and spiritual Messengers—according to a cosmic plan to which average humanity is not necessarily privy. It claims that there are guardians of racial evolution who channel the energies of the planet and direct human history towards ever-renewed opportunities for self-development, and who form the nucleus of what amounts to a hidden world government headquartered in Shambhala.

Numerous objections can be raised to this idea, but they rise only because the special nature and *modus operandi* of the Directorate are not yet understood. The obscurity surrounding the whole subject has lightened somewhat since the sixties, when a fresh dialogue on it began. At that time Idries Shah, scion of a prominent Sufi family of Afghanistan, established a Sufi school in England and disseminated a wealth of new information on the invisible Guardians; and in the same period John Bennett published his final volume of *The Dramatic Universe* in which he addressed this controversial topic in depth.

As he points out, writers of science fiction have debased the idea of superhuman beings responsible for human welfare to such an extent that many people find it not worth serious consideration. One objection is that if it is true, the state of the world hardly suggests that they are doing their job well. "A more serious difficulty," says Bennett,

> is that we should expect such a significant factor in human history to be better known. There is no obvious reason why the "Inner Circle" of humanity . . . should hide itself. Presumably, it requires cooperation from the uninitiated and one would expect that this cooperation would readily be forthcoming if only people were made aware of the help offered them and told what was required of them.[13]

However, not only is uninitiated cooperation a moot point, given human nature, but there is the additional point that, as Bennett says, if there is a conscious guidance in human affairs it comes from a level of being quite unlike that of people as we know them. "There is a certain naivete in the view that a higher level of being is describable in the language that is appropriate to the every-day world. . . . It may well be that the characteristics of a true 'Inner Circle' would be exactly the opposite of what we should expect."[14] Likewise its worldview and methods might be quite different from anything acceptable to reason from the uninitiated point of view, and therefore be the more easily overlooked.

Bennett himself believes that two different classes of humanity have probably always existed side by side. He visualizes two different genetic and cultural levels in Palaeolithic society, diverging from each other from the very earliest period of human history and resulting in the formation of what we would call an Inner Circle, an advanced master race of great magicians on one hand and backward subject races on the other, the two groups distinguished by the single factor of initiation.[15] And there is in fact growing archaeological and anthropological support for Bennett's hypothesis. Modern-type skulls with a large cranial capacity continue to be discovered among primitive remains as far back as 100,000 B.C.; and researchers like Charles Hapgood, whose maps of ancient sea kings have revolutionized thought on this subject, continue to unearth indisputable evidence of civilizations in periods that have always been regarded as primeval.

Hapgood, a professor of anthropology and the history of science at Keene Teachers' College in New Hampshire, has made a collection of medieval and Renaissance maps that have been authenticated by the Cartographical Section of the U.S. Air Force and studied with keen interest by Albert Einstein. Hapgood found that most maps and sea charts made in the Middle Ages were primitive, unskilled affairs that displayed a complete ignorance of geography or the principles of mapmaking. But among them he discovered some of a startlingly different caliber. Employing scientific methods of cartography as sophisticated as our own today, these old portolano charts showed the coastlines and interiors of lands that were unknown in the Middle Ages; for example, Antarctica, Greenland and South America. Copied again and

143

again through the centuries, some could be traced back to Ptolemaic and Phoenician times, others to times even more remote. As he delved deeper into their history he found that, treasured by generations of mariners for their detailed accuracy, these remarkable source maps had been faithfully preserved for thousands of years by seafaring races, and at last passed into the hands of pre-Columbian Europeans.

Hapgood believes they could only have been made by a maritime civilization that existed before the climatic and sea-level changes that occurred at the end of the last Ice Age. The maps show us lands subject to geographical conditions that have not existed there for many thousands of years at the very least—such as Antarctica and Greenland free of ice—and evince a knowledge of astronomy, nautical science, mapmaking, spherical trigonometry, the true circumference of the earth and a practical means of finding longitude that we have wrongly assumed was unknown until the eighteenth century. The evidence Hapgood's maps present in fact "appears to suggest the existence in remote times, before the rise of any of the known cultures [that is, the Egyptian, Babylonian, Greek, Chinese, etc.] of a true civilization of a comparatively advanced sort, which either was localized in one area but had worldwide commerce, or was in a real sense a *worldwide* culture."[16]

Hapgood traces this hypothetical civilization back by means of the charts to c. 6000 B.C. at the very least, but more probably to the depths of the last Ice Age, and points out that extensive social organization and economic resources are indicated in the drawing of the maps. They required many exploratory expeditions, many stages in the compilation of local observations and maps into a general chart, all under central direction, arguing some sort of global government. "Furthermore," he concludes, "it is unlikely that navigation and mapmaking were the only sciences developed by these people, or that the application of mathematics to cartography was the only practical application they made of their mathematical knowledge."[17]

He believes all the evidence points to an unknown race that achieved quite a high standard of civilization far earlier than we have thought possible, perhaps as far back as seventeen thousand years ago. Bennett reaches a similar conclusion. He envisages a race of great prehistoric sorcerers who were, both intellectually and in their feats of natural magic, unsurpassed masters of the spiritual realm, but also masters of the technology of the material world, becoming farmers and cattle-herders, astronomers and bridge-builders thousands of years before the Neolithic Age. Thus a ruling class segregated by taboo from the rest of Stone Age humanity (as occult lore avers) and possessing specialized spiritual techniques and genetic controls as well as the first natural sciences, formed a centralized governing "Inner Circle" that has persisted from the most distant times to the present day.[18]

Bennett's view accords with the one developed in this book, which proposes that under optimum conditions the awakening of kundalini undergone by the true shaman modifies his physiology and even his genetic programming in such a radical way that it actually functions as an evolutionary mechanism, refining his nervous system, sensitizing the body and its drives and forcing him towards a civilized state far earlier than the rest of his community. The higher energies are released, giving greater power of expression to the higher faculties of intelligence, altruism and will power; the creative and social urges flower and with them higher forms of religion. And in this way, by forming isolated communities and practicing careful genetic selection, over countless generations the most advanced shaman-masters of twenty to forty thousand years ago might well have developed into a civilized master race in the midst of a Stone Age population.

Furthermore, the nearer such adept communities lived to Central Asia and to the World Tree, the ultimate source of spiritual power, the more strongly would this process of forced growth operate and the more irrevocably would the few separate out from the rest of humanity. Under such conditions, a small governing Inner Circle of the kind Bennett envisages would be virtually inevitable, as would the enlightened mode of government from a distance that is actually always predicated of Shambhala.

In 1969 Bennett translated and published a paper by a Turkish Sufi writer, Hasan L. Shushud, which summed up Bennett's own conclusions distilled over a lifetime. The paper stated:

> Tradition asserts that for thousands of years there has been an "Inner Circle of Humanity" capable of thinking in terms of millenia and possessing knowledge and powers of a high order. Its members

intervene from time to time in human affairs. They do this, not as leaders or teachers of mankind, but unobtrusively by introducing certain ideas and techniques. This intervention works in such a way as to rectify deviations from the predestined course of human history. This inner circle, it is claimed, concentrates its activities in those areas and at those times when the situation is critical for mankind.[19]

And Walter Owen, another English writer on the same topic, says:

The members of the Fraternity are neither omnipotent nor arbitrary. Free will, the core of man's individual selfhood, is inviolable. They do no more than influence, prompt, persuade, impede. Their implements are natural law; and the materials upon which they work are the desires, hopes, fears, passions, appetites, antipathies and hatreds, the egocentric motives and designs of humanity that in the mass still bows down to the idols of the Stage, Den, Mart and Tribe, whose will is the "arbitrium brutum" of pathological reactions, and that is mentally little beyond the hunters of the mammoth.[20]

THE COMMUNITY OF THE BLESSED ONES

Despite the contemporary mental set towards egalitarianism, there seems to have been no period in history and no traditional culture in which superior Guardians of humanity have not figured in one occult context or another as belonging to an older and wiser and more advanced race than our own, to whom we owe all the humanizing and civilizing benefits of life. And one of the oldest and most widespread occult beliefs is that the souls of the Guardians are originally not even of terrestrial origin, but incarnate into our race from a much older one that lives among the stars.

Nicholas Roerich says that in Hindu-Buddhist mythology the Gods or Blessed Ones first came from the constellation Orion and made their soul-descent in Altai, probably on Mount Belukha, the highest peak in the Altai

Range, which has a name meaning "Orion-dwelling-of-gods." The lamas, adds Roerich, associate this legendary complex of ideas with Gesar-Khan, with Shambhala, and specifically with the world-mountain Meru. Herodotus too learned from the ancient Egyptian records that in the eighteenth millennium B.C. the souls of a race of godlike beings descended to earth from Orion and continued to do so, "taking mortal form" here for a further six thousand years, to the benefit of earthborn humanity; and that in the fifteenth millennium B.C. they appeared in Libya as the Ousir, the race later personified in Egyptian mythology as Osiris.[21, 22] All these legends from antiquity resonate significantly with Hapgood's theory of an unknown Ice Age civilization and with Bennett's parallel hypothesis of a master race of highly evolved magicians ruling a coexistent but vastly inferior Stone Age population.

The Gnostic tradition also makes an extraterrestrial claim for the Children of Seth. The Gnostics were a heterodox branch of early Christianity who asserted that their primogenitor Seth, the third son of Adam and Eve, was one who, unlike his quarrelling brothers Cain and Abel, enjoyed an unclouded connection with the divine realm and its celestial denizens and, incarnating among us, came as a messenger of light, a redeemer, into our imperfect world from one beyond it. Seth's descendants, says the apocryphal "Gospel of the Egyptians" recently found among the Dead Sea Scrolls, are "the vast imperishable race that came forth from three (earlier) worlds."[23] And Dr. Stephan A. Hoeller, a modern Gnostic, states that the Children of Seth "may also be understood as a body of enlightened Gnostic adepts present in the world in every generation who possess a distinguished luminous prehistory in their own right."[24]

The sacred *Book of the Great Invisible Spirit* known as the *Gospel of the Egyptians* was written by the Therapeutae, the Egyptian Essene school of healers and physicians who preserved much of the Hermetic wisdom of ancient Egypt and passed it on to the Gnostics. In the ancient Egyptian tradition, Seth was a sun or sky god, one of the twelve gods and goddesses of the Egyptian pantheon and the brother of Osiris, Egypt's primary god whom he slew and dismembered. For that reason Seth, of whom we shall hear more in the following chapter, figures in the popular mythology of ancient Egypt as an evil and disruptive force. The Hebrews incorporated Seth into their own mythology, gave him an Adamic pedigree and identified him with the rebellious fallen angels whose story is contained in the Jewish apocryphal books of Enoch and the Jubilees. These told how Azazel, chief of the Sons of God, fell from heaven with his angelic host through disobedience to the High God and intermarried with human beings, and how these angels became the forbears of a race supreme in knowledge and magical skills.

They were called the Holy Watchers or Rephaim (from the Hebrew word *rapha*, to heal) and, despite their moral ambiguity, were believed by many Essenes to be their spiritual primogenitors who had passed on their marvellous healing powers. In fact, the Greek word *Essenoi* is related to the Hebrew *Hazah*, "he saw visions," as well as to the Aramaic *Hasaya*, meaning "pious," and to *Asa*, "he healed," and is therefore cognate with the name of the fallen angel Asael or Azazel—which means healer or visionary one of God, a description which peculiarly fits the learned Essene sectarians of Jesus' day.[25]

The slightly later Gnostics of Nag Hammadi also placed their Seth tradition within this context, representing him as a Son of God who had come voluntarily from the heaven-worlds and fathered a race mighty in wisdom on the earth. But they believed him to be a being of light, not of darkness. The Hebrew priesthood, noted for its unsympathetic interpretation of the myths of surrounding races, excoriated the Sons of God as heinous reprobates, but Seth may perhaps be seen more truly as the Gnostics saw him, as equivalent to a Bodhisattva, an emissary of Light sent to earth to assist in humanity's evolution and to guide its faltering steps towards enlightenment.

The hierarchical implications in the Seth hypothesis have been in general as repugnant to the modern mind, suspicious of any form of elitism, as they evidently were to the ancient Jewish priesthood, and so we have consistently edited out of the collective consciousness the considerable weight of evidence in favor of the theory. Still less is it a palatable thought that the gulf between the higher race and our own may be unbridgable; yet so it is said. For unlike the majority of initiates who rise through the spiritual ranks of humanity through their own labor and devotion over many lives with the aid of whatever cycles of initiation our society has to offer, the Children of Seth are born into the world with a heritage of knowledge and power already gained during the life span of an earlier race. They are the Ancient Ones, already supremely enlightened and having access to psychospiritual powers that belong to a different world, a different time from our own, and which bestow on them the right and obligation to govern. In this they are constrained by only two things: the laws of the cosmos and our right to the exercise of free will.

In the *Antiquities of the Jews,* Josephus says that the Children of Seth were reputed to be great astronomers, "inventors of that peculiar sort of wisdom which is concerned with the heavenly bodies and their order;"[26] and here we are reminded of Pythagoras, the Egyptian-trained master of the Solar Mysteries, who had outstanding astronomical knowledge for his period and who, although he lived seven hundred years earlier, was even more explicit than the Gnostics about the extraterrestrial origin of both Gods and human beings. Pythagoras described the universe as an organism animated by a soul and infused by a supreme intelligence whose material and spiritual evolution were parallel and concordant movements; one was explained by the other, and together—and only together—they explained the world.

He was in possession of astronomical knowledge that would be utterly forgotten by the Middle Ages, understanding as he did that "the planets coming from the sun revolve around it, that the stars are so many solar systems governed by the same laws as ours, and that each has its appointed place in the vast universe."[27] As for the human soul, "it emanates from an unchangeable and higher spiritual order as well as from a former material evolution, from an extinct solar system,"[28] and has inhabited many other such solar systems. A visitor only on this earth for evolutionary purposes, it is humanity's destiny to evolve beyond it, beyond the moon, beyond the orbits of the outermost planets and beyond the Sun, and so to return to the true home-world lying far from this solar system in the depths of the universe.

The Pythagorean doctrines concerning the universe and humanity's eternal journeying through it, from star to star and in wave upon wave of races, those earlier helping to raise those coming later, were passed on in secret to subsequent Mystery schools and are reflected to this day in a wide range of esoteric writings from both East and West. A Sufi story, for example, recounts the occasion on which the teacher Muhiyuddin of Andalusia, perambulating around the Ka'aba in Mecca, glimpsed among the pilgrims an excarnate being doing the same. Accosted by means of a certain Sufi technique called "direct perception" and questioned, the being confessed that he was last in incarnation in a time before Adam. "While Adam is the father of the human race," he explained, "thirty other worlds preceded him."[29]

And another legend concerns the invisible guide of Sufis, the immortal Imam El-Khidr, whose cloak is of green fire and whom some Muslims identify with Elijah, the Hebrew prophet who was taken up in a whirlwind to heaven and has never died. One day an importunate dervish recognized El-Khidr in disguise. "I threw myself on the ground in front of him, crying: 'You must be the Presence Khidr, the Green One, the Master of Saints. Bless me, for I would attain.'"

"He said: 'You have seen too much. Understand that I come from another world and am, without their knowing it, protecting those who have a service to perform. You may have been a disciple of Sayed Imdadullah, but you are not mature enough to know what we are doing for the sake of God.'"

"When I looked up," the dervish recounted, "he was gone, and all I could hear was a rushing sound in the air."[30]

The blessed El-Khidr, whom the Koran cites as Moses' anonymous Guide in the desert, is the prototype of the Shambhalic Guardian. His legend goes back, according to the archaeologist Geoffrey Bibby, into Middle-Eastern prehistory, long before the Hebrew religion evolved, and links up with the even older worldwide legend of the Gods—the ultimate in the stratification of society. Guénon indeed refers to Shambhala-Agarttha as an undying organization through which Immortals like El-Khidr communicate sacred wisdom of nonhuman origin "across the ages to those capable of receiving it."[31]

Time and the corrupting hand of legend have blurred and confused the accounts of these superhuman adepts that the Mystery traditions have passed down to us, but the knowledge is never lost. It can be recovered and reinterpreted in contemporary terms again and again. It tells us that the initiate Hierarchy to which these beings belong is the central axis or *merudanda* of the whole human race, collectively performing the hidden evolutionary function of the chakric system in individuals. It is also in its formation and function an exact reflection of the World Axis; and both axes, the racial and the planetary, coincide in Shambhala. Thus Shambhala, the World Axis and the Hierarchy are in principle synonymous. This is why we find at the heart of all our mythologies the same archetypal complex of ideas, involving an assembly of wise beings who meet in judgment on the fields of Heaven, and always at the foot of a World Mountain, a World Tree or a World Pillar of Truth.

PART TWO

The Tree

Push on to the ultimate Emptiness,
Guard unshakable Calmness,
All the ten thousand things are
moving and working
Yet we can see the void whither they
must return.
All things, however they flourish,
Turn and go home to the root
from which they sprang.

—*Tao Te Ching*

Shambhala:
The Garden of the Tree of Life

In the lexicon of religious symbols the Tree of Life is one of the holiest and the most universal, as well as being arguably the most ancient. There is a tree, often represented as two, bearing the fruit of wisdom and eternal life in every one of the many versions of the Shambhalic myth, whether it be a peach, plum, apple, almond or date tree;[1] and as a symbol of the World Axis this fabulous wish-fulfilling tree sometimes replaces the mountain at the center of the kingdom, while at other times it grows on its summit or in the nearby garden of the King's or Goddess's palace. Basically it tells us that wisdom and longevity are the gifts of the axial experience, but it tells us in the mythological terms that have become the inheritance of the whole race. Even the festive Christmas tree is a part of that mythology, as Anne Baring and Jules Cashford point out:

> The evergreen tree we call the Christmas Tree, with candles flickering on its branches and gifts strewn around its roots, was once honoured as the Tree of Life, or the World-Tree. Uniting the dimensions of heaven, earth and underworld, it was the cosmic axis at the centre of the world, the *Axis Mundi*, through which the eternal energies of creation poured continuously into time. The greenness of the Tree of Life at this darkest moment was then, and is still under a different name, the sign and the promise of life eternally renewed. . . . Similarly, the silver star on the top of the Christmas Tree, the one the magi saw, is as a mythic image the pole star of the

world axis and the bright star of Inanna, Aphrodite and Venus, accompanying all the divine births all over the Near East.[2]

The peoples of classical antiquity worshiped the Tree of Life in the rites of a Pillar religion that appears to have once been universal. During the Bronze Age sacred trees stood in the innumerable garden sanctuaries of the Great Goddess throughout the ancient East, witness to her sacrificial Mysteries. In the Canaanite and Israelite high places a sacred tree stood adjacent to the *masseboth* or stone pillars that were a feature of these open-air sanctuaries; while in some cultures of the period the tree and the pillar were combined in a symbolic representation of what is quite clearly the *axis mundi*.

Thus a Syro-Hittite seal of c. 2000 B.C. depicts a sanctuary of the Goddess in which an icon of the World Pillar stands; it is guarded by the Mesopotamian hero Gilgamesh in dual manifestation as well as by a priestess and a cherub holding a branch, while at the bottom of the seal is a guilloche, a labyrinthine device that corresponds to the Hermetic caduceus. This particular sacred pillar consists of close serpent-coils that bear at the top a symbol of the sun, while around the sun-symbol are four little circles that symbolize four rivers flowing to the four corners of the world—the waters of everlasting life which flow from the World Axis and sustain the earth (Fig. 8). The owner of the seal is also present in this idyllic little scene, so it is probably a memorial to his initiation into the Mysteries of the religion.

We in the West are familiar with the Tree of Life primarily through its central role in the biblical myth of the Garden of Eden; but it has long been known that this Hebrew tale was culled from earlier Sumerian, Babylonian and Egyptian mythologies which Egyptologist Wallis Budge has traced to an even older unknown common source. It is probable that that source was Central Asia and that the Garden of Eden myth originated in remote times in the region of the Siberian shaman's World Tree, being later carried to every part of the world, and that Shambhala was in fact the first sacred garden. All the salient features mythologized in the Genesis story are present in Shambhala: the Tree in the center of the holy garden with its magical gifts and powers, the four rivers, the divine Presence and its serpent power, the husbanding of the garden by human initiates, the eating of the ambrosial fruit of the Tree of

Knowledge. Only *guilt* is absent. While these paradisial motifs are common to all the ancient Garden of Eden myths, only the Hebrew version has subverted the original meaning. As Baring and Cashford point out: "The Genesis myth is unique in that it takes the life-affirming images of all the myths before it—the garden, the four rivers, the Tree of Life, the serpent and the World Parents—and makes of them an occasion not of joy and wonder but of fear, guilt, punishment and blame."[3]

Figure 8. *Syro-Hittite Seal showing the Axis Mundi (undated).*

To Shambhala too may be traced the origin of the two primary esoteric systems that form the foundation of all religions from the Pillar cult to Islam: the Far Eastern Tree of Truth and the Hebrew-Cabalistic Tree of the Sephiroth. Ancient seals found in the ruins of the Indus valley cities give evidence of the existence there of a pre-Buddhist cult centering on the Tree of Truth (the Bodhi- or Bo-tree, meaning the "tree of awakening") thought to have come from Central Asia and still very much alive in India. Buddhism evolved from this old arboreal religion that has spread in various forms all over the Far East, providing the underlying basis of the tree-mythology of the folkways. And the Cabala, the initiatic system at the core of all the western Mysteries, is centered on a similarly abstract representation of the tree, the Tree of the Sephiroth, which is basically a diagram of the system of psychophysical energies in both human beings and the cosmos.

The ten luminous sapphire-like rays of the Tree of the Sephiroth are described in the Jewish *Sefer Yetsirah* (the Book of Creation) as a diagram of the spectrum of energies and powers underlying the manifested world. Ernest Scott has defined the Sephirothic Tree as "a cross-section of the Body of God, showing energy flows within it and the connections that exist—or may be made—between the various terminals."[4] The sephiroth, combined with the letters of the sacred alphabet, are the gateway to the secrets of Creation and are said to give rise to the world of matter. Like the eastern Tree of Truth, the western Cabala is a powerful system of self-transformation. "Given a knowledge of these energy levels and their lateral connections," says Scott, "a man may, beginning from his own level, ascend the whole diagram, identifying with and acquiring the properties of each, so retracing the road along which he was projected from the Ain Soph."[5] In either of these two systems he may in time creatively control all the forces of the universe, becoming one who, entering Pardes, learns the deepest mysteries of things and wins immortality.

These systems of initiation have evolved over thousands of years from the study of the World Tree by mystics in intimate communion with it; men and women who learned at first hand, in the environs of Shambhala, the secrets of the psychospiritual axis of the earth and correlated them with the axial secrets of their own bodies. The knowledge thus acquired was closely guarded and passed down in an oral tradition reserved for a very small elite; but in time it and the associated serpent-symbol of kundalini spread into the folklore of the world by the more open avenue of myth and allegory. And it is at this secondary level of understanding that the tree-and-serpent motif has attained its unique religious and occult significance, becoming the primary symbol at the heart of the Semitic religions.

In Neolithic cultures the serpent was symbolic of the creative generative source of the universe and signified healing, metamorphosis and the dynamic power of waters. At that early period the great serpent goddess of the abyss was worshipped, she who from the watery ocean of Being gave birth to earth and heaven; while later, in Sumer, the serpent became the wise consort of the goddess and was known as Ningizzida, Lord of the Tree of Truth. Always the companion of divinity, the serpent accompanies the Sumerian Tree of Life and later communes with Eve from the branches of the Tree of Knowledge in the Garden of Eden. Intertwining serpents form the hieroglyph of the Sumerian god Ningizzida as well as the spiral of the caduceus of Hermes, the Egyptian guide of souls; and a serpent winds round the staff of Asclepius, the Greek god of healing. In Aztec and Peruvian mythology too there is a cosmic tree which has an eagle at its topmost branch and a serpent at its roots, and in all cases, whether the serpent twines among the branches or the roots of the tree, it represents the fecundating energy of the universe.

THE TREE OF SACRIFICE

What becomes clear from an appraisal of world mythology is that, while there is a fundamental identity of the tree and mountain symbols, in the tree motif a deeper, more religious dimension is revealed: in it a play of opposites is darkly present. For however well hidden, the message of the tree is that the giver of immortality is also the giver of death. The mystico-religious associations the tree has always had with the idea of sacrifice and its redemptive power, and therefore with the great savior figures of history, has elevated it almost to a divine noumenon in its own right: it is the tau cross on which the god is sacrificed, the Tree of Salvation—but also of immolation—that tells us eternal life is won only through self-sacrifice.

In fact the sacred gardens of the Great Goddess were the places of human sacrifice. The Sumerians of Eridu revered a wonderful tree with roots of white crystal that "stretched towards the deep, its seat the central place of the earth, its foliage the couch of the primeval Mother. In its midst was Tammuz."[6] And Tammuz, who hung upon the tree, was the ever-living, ever-sacrificed god-king and son-lover of the great Mother Goddess who gave his body to the fertilization of the earth. According to the same principle raised to a higher religious dimension, Jesus Christ hung on the Tree of Redemption on the mount of Golgotha, died there and was resurrected to give eternal life to all: and this crucifixion, as depicted in a painting on the thirteenth-century English Eversham Psalter, took place on the crossed branches of a living tree whose other branches were cut back to the stem, rendering it the archetypal Tree of Life.

Likewise, under the Bodhi-tree at the Immovable Spot the Buddha, facing east and guarded by a mighty serpent-king, attained supreme enlightenment through surrender of self for the liberation of all sentient beings. So too the child-savior Mithra, like his Zoroastrian counterpart Gayomart, was born under a tree which then magically nourished and clothed him, after which it was his task to sacrifice the primeval bull—his own animal nature—for the benefit of all beings. And in the Icelandic Poetic Edda, which reflects the Gnostic mysteries of Mithraism, the Germanic All-Father Odin (Othin or Woden, the chief of the Aesir), tells of his immolation on the initiatic tree whereby he acquired the wisdom of the runes for his people.[7]

> I ween that I hung on the windy tree,
> Hung there for nights full nine;
> With the spear I was wounded, and offered I was
> To Othin, myself to myself,
> On the tree that none may ever know
> What roots beneath it run.
>
> None made me happy with loaf or horn,
> And there below I looked;
> I took up the runes, shrieking I took them,
> And forthwith back I fell.
>
> Then began I to thrive and wisdom to get,
> I grew and well I was;
> Each word led me on to another word,
> Each deed to another deed.[8]

In the Voluspa, the song of the Old Norse prophetess, the tree on which Odin hung is called *mjot-vithr,* the "measuring-tree," for it was believed that at the foot of that tree called Yggdrasil the laws were first brought into being by the Aesir and quantified, and it was therefore worshipped as the source of all higher knowledge. "With the idea of the supporting beam [that is, the heaven-pole or world axis]," says W. Hauer, "was connected that of proportion, hence of order and measure. . . . Thus the symbol of the world-pillar

160

expressed the belief in the firm foundation of the universe, in which measure and strict order ruled, and which was firmly upheld by an eternal support."[9] But since the higher wisdom energies are obtained only at the expense of the lower, involving a kind of death, tree-worship has everywhere been associated with sacrifice as well as with spiritual knowledge and regeneration.

Each race has considered a certain tree or species of tree sacred and has consecrated it to the sacrificial rites of its priesthood. In one of the Indus valley seals, the naked Earth-goddess, the great and terrible Kali, stands between the parted limbs of one of the consecrated pipal trees; in another seal a human sacrifice is being offered beneath the tree, deities of the garden in attendance. The Druidic oak groves of Britain and Brittany, the sacred Chinese mulberry groves, the Delphic laurel of Apollo and the oracular oak of the temple of Zeus at Dodona, the ash groves of Scandinavia and other cultic trees peculiar to the Persians, the Romans, the Hawaians and the Japanese, served once as local foci of reverence for the mystery of the World Tree. Thus in Christian folklore Christ's cross, like the frame of the shaman's drum, was made from the wood of that tree, even as in Greek folklore the steering timber of Jason's ship, the Argo, was fashioned from the magical wood of the oak groves of Dodona sacred to Zeus.

Sacred literature was written by initiates who were still in touch with the underlying mystical source of folklore and were able to convey its true meaning in wonderfully evocative poetry. Thus in the Voluspa, the World Ash Yggdrasil[10] is declared to be the greatest of all trees and the best; its limbs spread over the world and above the heavens, its shaft is the pivot of the ever-revolving sky and it stands on three roots. One is among the Aesir in heaven, "where there is the very holy well known as Urdr,"[11] whereby the gods sit in judgment over the souls of men; a second root stands over the Mist World, the sphere of human life in which lies the well of wisdom full of ancient lore; and the third root, gnawed by the great worm Nidhogger, is among the Rime giants, the guardians of the chthonic or material world below. These three roots stand for the three primary cosmic planes, the spiritual, the human and the chthonic; and through them streams the great current of divine life-giving energy in the symbolic form of a tree trunk with spreading roots below and spreading branches above (Plate 4).

Plate 4. *Yggdrasil, the Mundane Tree. The terrestrial plane in the center is encircled by the Midgard Serpent, its vital principle.*

Yggdrasil is presented as the embodiment of the suffering of self-sacrifice, for it is half-alive, half-dead, an image of the inextricable twining together of life and death, pain and bliss in the garden of Being as creatures everlastingly feed on its substance. In this image of death and initiation with its interplay of opposites, says Joseph Campbell, is the sense of an impersonal cosmic process that transcends the individual destiny. According to the Poetic Edda:

> The Ash Yggdrasil suffers anguish,
> More than men can know;
> The stag bites above; on the side it rots;
> And the dragon gnaws from beneath.[12]

Around Yggdrasil plays the entire drama that is also depicted in the Indian mahayugic cycle; as the World Axis it gives birth, rejoices and suffers death. It knows all the phases of the eternal merging and separating of the opposites, creating world unity at the beginning of things and proceeding through disunity to apocalyptic warfare at the end of every cosmic aeon. In that End Time it witnesses how the hellhound Garm breaks his fetters, how in the form of the Fenris Wolf the chthonic forces rise and run free across the earth, burning and devastating; how gods and giants do mutual battle. Then Thor engages the Midgard serpent, Odin fights the Wolf, good and evil contend and, as in the Kalachakra at the end of the Kali-yuga, the world ends in a fiery holocaust that shakes Yggdrasil's branches and wounds it to the death.

This is the world cataclysm called *Ragnarok*, the Germanic Twilight of the Gods that is said to recur again and again in cycles of degeneration and renewal throughout history. On each occasion "the fire leaps high about heaven itself,"[13] and with the union of the chthonic and heavenly fires the turmoil and the warfare cease; the opposites once again converge, Yggdrasil is at peace and paradise returns to the Ida fields of the Gods. So runs the Poetic Edda, written about a thousand years ago from a far older oral tradition, in a saga that tells us in metaphor that in the act of creation suffering and bliss are inseparably wedded and are at the heart of divine redemption. Those who are saviors cannot reject one without rejecting the other and cannot give life without accepting death.

Despite their philosophical depth, the sorrow of Ragnarok pervades the Scandinavian sagas and overshadows the whole of Germanic mythology. But the farther back the arboreal myths are traced the more innocent they are of grief and the more the emphasis falls on life triumphant and the power of death denied. Even the archaic rites of human sacrifice practised in the Sumerian gardens of the Goddess-Mother Inanna, culminating in the death of her divine consort, cast no shadow, but serenely affirm that death and self-renunciation are the ecstatic background to life and are woven into the bliss of being. It is as though the closer the myths come to their source, either in time or profundity of meaning, the more they partake of Shambhala's innocent purity and joy.

INITIATION AND THE WORLD TREE

Many of the seals and plaques of the late Bronze Age commemorate temple initiations in which the candidate underwent a three-day temple sleep and was led in his inner body, in a state of trance, through the gates of death into the spiritual world; and these memorials are outstanding for the impression they give of optimistic acceptance of death. Thus a gold Cretan-Mycenaean ring found at Pylos, dated to c. 1500 B.C. and showing the Tree of Eternal Life engraved on its oval face, depicts a garden scene of happy tranquillity that is situated in the blessed land of the dead, the Elysian Fields of Greek mythology (Figure 9). "The field of the design," writes Sir Arthur Evans,

> is divided into zones . . . by the trunk and horizontally spreading boughs of a great tree . . . old, gnarled and leafless. It stands with spreading roots on top of a mound or hillock with its trunk rising in the center of the field and with wide-spreading horizontal boughs. The scenes that its branches thus divide belong, in fact, not to the terrestrial sphere, but to the Minoan After-World. An obvious analogy is suggested with Yggdrasil, the Ash of Odin's steed and the old Scandinavian "Tree of the World."[14]

Here the human figures grouped round the World Axis are of a joyous vitality and are engaged in dramas of reanimation of the body, reunion of lovers after death and happy processionals towards the Halls of Justice.

Figure 9. *The Minoan Tree of the World engraved on the Mycenean gold "Ring of Nestor" (c. 1500 B.C.).*

The schools of the Greater Mysteries were the pivot of the early civilizations. It was believed that initiation was essential not only to the continuing evolution of the soul but to the further development of its intellectual and emotional instruments, and that at least once in the life of the individual he should have, through initiation, the opportunity of returning to his spiritual birthplace at the center of the world, there to receive transforming grace. And here again, although the neophyte encountered death, his initiation culminated in a joy that suffused his life thereafter.

Before his initiation, the Greek Apuleius was told by the officiating hierophant that the event would be like a voluntary death followed by a slow recovery, and in a fragment preserved by Stobaeus, Plutarch said in a passage that strangely echoes accounts of the Grail search and the search for Shambhala:

Thus death and initiation closely correspond. At first there are wanderings and toilsome running about in circles, and journeys through the dark over uncertain roads and dead ends: then, just before the end, there are all kinds of terrors, with shivering, trembling, sweating and utter amazement. After this, a strange and wonderful light meets the wanderer; he is admitted into pure and verdant pastures, where he discerns gentle voices, solemn dances, and the majesty of blessed spirits and sacred visions. Here he is free, being now fully initiated, and walks at liberty like a crowned and dedicated sacrificial victim, joining in the revelry.[15]

It was in such a state of trance that the candidate's soul was transported to a higher plane, as was Khamtul Rinpoche's in his Tibetan monastery, and there glimpsed for the first time some of the inhabitants of the upper spheres and kingdoms—the devas, dakinis, angels and heavenly animals that become visible near Mount Meru—as also the residents of the hidden kingdom. These are the Masters, the Lords of Shambhala, either incarnate or, as the Greek philosopher Proclus tells us, appearing as beings of light.

The initiate might meet in that sacred space his spiritual master or alternatively a celestial psychopomp such as Hermes, Mithras or Anubis, who would act as his guide and guardian; and there, in the company of the already perfected, he would be further purified and prepared for higher initiations still. For it is said that each branch of the tree is the gateway to a higher world and a further rite of passage of the soul, and at each gateway the Guardians appear. After such an experience death is never again feared but is met gladly.

Isis and Osiris: Shamanism in Egyptian Mythology

The farther back in time we trace the arboreal myths the more clearly we discern behind Bronze Age culture with its pictorial opulence and genius for clothing every idea in colorful dramatic metaphor, signs of the simple shamanic tradition from which it grew. Although shamanism enjoyed a revival during the classical period of Egypt and Minoan Crete, it was at its apogee much earlier, in the depths of the Ice Age, its archaic idiom prefiguring the later classical themes, its primary stamping-ground Siberia. A plaque found at Mal'ta, near Lake Baikal, and dated to c. 16,000 B.C., is inscribed on one side with the sevenfold spiral, the symbol of the cosmic Center, and on the other with three undulating serpents, traditionally regarded as symbolic of kundalini in the three worlds.[16] And in much the same area and Palaeolithic period, flying geese have been found carved on mammoth ivory and are regarded by Joseph Campbell as representing the shaman's astral flight, itself foreshadowing the mystic flight of the Buddha.

The vision of the tree as World Axis, Campbell observes, is a characteristic of Siberian shamanism, both then and now. Modern Tungus shamans say that a great religion once flourished in the Altai mountains and that although the tradition has degenerated since then, so that they now enjoy only a remnant of their former greatness, they still revere the mighty Tree Tuuru that grows there, its nine branches spreading over the world and reaching up to the zenith of heaven.

"Up above," one of the shamans told Ivar Lissner, who spent seventeen years with the Tungus tribes,

> there is a certain tree where the souls of the shamans are reared, before they attain their powers. And on the boughs of the tree are nests in which the souls lie and are attended [by sacred winged animals from the lower worlds] . . . The higher the nest in this tree the stronger will the shaman be who is raised in it, the more will he know and the farther will he see. . . . According to our belief, the soul of the shaman climbs up this tree to God when he shamanizes; and it is while in his trance of rapture that he performs his miraculous deeds. While in this trance he is flying as a bird to the upper world or descending as a reindeer, bull or bear to the world beneath.[17]

The nest in which the shaman's soul is specially reared is in one of the upper bardos or heaven-worlds familiar to Buddhists, and beneath it lies the Middle World or Middle Earth of human embodiment into which he will be reborn; while below Middle Earth are the three nether-worlds of the sacred animals. And so, despite his naive imagery, the shaman's cosmology conforms in all respects to the spectrum of heavens and hells known to all the later religions and metaphysical systems as well as being woven into many of the myths of the Bronze Age world. Some of these, such as the Homeric myth of Artemis, goddess of the hunt, are frankly shamanistic in tone; but there is probably no legend from that period which in its arboreal imagery so betrays its debt to Siberian shamanism as the myth of Isis and Osiris. It is here that the hidden meaning of the tree-mythology fully reveals itself, lifting it above duality into a wholly spiritual realm in which life and death achieve union.

The many oral versions of this predynastic Egyptian myth Plutarch collected and wrote down in the second century C.E., but, although it is set in Egypt of the Bronze Age, it may well be as old as Egypt before the sands, perhaps one of the oldest myths in existence. For that very reason it is more transparent than most to the shamanism underlying all of them. On one level it recounts the drama of the lovers Isis and Osiris and their antagonist Seth. These were three of the nine gods and goddesses of the Ennead, which was the Egyptian assembly of divine rulers of the world descended from the supreme God and which corresponded to the Greek pantheon of Gods, though the latter numbered twelve. But on another level the myth is an account of the two degrees of initiation of a shaman and gives us a unique glimpse into the direct relationship of the World Axis to the shaman's transformations of consciousness in which life and death are no more than alternating phases of eternal being.

As we have already learned, Osiris was identified with the constellation of Orion and therefore has a connection with Shambhala, or more specifically, with the divine race that first appeared in Altai and then, about two thousand years later, in northern Africa. He was worshipped as a god of the "dark mysteries" who knew the secrets of the stars, and was etymologically related to the world family of Gods. Schuré points out that the Etruscan Aes or Aesar, Gallic Aes, Scandinavian Ase, Copt Os (Lord) and Egyptian Osiris have the same root;[18] and so probably has Azara the name of the guardians of Shambhala. The true hieroglyphic name of Isis, says Wallis Budge, was Às or Às-t, meaning a throne or pillar; that of Osiris As-àr or Asar, sometimes rendered Asaru (a form of Osiris worshipped in lower Egypt).[19] Osiris is thus related to the gods of the north, for in Old High German *às* means the central post, beam or pillar of a house, whose plural is *aesir*; therefore the race of the Aesir were immemorially called the pillar-gods.[20] Again Osiris is often referred to as An. In a hymn to Osiris he is called "the god An of millions of years" and also as "An in An-tes, Great One, Heru-Khuti, thou stridest over heaven in long strides."[21]

This name is specifically connected with the idea of the heavens, and the appellation relates him to the Sumerian god of heaven, Anu, and to the mysterious Annunaki of Sumerian mythology (of whom Anu was the chief god), as well as to the Igigi, a dominant branch of the Annunaki specializing in astronomy.[22] Osiris may also be linked to the Ojin, the primeval gods of Japan who settled in the Hida mountains and gave that land its early arts and sciences and its Shinto religion. And through Orion he is, of course, related to Siberia and Altaic shamanism.

The founding myth of the Egyptians recounts how Osiris came to their land from the direction of Libya to teach them the arts of cultivation and the honoring of the gods, and to "establish justice throughout both banks of the Nile;"[23] and how he married his sister Isis and reigned as the first king of Egypt. He traveled to many other distant lands to give their people civilization, and while he was away Isis ruled peacefully in his stead. But his brother Seth, jealous of his fame and good fortune, sealed him in a casket and flung it into the Nile. There it drifted into the open sea and was carried by the tides to a far country—Byblos in Phoenicia in Plutarch's version—where it came to rest in the roots of an erica tree that grew up around it and finally enclosed the coffin entirely in its trunk, hiding it from view.

Now the queen of that land, discovering the fragrance of the erica tree and becoming enchanted by it, had it cut down, made into a pillar and erected as the central beam of her palace; and it was to that pillar that Isis, mourning, traced the body of her beloved husband. Acting as the nurse of the youngest royal child, she secretly placed him every night by the pillar, which burned away his impurities as in a holy fire, while she, in the form of a swallow, flew round and round it, singing a mournful song. But the queen, coming upon this scene, snatched the child away in horror, thus depriving it of the opportunity of eternal life. Then Isis claimed the pillar, had it cut open and rescued

Osiris; and, turning into a kite, she fanned him with her great wings until he was brought back to life. According to some versions of the tale, it was then that she conceived Horus, her divine son by Osiris.[24]

We have here a classical account of the preliminary purification in the initiation of a shaman, in a far place, away from kith and kin and concealed within the "darkness" of the trance state. We have the presence of water, the emotional medium that facilitates initiation; the Tree of Life that is the spiritual fire in which the infantile soul with its base desires and appetites must be sacrificed; the transformation within that fire of the divine part of the soul; and finally the soul's resurrection or rebirth to new and more effectual life. In Isis's birdsong, piping and mournful, we recognize the song of the entranced shaman that so many ethnologists have reported and that harks back in time to the bird-figures of shamans painted in the Ice Age ritual caves of southern France. Isis's flight around the erica pillar recalls the flight of the shaman around the World Tree, encircling it as he weaves his ecstatic spells and utters his strange bird cries; and in Seth's action, which seems to do such violence to human hopes and joys, is to be found the shaman-master's call to Dharma, to spiritual duty, when the time is ripe for the further evolution of the soul.

Seth is perhaps the most mysterious figure in Egyptian mythology, the alter ego of Osiris, who is the Lord of light, consciousness and order. Like the Siberian shaman's trickster-god, Seth is both the epitome of the principle of darkness and chaos and the culture-bearer, the creator. He symbolizes the potential energy of creation, raw, chaotic and untamed, that lies at the deepest and darkest level of the psyche in the unconscious, and which erupts again and again at the call of evolution to destroy our finest works in its inferno. Yet it does so only in order to sow new seeds so that, in rebuilding, we may redeem it, harnessing and controlling its unpredictable powers in the service of an even greater good. At that point the cruel shaman-master, Osiris's dark brother, becomes the willing servant of the new order and thus reveals himself as the divine reconciling and creative force in the universe.

Just as the sacred tree in the story of Isis and Osiris was transplanted to the center of the royal palace in Byblos, so at each tribal seance the Siberian shaman plants a tree in the center of his tent in memory of the great Tuuru, and the symbolic tree is also called Tuuru. At the annual Isyack or Wesak festival a sacrificial ceremony called the Uplifting of the Soul of the Horse is conducted, after which the shaman hangs the pelt of the sacrificed animal on the symbolic Tuuru, even as the golden ram's fleece that Jason sought was hung on the sacred oak at Colchis. Therefore Tuuru, like Osiris's erica tree, is a tree of sacrifice; on it the shaman is purified by the shedding of his infantile desires in exchange for the divine knowledge that gives him the ability to communicate with the dead. Like Osiris, who was elevated to become the Lord of the Dead, the judge and savior of souls in the underworld, the shaman is transformed into a mediator between the living and the dead; he too becomes a Lord of the Dark Face.

Now after the events at Byblos Isis returned to Egypt, where she hid her husband's body temporarily in a chest and placed it in the rushes of the Nile Delta while she returned to Buto to care for her little son. This suggests that the process of divinization was not yet complete. Sure enough, while Seth was out hunting the wild boar, he came upon the chest and, opening it, tore the body of Osiris into fourteen or sixteen pieces, which he scattered up and down the shores of the Nile. Once again Isis was bereaved and once again she sought her husband, this time down the length of the mother-river; and although in time she recovered the pieces of his dismembered body and reassembled them into the living Osiris, one piece was never found. The lost piece was Osiris's penis, which some traditions say was swallowed by a fish, the symbol of godhead; the meaning being that it was sacrificed to his awakened divinity.

The Egyptian priests believed that wherever a piece of Osiris's body fell a cache of esoteric knowledge was buried, awaiting a time when humanity would be mature enough to receive it. Each cache was a terma concerned with a particular aspect of knowledge; one with astronomy, another with medicine and so on; and wherever it lay, there a temple was built and priests were set to guard the treasure. But at a deeper level Osiris's dismemberment was a description of the second degree of initiation of which all shamans speak that raises them to the highest level of proficiency, of adepthood. Of a similar initiatic ordeal a Tungus shaman called Semyonov Semyon said:

My ancestors stood me up like a block of wood and shot at me with their bows until I lost consciousness. They cut up my flesh, separated my bones, counted them, and ate my flesh raw. When they counted the bones they found one too many. . . . The same thing happens to every Tungus shaman. Only after his shaman ancestors have cut up his body in this way and separated his bones can he begin to practice.[25]

This visionary experience with its peculiarly psychosomatic component is still undergone by some Far Eastern mystics. In it the redundant or missing genital member of the shaman is replaced by one of quartz crystal, a classic metaphor for the process of kundalini awakening. Thereafter he is the denizen of the three worlds. He is empowered to fly to the nether worlds to rescue the souls of the sick and dying from the chthonic grip of the Lord of Death, even as Isis rescued Osiris, or to fly up to the heaven-worlds with intercessory messages to and from the ancestors and the Lord of Life, the great Invisible Spirit—by which same means Osiris's apotheosis was achieved.

Hovering over him, Isis fanned his body again with her great wings of the spirit and he revived to become the Ruler of Eternity, his Passion benefiting the whole universe. "He now sits in the underworld with all power and majesty, in the Hall of Two Truths," Plutarch writes, "where he judges the souls of the dead, which are weighed in the balance against the feather of truth of the Goddess Maat, she in whose care are the laws of the universe."[26]

As for Seth, the wild creative impulse was now willingly yoked to its creation. "The time of the confusion past . . . the unregulated, chaotic powers of the universe were now mastered," say Baring and Cashford, "and, further, brought into relation with the new order by being required to help sustain it. In the festivals of Osiris along the Nile, Seth was the boat that carried his effigy, just as he carried the sun through the watery abyss of night."[27]

As an allegory of the shamanic Mysteries the idyll of Isis and Osiris probably evolved over an enormous period of time. World religions rework a very few basic themes which they express in terms adapted to the age and culture in which they arise, and the love that divinity has for the human soul is a theme that has been told again and again around the world, although never more beautifully than in the love story of these two deities, once no doubt rulers of prehistoric Egypt. Their age-old story helps to throw light on the origin of the Pillar religion in the shamanic mysticism that emanated from Central Asia. It belongs to the world's remote presacerdotal past, when priests wore the animal masks and pelts of the shaman, as Egyptian murals testify; when religious experience was focussed on spirit-possessed trance states and was deeply bonded to the natural kingdoms, and when spiritual vision was keener than at any other time in human history.[28] Only in such a clairvoyant age, before the growth of technological societies, could such a direct knowledge of the World Tree have developed and its mysteries have been so simply and yet so profoundly understood.

WHERE IS THE WORLD AXIS?

The Pillar religion developed its more theistic and institutional features around the sixth millennium B.C., when Central Asia entered a period of great climatic change. Searing wind storms and drought scoured the rich grasslands that had teemed with game, turning them into desert and bleak tundra and forcing unusually large migrations of nomadic peoples into more settled lands to the south, where they seeded anew their cult of the World Pillar. In that period, says Guénon, Shambhala became an underground organization and the age of Mystery religions and secret societies began. Sacrificial altars were erected on the Goddess Mother's altars, and her consort the god-king became known as the Heaven-Bearer, the god of the pillar whose ritual sacrifice and resurrection remained the central mystery of the faith for as long as it endured.[1]

Although the idea of the World Tree is implicit in the tribal totem-poles found in all early shamanistic societies, it was not until the early Bronze Age that the ubiquitous votive pillar descended from them developed an arboreal style and was embellished with finely worked ornamentation, being usually mounted on a three-tiered pyramid or an altar stone. The top of the pillar was modeled in the shape of the Tree of Life, having outstretched arms with rounded or rolled-up ends representing its two widespread lower branches, and was known as a volute (Figure 10). The wedge-shaped point between the two arms was called the resting-place of the heavens, which the Assyrians located "in the amber land of Kaptara on the Upper Sea, where the pole star stands at the zenith,"[2] while above the point of the wedge were light symbols;

the pole star for the night sky, the sun for that of the day.

The volute design occurs in the most diverse cultures. Archaeologists have uncovered many examples of it embellishing sacrificial altars in the *bamoth* or high places of biblical Palestine and on the island of Malta. A scarab with the seal of Ramses IV shows the volute design; so does an Assyrian cult pillar and a god-seat in Malta, and so do drinking vessels of the Philistines of biblical fame, whom the Hebrews called Kaphthorites or pillar people. The Saxons too worshipped the Irminsul, sacred to all early Germanic races as the All-Pillar that holds up the universe and as the seat of the gods. A column that displayed the volute as a symbol of the north, the Irminsul is probably related to the Roland pillars still found in many market-places in northern Germany: in medieval times the seat of the magistrates was beside these pillars of justice and equity, where trials were held and oaths sworn.[3]

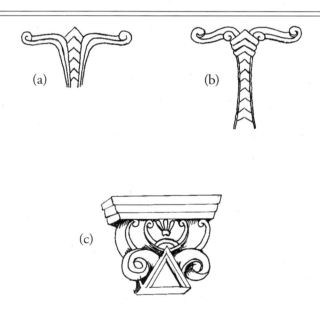

Figure 10. *Three Examples of the Volute. The Volute: (a) On a Philistine Bowl, 1160 B.C. (b) Old Saxon Irminsul (c) Stone Capital from Cyprus; (heaven-pillar with sun, half-moon and stars.*

The volute has passed into the symbolism of the later world religions and has been called "the god-symbol of a sacred principle of world-organization."[4] Professor W. Wirth, a Scandinavian scholar, claims that the consistency of its form, the religious significance it always displays and the extent of its distribution over all continents point to it as being one of the oldest symbols of an early religious worldview, one of the first great conceptions of a world order. By "early" Wirth is no doubt implying something primitive. But in fact the volute design as a development based on the Tree of Life, far from being a primitive cosmological conception, a first crude attempt by early humanity to explain the world, bears the timeless authority of a fundamental truth about the structure of the cosmos: one that has been passed down through the ages to every race whose faculty of psychic vision has not entirely atrophied and which still survives in the esoteric brotherhoods.

To this day the symbolism of the pillar or twin pillars is familiar in such circles.[5] Two pillars, for instance, are normally found side by side in any Masonic temple, where they form the two basic symbols of medieval craftmasonry. One is known as Boaz, the pillar of strength, the other as Jachin, the pillar of wisdom; but essentially they are one. Identical in construction and design, they represent the Tree of Life. Trevor Ravenscroft likens them to "the Yggdrasil tree of Norse mythology, the world-Ash which binds together heaven, earth and hell. The crown of this tree," he says, "comprises the twelve constellations of the Zodiac, the spiraling branches symbolize the planets and the roots of the trunk dig deeply into the elements of the earth."[6]

Behind the Masonic symbolism lies the concept of a supra-planetary galactic order. The great chain of cathedrals which Ravenscroft describes as running from Scotland to Portugal, following a line of earth-chakras, is marked at each end by one of these identical pillars, and part of the archway that unites the whole is the English Great North Road, "which was called by the Romans Lactodorum, meaning the constellation of the Milky Way."[7] Like the serpent that bites its tail, the length of the chain of spiritual centers returns to itself, unified like the zodiacal wheel of the galaxy and locked into an abstract figure in which the two pillars are dual aspects of a single World Axis.

The life-giving poles or perches that once existed throughout the known world in the sanctuaries of the Goddess Mother emerged in ancient Egypt as the Djed pillar, which was carved from a tree-trunk and erected on an altar in the temples of Isis. It was sometimes represented in murals as a tree with four horizontal branches like those L.C.W. saw, and its raising from a horizontal to an upright position marked the dramatic culmination of the New Year harvest celebrations and the day of the Sed festival, when the periodic rites of Egyptian kingship were renewed.[8]

The word *Djed,* which meant "stable" or "durable," was a synonym for Meru, for it had the further meaning of Osiris's backbone. Seth's killing of Osiris had "laid the Djed on its side,"[9] but Osiris had prevailed in the end; his backbone had stood up again; life had vanquished death and had, literally, risen up Osiris's spinal column, rejuvenating him. The ceremony was therefore a hidden allusion to the dauntless power of kundalini over the forces of destruction as well as to the ever-living spirit of the corn, which is cut down yet grows again towards the light. And the raising of the Djed had a further planetary meaning, for it also celebrated the rising of the sun each morning.

Figure 11 shows the goddesses Isis and Nephthys kneeling on either side of the Djed, assisting in the creation of the sun out of the womb of cosmic life. Here the sun, say Baring and Cashford, "rests between arms forming the sign of *Ka*—the divine embrace in which each thing, person and god is held—coming from the *ankh* of imperishable life, itself coming from and generated by the Djed column."[10] This formulation of the world process of creation reminds us that every individual alive is connected by gravity to the center of the earth and therefore to the World Axis, and is, however unconsciously, held in the loving and divine embrace of the same power that upholds the sun. Something of this esoteric mystery must have still been known to the Egyptian priesthood when they celebrated the rites of the Djed pillar.

However, it is likely that by then their knowledge was largely derivative and that they had only a limited understanding of the location or deeper significance of the prototypic World Pillar. According to the Medinet Habu texts, the early Egyptians were aware only that it stood in the far north under the pole star, in the uttermost northern darkness where the sun had its resting-place. The Heaven-Bearer, they said, lived in the northern "midnight" from which the sun rose each day, for there eternal night reigned. In the Pyramid texts he was called Tat, the god of wisdom "born in the distant darkness."[11]

This pillar-lore the Egyptians connected with the amber traders from the Baltic region, the Haunebu, who came south bearing costly gifts of amber for the pharaoh. They called the Haunebu "the people of the pillar" because, according to the pylon of the pharaoh Horemheb (1333–1310 B.C.) they lived in the north where the true Heaven Pillar stood.[12]

Figure 11. *Isis and her sister Nephthys kneeling at the altar helping the Sun to rise from the Djed pillar (Papyrus of Ani, c. 1250 B.C.).*

In China a symbolic World-Pillar called the Heaven-Earth Axis stood at the center of the Ming T'ang, the imperial residence at the center of the kingdom, and the god of the Pillar was called Wang. The Germanic races called him Irmin or Iormin, the Greeks Atlas and the heaven-pillar he supported the *stele boreios* or the north pillar. The Indo-Europeans who had invaded pre-Hellenic Greece, adapting their gods and mythology to their new

Mediterranean home, brought with them from northern lands the cult of the Pillars of Atlas, the god who held up the sky by means of a pillar and who persuaded the hero Heracles to take his place. But they too, like the Romans and other races of antiquity, knew the World Axis only as a pillar or pillars somewhere in the remote north.

The Pillars of Heracles were not originally associated, as they now are, with natural rock formations on either side of the Strait of Gibraltar, but were known to be man-made votive pillars that appeared in many lands settled by Indo-European migrants: among other places as far east as Sogdiana, between the Jaxartes and the Oxus rivers, and at the mouth of the Hellespont in Asia Minor. Alexander the Great erected such pillars at the easternmost point of his conquests, and the Greek historian Posidonius, who in c. 90 B.C. spent a month studying the tides at Gades, now modern Cadiz, spoke of two man-made Pillars of Heracles standing there before the temple of Heracles, about one hundred kilometers north of Gibraltar. But Apollodorus of Athens stated emphatically that it was not the Pillars at Gades that Atlas gave Heracles to hold but those in the far north. "Atlas," he said, "stands among the Hyperboreans,"[13] by which he meant the race of sages believed to live in the extreme northern latitudes. In the *Aeneid* Virgil is equally explicit that the North is where "Atlas, the Heaven-Bearer, holds on his shoulders the turning spheres inset with blazing stars."[14]

However, there is no evidence that the people of antiquity equated the World Axis with what we know as the rotational axis that emerges at the North Pole, despite our ready assumptions in this regard. As Spanuth points out: "It is a basic fault in historical method, but an extremely common one, to attribute to ancient people modern geographical knowledge and conceptions, and to equate the names and phrases used by the ancients with those of modern geographers."[15] This is precisely the mistake we make when we try to understand the classical conception of the World Axis from our own point of view.

For one thing, it evidently had a much broader and more metaphysical meaning than anything with which we are familiar today. "According to one particular form of symbolism common to most traditions," says Guénon, "it is the 'bridge' connecting Earth to Heaven; or connecting the human state of existence with other, supra-individual states; or linking the sensory world to the world beyond the senses. Each of these possibilities is just a different expression of the same fundamental idea of the 'World-Axis'. . ."[16] The stress he places on the psychospiritual nature of the World Axis in both the Eastern and Western traditions should warn us that any simplistic physical assumptions about it would be wide of the mark and a gross undervaluation of the subtlety of the classical mind.

As for Classical geography, we can learn little from the ancient geographers (of whom the Egyptians were the most advanced) that does not suggest that for them the World Pillar stood considerably south of the North Pole—as did the pole star in antiquity. As may be seen from an Egyptian world-map drawn up c. 1200 B.C. (Figure 12), only a portion of the upper half of the Western hemisphere was known. This region is shown as a flat disc surrounded by a great water-circle, the *sin wur*—that is, the northern Atlantic Ocean—bisected by the Mediterranean Sea, then called the Great Green, and divided into nine divisions called bows, which roughly correspond to our modern lines of latitude; and the Heaven-Pillar stands in the land of the ninth bow, whence came the trading Haunebu. Evidently the north pole was not known, nor the rotation of the earth.

The Greeks and Romans knew no more of the world than the Egyptians. They adopted the same system of bows, which they called *paralleloi* and *circuli* respectively, and the whole world ending at the equator as "all the nine bows." The tenth bow was conceived to be in the northern sky, at the apex of the Heaven Pillar where the sun rested at midnight. Pliny the Elder, the Roman scholar of the 1st century C.E. said the ninth division of the world "goes across the Hyperboreans [i.e., the lands in about the same latitude as present-day Jutland] and Britain with a 17-hour day (at its longest)."[17] The ninth bow, therefore, according to the Romans, corresponded to the area of the globe between latitudes 52 degrees and 57 degrees north, passing, as can readily be seen, through Ireland, Britain, southern Scandinavia, northern Germany, southern Siberia, Japan's Hokkaido Island and Hudson Bay. These, then, were the lands, all well below the Arctic Circle, in which the peoples of antiquity located the mysterious Heaven Pillar and where they also sited the paradisial kingdom in the north.

Figure 12. *Egyptian World Map (1200 B.C.).*

Clearly they recognized that the World Axis was connected with the rotation of the heavens in some manner not then known to them; but it also had connotations which seem to distinguish it absolutely from the earth's spin axis, almost as though two separate systems have been confusedly presented as one. There are in fact many lacunae, contradictions and ambiguities in the ancient geographies which suggest just that. What emerges from a close study of them, such as Charles Hapgood conducted in his survey of very old nautical maps dating from pagan times, is that the ancient geographies are all thread-ed by a secret tradition of superior scientific knowledge, presumably emanat-ing from the temples and initiatic schools of the day.

It is this covert stream of learning, on which Hapgood comments, that provided the basis for a truly informed metaphysic concerning the World Axis, and from which garbled fragments, imperfectly understood, were leaked to profane geographers. Far from clarifying the material, however, uninitiated minds succeeded only in burying still deeper a significant body of truth by trying to incorporate it into an inadequate and crudely physical worldview. Nor does the metaphysic of the World Axis yield its secrets any better to modern geographers, however sophisticated their science has become in the last three hundred years. Guénon makes that abundantly clear. Opening up the secret scientific tradition of the Hierarchy, he proposes that nothing less than a new model of the world is needed if we are to understand the true nature of the World Axis.

TOWARDS A NEW VIEW OF THE COSMOS

According to Guénon, Shambhala originally lay at the North Pole, but has shifted its location several times in the course of human history. He is unequivocal about this circumstance. "There is every reason for supposing," he writes, "that there have been several successive locations [of Shambhala-Agarttha], each corresponding to different cycles, themselves subdivisions of another, more drawn-out cycle. Were the whole cyclical content somehow placed outside of time, there would be seen to be a hierarchical order in this determining of position," whereby the various spiritual centers follow each other in succession.[18] Does this mean the World Axis shifts?

Guénon's treatment of Meru and its changing relation to the terrestrial world is the most abstruse and difficult part of his entire thesis. His vision is a vast one, involving as it does a sacred geography and a sacred history of whose principles we are ignorant, but which sweepingly correlates great continental movements of the earth with cycles of human evolution. Perhaps for reasons of esoteric security, he touches on the subject only lightly and passingly, yet sufficiently to remind us that we are in the presence of a cosmological science that has never yet been fully aired. In fact, Guénon offers little information of a practical kind about the changing geographic location of Meru other than preliminary glimpses into an unfamiliar landscape demanding centuries of exploration.

According to his thesis, behind the physical body of the earth lies its energetic template, a permanent prephysical web of forces delineating the planetary structure in its essential form. In this inner light-body or *vajra*-body is located the World Axis, the source and regulator of all the energies of the planet. At the beginning of each great temporal cycle—and by a great cycle Guénon means at the very least one round of the Zodiac, one Sidereal Year of 25,920 years—the two bodies are in virtually perfect alignment, but as the cycle proceeds, a separation occurs and the physical body falls increasingly out of alignment with its inner template, creating all the earthly stresses and vicissitudes of time and change.

Guénon's universe as a whole is at rest and in a state of ideal harmony and order, and is never disturbed in the higher dimensions. But with the separating out of the physical plane, *motion* is created and the suffering of change begins.[19] In other words, the process of increasing differentiation of the physical from its background spiritual context inflicts on the planet and all its lifeforms a local disturbance, the *angst* of movement, of disequilibrium, of continual readjustment to new conditions. The spiritual world of Being is changeless; but the natural state of its reflection on a lower plane, even at its least displaced, is to be "off-center" in relation to it and therefore in perpetual compensatory motion.

There is an echo here of Neoplatonic theory in which a perfect and timeless sphere of Being is reflected in an imperfect sphere of Becoming, whose nature it is to create time and illusion. The action of differentiating becomes the source of geophysical changes and temporal cycles, and effects a kind of local warping or distortion of the fabric of reality. And the greater the differentiation, the more the distortion; the faster the rate of change, the more intense the stress; the more solid the illusory or, rather, relativistic features (such as flux, conflict and decay) that seem to rule the phenomenal universe, the more nearly a state of crisis is approached, leading to human premonitions of catastrophe. This suffering of change—and it is a true suffering—is a natural condition of our world, as the Buddha recognized, an inevitable concomitant of coming into material manifestation.

Guénon's work further suggests that one of the geophysical expressions of this process is the separation of the poles, leading to great changes on the surface of the earth. The theory may be summarized as follows: The World Axis is not necessarily coincident with either the spin axis or the magnetic axis of the earth, although it may be on occasion. Essentially it has an independent existence. At the beginning of the great temporal cycles, the North Pole and the magnetic pole are in virtually perfect alignment with the World Axis and with each other. All three stand at that time apparently united at true North, so that the supreme spiritual center is in a literally polar location; but as the cycles proceed, the poles fall progressively out of alignment with the World Axis and terrestrial changes develop. Thus according to Guénon, although at the beginning of the present great cycle, Shambhala lay at the North Pole under the name of Tula, it has relocated southward over the millennia and is now situated in Middle Asia, where it has been for thousands of years. But more about its movements than that cannot be said with any degree of certainty.

For Guénon the whole of the phenomenal world and everything in it is dependent on the activity of Meru, that is, of the World Axis. It is the true center of the world wherever it is located, the absolute referent in relation to which everything else moves, itself unmoving. He equates its regulatory function with that of Chakravarti, the universal monarch of Hinduism, whose palace, symbolically speaking, rests on the summit of the sacred mountain; he is the one who "makes the wheel turn, that is to say the one who, being at the center of all things, directs all movement without himself participating in it, or who is, to use Aristotle's words, the 'unmoving mover.'"[20] To determine in any absolute sense the geographical location of such a supra-physical creative principle would require, as Guénon says, an expert's knowledge of the science of sacred geography, which we do not have.

Traditionally, sacred geography is based on an *open* model of the world. Our present scientific world model is closed: its referent system is not open to any dimension higher than itself; and this is much easier for scientists to deal with. But the reality is that the earth incorporates a principle that connects it at all times to a greater spiritual world. By virtue of the World Axis it *is* open to a higher dimension, and this fact radically modifies everything we can say about it, the way we can measure and describe it. Under such circumstances, reality becomes characteristically multidimensional and processive rather than static.

Guénon is reiterating ancient Taoist wisdom when he says that the physical world is a part of a greater whole that is one and indivisible, perfect, changeless and at rest, but that to come into phenomenal existence, it has to separate out from its spiritual background. Yet to thus differentiate the part from the whole is to establish a displacing motion, from whence comes duality and imperfection. Earth separates from Heaven and from the axial power that connects them; forces separate out in seemingly polar opposition to each other, and from that separation come all manifested things. Chuang Tzu, a Chinese Taoist of the seventh century B.C. expresses a similar idea, although he calls the World Axis by its Eastern name, the Heaven-Earth Axis.

> Once the two modalities of being [yin-yang] had become differentiated within primordial Being, their revolution began and the Cosmos was modified accordingly. . . . The binomial Heaven-Earth [the World Axis] is an invisible force; its action-and-reaction produces every modification. Starting and stopping, fullness and emptiness, astronomical revolutions [time cycles], phases of the Sun and Moon [seasons]; all these are brought about by that single cause that nobody perceives but which functions perpetually.[21]

Guénon quotes Chuang Tzu in *The Great Triad* in order to illustrate his own thesis, which goes far beyond traditional Neoplatonic conceptions. Within the limitations of our sadly outdated language system, he attempts to express the dynamics involved in this notion of a greater cosmic order from which the physical world separates out, creating as it does so a certain cyclic sequence of changes within the timeless and changeless whole. The multidimensional picture that emerges bears a striking resemblance to David Bohm's quantum theory of the implicate and explicate order. Bohm claims that the manifest three-dimensional world that we inhabit is an explicate order that unfolds from an unmanifest implicate order underlying it. He calls this unmanifest ground the holomovement or "ocean of energy" whose motion is a rhythmic folding and unfolding of the physical world. The idea that these two orders together constitute the ultimate evolving supra-sensible reality emphasizes, says the physicist, "the unity of unity-and-diversity" and the oneness of the whole-and-the-part.[22]

Guénon has a like vision in which he construes the underlying field analogous to Bohm's holomovement as related to the pulse of time, whereby rhythmic temporal cycles are established in the unfolding of the physical world from its primal matrix. Shambhala's shifts of location on the surface of the globe reflect, then, its cyclical adjustment to the geological changes such as pole shifts that may accompany such an unfolding,[23] perhaps also its adjustment to reversals in the earth's magnetic field. By such shifts it preserves unchanged its vital link with the World Axis. For although change occurs on one plane of the universal spectrum, on the highest planes the universe itself is unchanging, is motionless, blissful and forever at rest, and it is Shambhala's unique function to keep the earth connected to that primordial source of bliss.

THE ETERNAL RETURN

To sum up, change is a symptom of *local* imbalance, of *local* asymmetry, and has its natural term. The trajectory of time is not endless, but will cyclically return to its beginning. Our world is but a part of a greater self-organizing whole in which the mechanism of correction is built into the World Axis at the center. We may call that Axis Meru or the Absolute Norm, or, as Guénon does, the path of the Shekinah or Holy Spirit, or again Tao or the Way of Heaven. These are simply the names various races and cultures apply to the same subtle phenomenon, the life-giving flow of spiritual energy through the core of the planet. But in all cases the reality is that, in the context of eternal Being, the errors of time must always be resolved. And, as an adjunct of the World Axis, Shambhala is the avenue through which this corrective activity can happen, no matter where it is on the face of the earth in any given era.

Without wishing to enter too deeply into the metaphysical principles on which all these deductions from Guénon's work have to be based, it may be said that they rest on the premise that the universe is in all respects benign. The paradox of the existential suffering of change, of the progressive loss of harmony in a divine Creation, loses its terror when contemplated from the standpoint of a higher harmonious order of reality that never changes or decays. So too in a temporal sense, the possibility of planetary instability that such a hypothesis confronts us with is in reality contained within a higher order of unchanging paradisial repose that will manifest anew at the end of each great cycle. The *angst* is temporary; at the end of the cycle terrestrial balance will be restored, the three poles will draw together and resume their primordial approach to unity, and Shambhala will return to the polar station which in the spiritual world it has never really left.

The above gleanings from a sacred metaphysic that preoccupied the thoughts of countless adepts of traditional cultures cannot do justice to the range and profundity of their insights into the nature of the cosmos. We have touched only the periphery of a metaphysical system so prodigious that it has occupied almost the entire span of human history, dwarfing to a mere flicker of time the past three hundred years of modern science and leading to practical realizations of which our sciences are as yet barely capable. Guénon asserts that this body of wisdom is preserved in its entirety in Shambhala and that initiates continue clandestinely to feed into our general stock of knowledge keys to its far-reaching doctrines. The Pillar religion with its worship of the miraculous all-giving Tree of Life provided antiquity with one such key. Another was the myth of Gaia, the Earth Goddess.

In Classical Greek mythology the earth was still regarded as a living being, but Gaia was nevertheless subordinate to the laws of the Sky God Zeus and no longer the supreme mother of all that lived. But in the earlier Minoan, Sumerian, and Neolithic cultures, the Earth Goddess had not been one of a pantheon of gods and goddesses; she stood alone, the supreme originator of life, reverenced as "mother of all, foundation of all, the oldest one,"[24] in the words of the poet Homer. In those days the sense of a united cosmos was still strong. Thus the Greek historian Hesiod, writing in c. 700 B.C., said of the folklore of the past that his mother had learned: "Not from me, but from my mother, comes the tale of how earth and sky were once one form."[25] This sense of the oneness of all life, of the unity of heaven and earth, of spirit and matter, of earth and humanity, was lost by the time Greece came of age, as Baring and Cashford remind us.

> In the Homeric Hymn . . . Gaia is still invoked as 'Mother of All', but she has also become 'bride of starry Heaven', and no mention is made of the fact that in other myths Ouranos, Heaven, was once her child, as was everyone else whom she brought forth from herself. Here, she is the one who feeds everything in the world; she gives life and she takes it away.[26]

Today we are being given keys that bring us closer to the holistic awareness of that archaic world. Among them are further insights into the mystery of Gaia's psychoid nature that intimately relates her climatic, ecological, and even geological condition, not only to the play of forces in the greater cosmos, but also to the human thought-field that surrounds the globe and to the moral and spiritual condition of human society in general. In the body of Gaia, every organ, including the human, is wedded to every other and bears reciprocal responsibilities. And thus the psychically healthy or diseased state of humanity is a critical factor in the severity or otherwise of such convulsions of nature as may occur at the end of the great cycles. These convulsions are Gaia's way of periodically purifying and regenerating herself, a kind of spring-cleaning, and as a functioning part of Gaia, the human moral condition has the power to modify the process for good or ill.

It is said that a record of the earth's geological history is stored in Shambhala's archives and details the great movements of human-planetary evolution whereby Gaia maintains herself. In this way the Directorate monitors life on earth, anticipates its future development, and plans such action as will cooperate with the greater whole. For in the World Axis we may visualize Gaia possessing a higher governing center analogous to the human cortical governing center, by which she is able to organize her domain according to conscious, rational, psychospiritual principles in ways that promote benefit to all. From this perspective, the global convulsions of nature at the end of the great cycles are natural and organic events designed by a benign World Spirit to stabilize the planet and to bring all things on it back to their original state of perfection, repose, and high creative energy, and so to herald the onset of a new golden age.

Atlantis and the Hyperboreans: Seedbeds of Civilization

$\mathcal{G}$uénon claims that long before the Indo-European races arose the tropics were differently distributed and that a great Hyperborean culture flourished around the Arctic Circle. Shambhala was then known as the "white island" and the "sacred isle," and Meru as the "white mountain" that stood in the middle of the island, a triangle of light— "the initiatic triangle"[1]—radiating at its summit. At that time Atlantis lay to the west.

Numerous sources support the tradition that Shambhala once lay near the North Pole. The Scythians, a branch of the Vedic peoples who roamed the Central Asian steppe in the first millennium B.C., told of a wonderful place similar to Shambhala that lay far to the north. They said that if one traveled far enough, one came to lands of mythical and fantastic tribes and beyond them, to the Ripean mountains, which lay in a desolate waste of snow and darkness that no mortal could cross. Beyond that barrier lay a beautiful country, warm and sheltered from the icy winds outside, where the sun rose and set only once a year, as it does within the Arctic Circle, and there a happy race lived in parklands full of flowering trees.

According to the ancient Greeks, this was the northern station of their Delphic god Apollo and the land of the legendary Hyperboreans to which Apollo returned every nineteen years, riding the sky on a chariot drawn by swans. It was a secret paradise where the heavens turned on the polar axle, which the Hyperboreans revered as the Pillar of Atlas the Heaven-Bearer, and it belonged to a wise and prosperous people who lived for a thousand years in harmony with each other, free from suffering, sickness and old age. To the Greeks these semi-deified sages were the stuff of myth, for their land was accessible only to gods and heroes, not to mere mortals, and could only be reached by an aerial way. The poet Pindar wrote that "neither by ship nor foot couldst thou find the wondrous way to the assembly of the Hyperboreans."[2]

In the seventh century B.C., a Greek called Aristeas of Proconnesus, a priest of Apollo, traveled north-eastward towards Central Asia in a vain search for his god's Hyperborean home. Returning safely to Greece, he wrote a poem of which only fragments have survived, but which show he seemed to have got as far as Siberia. It was from this poem that the Hyperboreans received their Greek name. It speaks of lands and strange tribes beyond the ken of the Scythians, of a country rich in gold (probably the Altai mountains) and far to the north of that land a cave in which the cold north wind Boreas blows. The Hyperboreans, Aristeas said, were so called because they lived on the far side of that cave, in an Elysian country that his later countryman Herodotus located by hearsay on the shores of either the Arctic or the Baltic Sea.[3]

The tradition of a great Arctic Wisdom center that could have been Shambhala has taken a number of forms. John Bennett cites the theories of B. J. Tilak, a Hindu historian whose study of the earliest Vedic hymns led him to conclude that the Vedic people must have originally come from within the Arctic Circle, carrying their sacred hymns to the sun into Central Asia in postglacial times. Adopting Tilak's view, Bennett is of the opinion that a major center of initiation existed on the shores of the Arctic Sea in the distant past and that its adepts were the so-called Titans, the "old gods" of whom Hesiod tells, who went north after being defeated by Zeus and his new pantheon of gods and lived with "their hearts free of anxiety in the Islands of the Blest on the shores of the Ocean where the great maelstrom whirls."[4]

Bennett considers the Titans (one of whom was Atlas, later assimilated to Zeus's Hellenic family) were shaman adepts who were defeated in an apocalyptic power struggle that broke out between the clans of ruling magicians during the last Ice Age and who retreated to the Siberian Sea, a region of the Arctic that has never known ice. There they evolved the rudiments of the Indo-European language we know today. "There are," he says, "numerous . . . evidences of a Hyperborean origin to the Vedic hymns. The same is true of the

Avestan hymns and the Norse sagas. Even in Homer some passages suggest that his hymns must have come from the Arctic region."[5]

Behind all these old legends of a polar Elysium lie prodigious vistas of human history going back perhaps seventy thousand years or more to a time when Cro-Magnon people, the true Hyperboreans, were increasing in numbers and spreading around circumpolar Eurasia, gathering in Central Asia where their culture chiefly evolved and dispersing again ever farther across the world. Over a period of more than forty thousand years they migrated eastward across the Japanese Sea and the Bering Strait to the Japanese islands and the American continent, westward to the Atlantic Sea, the Canary Islands, northern Africa and the length of the eastern African coast, and crossed the Caucasus mountains into Asia Minor. But their habitat was always mainly in the vast temperate Eurasian corridor, with a strong concentration in northern Europe; and the type consequently tends to be more identified with Europe, where it was first discovered, than elsewhere.

Cro-Magnon man has been called the "signature" of the Aurignacian culture period, the typical figure of the time, but his race was not the only one to appear as the first true example of *Homo sapiens* and the forerunner of our modern race. Grimaldi man, a type resembling the Italian, appeared at the same time, as well as another one resembling the modern Eskimo, and another, the Caspian type, a smaller long-headed people, arrived in northern Africa, while a further strain resembling the bushman also appeared on the scene.[6] Over the millennia all these strains ceaselessly migrated, mingled and interbred, forming a more or less homogenous genetic pool from which our modern race has evolved.

At the height of his powers, about thirty thousand years ago, Cro-Magnon man was a magnificent creature: straight and tall—about six feet, four inches in height—larger, stronger and arguably more intelligent than modern humans, with a larger cranial capacity, a broad, rugged, handsome face and fair coloring. But by the end of the last Ice Age both his stature and his intelligence had diminished—he was only about five feet, four inches high—and he was approaching extinction.[7] His strain died out about ten thousand years ago, although it survived for a while in pockets here and there until c. 2000 B.C. and an Ainu remnant still lingers on in Japan.

Contrary to the findings of late nineteenth-century historians on which many erroneous and romantic racial theories have been built, the Cro-Magnon culture bears no relation to the myth of a superior Aryan or Indo-European master race that gained currency at much the same time that Cro-Magnon remains were found in southern France. Scholars proposed at that time that an Aryan race of exceptional physical and intellectual endowment, its birthplace in the region of Germany, was behind all the greatest and most noble human achievements and that its pure line could be traced back deep into prehistory to the European cave artists and even to Atlantis. This misconception was taken up with passionate enthusiasm by the German people and was woven into a declaration of mystical Germanic racial destiny, later popularized by the Nazis; but the theory has since been thoroughly discredited.

We now know there is no such race, only Aryan-speaking peoples from different racial groups. The nomadic forbears of the Teutonic race, steppe-dwellers of the Eurasian corridor, are a mixture of a number of races of hybrid stock and share little except their common Aryan lingual roots, which a prodigious philological study by A. Meillet and Marcel Cohen has traced to southern Russia and ultimately Central Asia.[8] There the Aryas, as the Vedic pastoralists called themselves, roamed for several thousand years, bequeathing their Sanskrit tongue to the medley of migrating and intermarrying tribes who passed that way, and so provided the basis for our many Indo-European languages. In fact modern historians, now more aware of the historical realities, are increasingly dropping the use of the terms "Aryan" and "Indo-European" altogether, as being more misleading than useful.

Cro-Magnon artifacts are not numerous and so culturally this Ice Age race remains something of a mystery. The little goddess-figurines and the skillful designs incised on antler, bone and stone dating to c. 22,000 B.C.—spirals, meanders, labyrinths, chevrons, serpents, fish, birds' wings, water, leafy branches; many of the more abstract symbolizing, as Baring and Cashford say, the intricate pathways the souls of the dead take to the invisible world beyond—testify to a peaceful society with a rich mythology of the sacred. They testify too, as these authors say, to "a surprisingly unified culture—or, at the very least, a common nexus of belief. . ."[9] But the beautiful Cro-Magnon art, the use of a harpoon for fishing and a bone needle for sewing are almost all time has bequeathed to us of their culture.

Nevertheless, after twenty thousand years and major coastal inundations, all traces of even the most advanced technological culture can vanish, particularly if confined to a small percentage of the population; and therefore, despite the poverty of evidence, it is by no means beyond the realm of possibility that Hapgood's hypothesized Ice Age civilization was a Cro-Magnon one. Indeed it is by far the most probable explanation. With such a highly stratified society as has already been postulated, the majority of the Cro-Magnon population would have been simple hunters and gatherers while the small clans of adepts led an entirely different way of life, settled, civilized and literate. The Hindu historian Sisirkumar Mitra shows that a similarly stratified social pattern existed in early Vedic community life, in which closed dynastic family groups of Rishis lived in forests outside the cities, apart from and outside Indian Vedic society.[10]

One thing that indubitably relates the Cro-Magnon race to that of the Hyperboreans is the evidence in both cases of a megalithic Pillar cult. Just as the original pillar or pillars of Atlas were said to hold a central place in the religion of the Hyperboreans, so archaeologists have noted that wherever the Cro-Magnon race has settled a Pillar culture has left its trace. The remains of countless stone circles, menhirs and troy towns are scattered throughout Eurasia and the Pacific lands, memorials to great crisscrossing migrations of Cro-Magnon people. Roerich saw thousands of such megalithic works in the highlands of Tibet, and Cro-Magnon skulls and skeletal remains are associated with a profusion of megalithic pillar-works from the Baltic to northern Africa, where the blond Tamahu worshipped the Magna Mater and her spouse the Heaven-Bearer, as did their cousins in Brittany.[11] In the Canary Islands the Cro-Magnon Guanches, now extinct, were megalith-builders who worshipped with sacrifices the god of the World Pillar whom they called "the God who Holds the Heavens," and who thus prevented the collapse of the foundations of the world.[12]

Even though these stone circles and fortifications (such as those found on many Mediterranean islands) testify to a sophisticated level of geometry and land surveying as well as a highly organized and centralized society capable of coordinating massive works, the Cro-Magnon people at their height could have achieved an even higher order of civilization. Commenting on the wonderful Ice Age cave art at Lascaux and Altimira, Baring and Cashford speak highly of the unplumbed capabilities of the Cro-Magnon race. They believe the recent discovery of a sophisticated system of lunar notation carved by Palaeolithic men on bone, stone and antler as early as 40,000 B.C. "urges us to value their intelligence more highly than we have."[13]

Citing all the evidence for a unified world culture in prehistoric times, John Michell urges a similar reevaluation:

> The entire surface of the earth is marked with the traces of a gigantic work of prehistoric engineering, the remains of a once universal system of natural magic, involving the use of polar magnetism together with another positive force related to solar energy. Of the various human and superhuman races that have occupied the earth in the past, we have only the dreamlike accounts of the earliest myths. All we can suppose is that some overwhelming disaster, whether or not of natural origin, destroyed a system whose maintenance depended upon its control of certain natural forces across the entire earth.[14]

In the enigmatic vestiges of this ancient system we can glimpse the recurring motif, repeated in countless contexts, of a cosmic marriage between heaven and earth that was perceived as the fundamental function of the World Pillar and that enabled Cro-Magnon adepts to bind the earth fast in a web of cosmic energy that ran north and south, east and west, but converging always on a supreme power center in Central Asia. And we see that the same cosmic-marriage motif, inherited from that mythic depth of time, pervaded the institutions and arts, cults and customs of all the civilizations that followed, repeating the same eternal theme of unity in diversity.

The universality of the Pillar culture has been obscured by the fact that the religion metamorphosed as it spread, developing in time distinctive local characteristics that seemed to bear little relationship to its Asiatic source. Achieving instead a high degree of autonomy and differentiation, Western religion has appeared to deny the possibility of a unified world culture such as Michell has visualized, and to present only a fragmented patchwork of cultic beliefs and customs peculiar to the West. The sheer density and chiaroscuro of intervening history has made it difficult for historians to envisage a universal Cro-Magnon culture and religion that could have existed across the earth for scores of thousands of years, encompassing many variations of style without loss of cohesion, and even more difficult to imagine that this unified state might be the norm for humanity in an enlightened world. And yet many philological and archaeological studies, as well as those conducted by Hapgood into cartographical history, have pressed the logic of just such a universal prehistoric picture.

ELECTRIS: A HYPERBOREAN WISDOM CENTER

Whether we think of it as Hyperborean or Cro-Magnon in origin, we must assume that Shambhala shifted at some point from the Arctic Sea into Central Asia, but we do not know when this happened. According to Guénon, the same people founded both Atlantis and Shambhala; but the time scale on which these events occurred and the movements of the initiate communities concerned in them is amazingly varied and ambiguous in the different occult traditions available to us, ranging from millions of years (Blavatsky) to mere thousands (Bennett) and making any definitive chronology impossible. But if Guénon's theories are correct—and he is probably our most reliable guide—we must think at the very least in terms of the last glaciation, possibly as far back as twenty-five thousand years, when determining Shambhala's shift into Central Asia.

At the same time, Greco-Roman sources confirm another long-held occult tradition to the effect that a Wisdom sanctuary called Electris was also established in the Western hemisphere; a sanctuary which the early Greek historian Hecataeus claimed had been built by the sea-god Poseidon, the father of Atlas. This was the home of the Hyperboreans so revered by the ancient Greeks. According to the report of Diodorus Siculus of the first century B.C., quoting Hecataeus, the sanctuary existed on a large island "no smaller than Sicily" and presumably off the coast of Europe, since it was "opposite the land of the Celts."[15] He tells us it was built as a troy town after the pattern of the spheres, by which he meant an astronomical design similar to that of Stonehenge and other ancient sun temples, in which the scheme of the heavenly spheres or astral shells surrounding the earth was represented diagrammatically by a series of concentric circles marked by walls, ditches or moats around a central pillar-stone.

Diodorus said that the Hyperborean island was an especially holy place, rich in precious metals with which the people adorned a magnificent temple dedicated to the worship of Apollo, and where they passed their days in feasting while beautiful maidens danced and sang to the music of lyre and lute. Within the temple complex stood Atlas's heaven-bearing pillar and there also the *hieros gamos* or divine marriage rite was celebrated between gods and mortals, which the anthropologist Robert Heine-Geldern has called one of the sacred mysteries of the Megalithic Age. The Greek poet-dramatist Euripides named the island the marriage-bed of Zeus, for in the enclosure at its heart Leto, a mortal maiden born on the island, according to one version of the tale, bore him twin children, Apollo and Artemis. In another version Leto was a Titan, one of the old goddesses of pre-Hellenic Greece.

There can be little doubt that at some time in antiquity the sanctuary that the Greeks called Electris was, like Shambhala, part of a global web of initiation centers and that at a secondary level it influenced the whole of the Western Hemisphere. Bernbaum points out the many significant ways in which it is similar to the Asiatic center. It was in the land of the Hyperboreans, he reminds us, that the Hesperides were said to guard the golden apples of immortality that grew on the World Tree; and it was there that the Greek hero Perseus sought the magical means for the slaying of Medusa, the terrible Gorgon with hair of snakes. In Bernbaum's words:

> The journey to both places gives one magic powers, embodied either in objects such as winged sandals or else in the effects of mystical practices. These powers help one to overcome the forces of evil; they enable Perseus to slay Medusa, and the King of Shambhala to kill the tyrant who takes over the world. By turning people to stone, Medusa symbolizes the forces of bondage that work against liberation; we find a similar motif in the journey to Sham-

bhala where the traveller must cross a river whose touch would turn him to stone.[16]

And in both cases, after many difficult adventures getting to the northern paradise, "the Hyperboreans go on to a better world, and the inhabitants of Shambhala proceed towards Nirvana, which lies beyond any earthly paradise."[17] Moreover, in the annals of mythology both sanctuaries have been accorded a culture-bearing role, for classical Greece regarded the Hyperboreans as models of wisdom, tranquillity and the aesthetic virtues and revered them as the founders of Greek civilization, even as the adepts of Shambhala are revered still as the founders of Asiatic civilizations.

The Orphic Argonautica, which dates from the sixth century B.C., reflects the mystical power of the island of Electris when it refers to it as the seat of the gods "which lies under the pole star in the furthest waters of Tethys."[18] Taboo wisdom centers of such note, looked to as the divine home of gods and demi-gods, must have been imbued with terrible mystery and fascination, presenting to the surrounding populace a face veiled in wondrous legends that changed with the changing periods of history. Electris was doubtless a barbaric settlement in the beginning, a center of high shamanic magic inhabited not by the common run of prehistoric tribesmen but by families of divine Cro-Magnon stock, powerful shaman-masters and pole lords like their cousins in Altai; guardians of a sacred place forbidden to the tribes of wandering hunter-gatherers and generating unearthly and awesome tales of the supernatural. Thousands of years must have passed before its reputation, still charismatic, acquired the rich Hellenic patina that Diodorus extolled.

Yet from the beginning all such sanctuaries seem to have been modeled on a single architectural prototype, as instantly recognizable as Muslim mosques are recognizable the world over and in all periods as emblematic of Islam. It is probably due to this basic similarity of architectural design that from the fourth century B.C. onward some scholars have equated Electris with Plato's Atlantis, despite numerous discrepancies, and the Hyperboreans with the much-debated and ill-fated Atlanteans. Guénon states explicitly that the Atlanteans were Hyperboreans, and as we shall see later, there have been several allusions in our literature to the possibility that Shambhala and Atlantis were once Hyperborean sister-centers of initiation, one in the eastern mountains and the other in the western sea. Centuries of devoted research into the Atlantis story have in fact uncovered a significant number of parallels between the Atlantean legend told by Plato and the Greek Hyperborean one.

ATLANTIS: "A PRIMORDIAL GLORY THAT WAS LOST"

Plato's tale of Atlantis and its tragic end are as famous as it is baffling. The priests of Sais on the Nile Delta told it to Solon, a distinguished Greek lawgiver, when he visited Egypt in the sixth century B.C. Returning to Athens, Solon wrote down the account he had been given, which was derived from original records contained in ancient Egyptian temple inscriptions and papyrus texts. The unpublished manuscript passed into the possession of his family, and a hundred years later is reputed to have found its way into the hands of his kinsman Critias and from thence into Plato's hands. Plato then included the dramatic and poignant story of the lost kingdom in *Timaeus and Critias*, although he was never to finish it.

His story of Atlantis as it has come down to us is of a high civilization founded by the gods and centered on a royal city called Basileia which lay on an island somewhere outside the Strait of Gibraltar, but which in a single dreadful day and night sank forever beneath the waves. This vanished land, says Geoffrey Ashe, "is the noblest setting ever conceived for a drama that has haunted imaginations through the centuries; the drama—the tragedy—of a primordial glory that was lost."[19]

Atlantis was the size of a continent, fertile, an earthly paradise; and like the Hyperboreans, the Atlanteans were said to be of unparalleled spiritual and creative genius, skilled in the sciences, with an aristocratic society and wise laws written on a god-pillar dedicated to Poseidon that stood in the middle of the sacred enclosure at the heart of the metropolis. In 1882 Ignatius Donnelly, an American lawyer turned author, characterized Atlantis as the world's first and finest civilization, which pioneered medicine, the use of metals and alphabetical writing, theorizing that its rulers became the gods and goddesses of Greek, Hindu, Phoenician and Scandinavian mythology.[20]

Again like that of the Hyperboreans, the Atlantean influence, so Plato tells us, dominated a large part of the Mediterranean world. Its ten districts, which in time included surrounding islands and parts of Europe and Africa, were ruled by ten kings, five sets of twins born to Poseidon and Cleito, a mortal woman born on the island; and the children were reared in the city's inner citadel, which was forbidden to all save the royal family. The eldest twin of the five pairs traditionally mounted Atlantis's throne, his nine royal brothers swearing fealty to him.

Like Electris, Atlantis was originally built as a troy town which grew into a large city. Plato's narrative states that on the hill that lay in the center of Basiliea, the Atlantean capital city, stood a holy shrine of "somewhat outlandish [i.e. barbaric] appearance,"[21] with Poseidon's pillar at its midpoint; and around the hill were built five concentric circles of sea and land equidistant from each other. They formed three moats separated by two rings of land and protected the Great Mother Cleito from all possible harm. Poseidon had laid them out in the beginning of things at the very dawn of time, "when there were still no ships or sailing";[22] from which we can deduce that, like Electris, the citadel was built in a very early period indeed. But with the passage of time a great city grew up around the outer canal, busy harbours were built for the fleet of ingoing and outgoing trading ships, and a covered causeway was constructed between the outermost harbor and the inner citadel (Figure 13).

As has been said, it was a ground plan familiar to the ancient world. In the Prose Edda it is said of Asgard, the most holy shrine of the Aesir, that "men call it Troy," and we may therefore surmise that the fabled city of Troy that the Achaeans destroyed was built on just such a plan, as Homer's *Iliad* suggests, and provided the name by which these pillar-enclosures became universally known. Like Atlantis, like Asgard and like Electris, Troy too was probably an ancient Wisdom center.

For a long time, said Plato, the Atlantean priest-kings, heading a loose confederation of kingdoms, ruled benevolently over their empire; but at last the divine strain was weakened by continual miscegenation and, corrupted by love of power, greed and other "mortal" weaknesses, they began to tyrannize over their subjects and overextend their dominion, "arrogantly advancing from their base in the Atlantic Sea to attack the cities of Europe and Asia."[23] Then the nations rose up against them and in a great battle they were defeated by a coalition led by the Athenians.

It was at this point that a great convulsion of nature destroyed both the Greek armies and Atlantis, which in earthquake, flood and fire was submerged beneath the sea. According to the Egyptian priests, this cataclysm took place nine thousand years before Solon's visit to Egypt in the sixth century B.C. Thus the Atlanteans suffered divine retribution according to a judgment already passed on them by a tribunal of their fellow Titans and were destroyed. Since then no trace of the Utopian splendors of their mother-city has ever been found save a sea of mud impassable to sailors where once land stood.

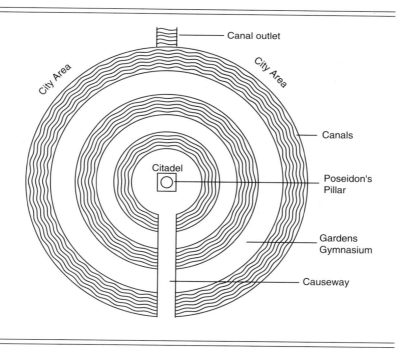

Figure 13. *Atlantis: A Troy Town.*

Plato's countrymen gave little credence to his tale. Nevertheless, it was a fact that they had called the holy island of the Hyperboreans Electris, after Electra the daughter of Atlas, Poseidon's eldest son; and Atlas, as Plato tells us, was the first king of Atlantis. Indeed Atlantis and Electris have the same meaning, according to Eberhard Zanggar. Atlantis took its name from Atlas, or rather from Atlas's daughter; for the name is a *patronymikon*, a word that describes a father/daughter relationship, so that, literally translated, Atlantis means "Atlas's daughter"—as does Electra.[24]

Underlying this genealogical detail are hints of the great dynastic order that must have once maintained a worldwide network of Wisdom centers and provided the channel for their chain of spiritual transmission down the ages. The *modus operandi* of this dynasty was the *hieros gamos*, an institution that was probably begun towards the end of the last Ice Age, when kingship first came into being, and that offers one of the most important clues to humanity's transition from a Palaeolithic to a Neolithic level of culture.

Archaeological traces of the *hieros gamos* are found in every part of the world. Sumerian seals found in the city of Lagash, which flourished in the third millennium B.C., show that a temple priest officiated with all due ceremony at the sacred coupling of what appear to be a high priestess and a king.[25] For the latter, the act, when knowledgeably performed, would have had the effect of a spiritual initiation. Behind it lay a long tradition of sexual yoga. The transmission of higher energies by such a method, undertaken by an adept for the purpose of improving the royal stock, had the effective power of a genetic science and was capable of creating deep physiological and psychological changes in the royal line.

Little is now known of this most secret aspect of Yoga Tantra, but it is recognized in initiatic circles that the exchange of energies entailed, while of great benefit to one of the partners, is disadvantageous to the other. For the adept it is a self-sacrifice and an act of compassion. It was therefore in a spirit of altruism that in post glacial times the divine race relaxed the taboo that had traditionally surrounded adept communities and began to offer spiritual initiation to selected members of inferior races through the practice of the sacred marriage, thereby eventually creating a new and improved human stock and securing divine dynastic succession in the royal houses thus founded.[26] The mixed communities that then became possible led to the breaking down of old tribal patterns, to a class system, institutional religion, trade, urbanization and the modern world.

The theme of kundalini awakening in all its richness and human pathos has threaded its way unseen through all our mythologies. The biblical allusion to the Sons of God who mated with the daughters of men is a distant echo of this secret practice whereby great men of renown were born to high initiates and women of lower uninitiated stock and became priest-kings mighty in knowledge. A similar legend is current in Asia concerning the Nagas of India, the mysterious order of shaman adepts whose totemic animal is the serpent, and who are reputed to have mated on occasion with members of the Indian royal families in order to improve the ruling stock.

Of such a mixed lineage is Atlas. In Greek legend he takes his place in a line of ten divine kings or queens beginning with Uranus and continuing through Poseidon, Atlas, Electra and six further descendants. Each one is said to have been born of a god and a mortal, to have built a city and brought the arts of civilization to nomadic tribes sunk in ignorance. As we can see, the Atlantis story picks up a theme that in Hyperborean guise was well known to the Athenians and repeats its same timeless motif of miscegenation and self-sacrifice in the interests of evolution.

Thus Leto, the Hyperborean maiden who conceived Apollo and Artemis by Zeus on Electris, is philologically related to the Great Mother Cleito on the island of Atlantis, she who was the spouse of Poseidon and the mother of Atlas. Both Cleito and Leto were earth-born (i.e. uninitiated) maidens born on a holy island; both became mother-goddesses by union with a god; both bore lesser gods or semi-divine offspring. The name Cleito, says Jurgen Spanuth, became Leto with the passing of the Hyperborean story into the Greek language, and both names refer to the great Goddess-Mother who ruled the ancient world for more than thirty thousand years, until the patriarchal Hellenes reversed the old mythological order.[27]

The Athenians also assigned to the Hyperboreans just such a priestly culture-bearing role as Plato gave to the gods who founded Atlantis. Bearing in mind Socrates' tragic fate as a heretic, Plato was in general guarded in his treatment of the gods, but he knew they were human like ourselves and on occasion quoted Hesiod, who in an earlier and more liberal age had referred to them as both "the golden race that came first," and the First Race, initiates and philosophers who, wise and caring, had in remote times guided the development of the simple uninitiated tribes who fell under their care.[28] So too

Plato speaks in *Timaeus and Critias* of this senior race who had founded Atlantis and equates them with the Titans, the "old gods" who ruled universally before the Olympians and who at the very dawn of time had divided the whole earth up between themselves, so that each god-clan ruled a portion of it.

The Critias narrative continues by telling how the sea-god Poseidon took Atlantis for his own:

> Once upon a time the gods divided up the earth between them. . .
> Each gladly received his just allocation, and settled their territories; and having done so, they proceeded to look after us, their creatures and children, as shepherds look after their flocks. They did not use physical means of control, but brought their influence to bear on the creature's most sensitive part, using persuasion as a steersman uses the helm to direct the mind as they saw fit and so guide the whole mortal creature.[29]

By this we can assume Plato meant the teaching of philosophical and religious principles and ethical practices. And his narrative indicates that the religion the Gods propagated was the Pillar religion, the same as that practised by the Hyperboreans.

In the Critias dialogues it is recounted how the ten priest-kings gathered together periodically to celebrate the bull-sacrifice, the centerpiece of their cult:

> Their rule and community were governed by the injunctions of Poseidon, enshrined in the law and engraved by the first kings on an orichalc pillar in the temple of Poseidon in the middle of the island. . . And before any prospective judgement they exchanged mutual pledges in the following ceremony. There were in the temple of Poseidon bulls roaming at large. The ten kings . . . entered alone and started a hunt for the bull, using clubs and nooses but no metal weapon; and when they caught him they cut his throat over the top of the pillar [in the Greek text *kata koryphen autes*] so that the blood flowed over the inscription.[30]

There followed a feast in which the limbs of the bull were consecrated to Poseidon, after which the ten kings sat in judgment at the foot of the pillar; a practice that reminds us of the Aesir who sat in judgment at the foot of Yggdrasil.

Now, in the Greek text *koryphe* means the volute at the top of the pillar of sacrifice, and so presents us with yet another example of the correlation of Atlantean and Hyperborean religious symbols and practices. In Old Norse both the volute and the center post supporting the roof of a dwelling is called às; and às, it will be recalled, was the hieroglyph of Isis, às-ar that of Osiris. From às also comes the name Asgard for the holy island in the Eddas on which the Aesir foregathered for their royal ceremonies. From this widespread association of the cult pillar with royal judgment as well as sacrifice stems the volute's original meaning of a throne, of kingship, of supreme authority both spiritual and temporal, which it has retained from Neolithic times. The kings and leaders of Western nations have carried the volute up to the present day as a scepter or sacred emblem, and the royal lily emblem of France, evolved from the Irminsul, is prefigured without change in Hittite, Assyrian and Scythian examples and, as we now note, in the Atlantean example as well.

The Lost History of Ancient Greece

It is clear that the Atlantean culture shared many significant points of similarity with that of the Hyperboreans, and that hieratic centers like these, governed by great dynasties of priest-kings, were once a prominent feature in the landscape of early civilization. If the Athenians had not forgotten their former Achaean world, they would have recognized the striking parallels between Plato's lost city and the homeland of the Hyperboreans and would have understood their factual basis. But Athens was a city-state shipwrecked in time; it had no past. To its populace even Homer's reminiscences of long-gone historical sagas had acquired by the sixth century B.C. no more than the cultic gloss of myth. Their Bronze Age world had been forgotten.

Historians have frequently noted that it is almost impossible to pierce the dense pall obscuring the past beyond the sixth century B.C., when civilization was first re-emerging from a Dark Age that had lasted for six hundred years; and it is no doubt due to this circumstance that we must at least partly attribute our strange ignorance of history prior to the rise of classical Greece.

A number of scholars have theorized that some kind of geological disaster must have visited the earth towards the end of the thirteenth century B.C., causing a spontaneous outbreak of volcanic activity of an unusually violent nature, followed by earthquakes, floods and fires across much of the globe; and there is some archaeological and climatological confirmation of this theory. Although disputed by others, it has been put forward to account for the otherwise inexplicable and sudden destruction of so many flourishing civilizations at that time, which swept away historical knowledge and plunged much of the known world into darkness, causing to our certain knowledge the precipitous decline of Bronze Age Greece.[31]

The roots of its culture had lain in the Egyptian, Minoan and Mycenaean civilizations, but by 1200 B.C. the Minoan world had vanished. After that date the light of the Mycenaean civilization too was extinguished forever, and Greece descended into barbarism. It was cut off from Egypt; links with the north were broken as the old trade routes ceased; written records were destroyed and with them the art of writing itself, and as historical scholarship declined the Greeks mythologized history and invented their own past on the rubble of a ruined world order.

Greek adventurers plundered the treasure of dying cities, and Greek poets recalled a lost world of gods and heroes, of fallen empires and a blissful seat of the gods where the dead rested at ease; but vaguely, imaginatively, without genuine historical knowledge, for much of the past had been irretrievably lost. It was not until the sixth century B.C. that a galaxy of writers and philosophers like Pythagoras, Hesiod, Aeschylus, Democritus and others down the centuries were able to knit anew the fabric of civilization in a reinvented form. The renaissance came from Central Asia, when Hyperborean missionaries of Apollo founded a sanctuary first on the island of Delos and then in Delphi, bringing Greece the arts and sciences of a new age.

Hyperborean Apollo did not belong to the Olympian pantheon; he came to Asia Minor from an earlier age and a region in which shamans and adept-magicians worshipped a Supreme Being who, says Schuré, was originally known under the name of Ap Olen or Ap Wholen, meaning Universal

Father.[32] But when Apollo's cult took root in Delphi he was turned into a Sun God and given a new birth-story that enabled him to be absorbed into the Hellenic pantheon of Zeus, although never entirely losing the imprint of his circumpolar origins, as Guthrie shows.[33] Apollo brought the Athenians new tidings from the heart of Asia in a form best suited to their reborn culture.

Wherever we turn in this story of the ancient Mediterranean world we come upon tantalizing echoes of a larger ambience and of currents of cultural communication and fertilization that had their epicenter far from Greece in the Altaic zone, among masters of trance and ecstasy. The essential point of the Atlantean story, and one that is still too often overlooked, is that Plato presented Atlantis as a prehistoric Wisdom center that became, according to the Egyptian priests who enlightened Solon, the hub of a great quasi-religious Western empire. It probably sheltered many different races and communities under its wing in much the same way as during the Middle Ages the Holy Roman Empire of Christendom, centered on the papal city, asserted its hegemony over most of the kingdoms of Europe. And yet that Atlantean empire, Plato said, was only one nexus established by the gods in a greater network of Wisdom centers whose capital was elsewhere, "at the center of the Universe,"[34] under the sovereign rule of Zeus. And so we come once more to the idea of a supreme center of cultural propagation senior to Atlantis and with world-embracing powers like those of Shambhala.

The part such centers of the Pillar religion played in prehistory as seedbeds of civilization has been almost universally ignored by modern historians, to the great detriment of our understanding of the past. Yet there is ample evidence of the impelling civilizing power of great religions. We know that King Asoka of the third century B.C. united much of India under a Buddhist culture centered on his royal capital; papal Rome built a chain of monasteries across the whole of barbarian Europe that gave it learning and religio-political stability; and militant Islam subdued a vast domain from its Baghdad base and became the channel for a brilliant, far-reaching Muslim civilization.

The Scottish archaeologist Euan McKie contends that the same phenomenon occurred much earlier in the age of the European megalith-builders. He believes on the evidence that the earliest of the megaliths, which may be up to ten thousand years old, were the work of a missionary culture-bearing priesthood from elsewhere whose shrines were centers of both religious and scientific learning. Drawing nomadic populations to constellate around them by bartering knowledge for food, they spread the process of agricultural settlement with its arts and sciences throughout Western Europe, so giving cohesion to a thriving Neolithic society.[35]

But despite the clear testimony of history, the bonding power of religion rather than politics in the formation of a great hegemony such as Atlantis is still not sufficiently acknowledged. Consequently, many people now too readily dismiss the Atlantean story as a mere product of Plato's imagination, as his fellow Athenians did. For the past was virtually closed to them, standing as they were at a turning-point in history. The Pillar religion was dying. In the older world of their Achaean past, the great Wisdom centers were gone, the gardens of the Great Goddess reverting to wilderness, the courts of the god-kings silent. The world had shrunk to the Aegean, and in the Athenian memory all that had constituted the celebration of the World Axis had passed irrevocably into myth and by Plato's time was honored only as myth.

THE PYTHAGOREAN "Y"

 I n folklore Atlantis and Shambhala are implicitly linked together as charismatic images of heart's desire, two shining mirages that lie on the farthest horizon of human longing, unattainable, always receding as we reach for them; at best no more than symbols of ideal states of consciousness never realized. But their association seems to have a far more real and historically concrete basis than that. Initiatic tradition affirms they have both genuinely existed, one in the western sea, the other in the eastern mountains, as lynchpins of what was once a network of Wisdom centers located on a great power-grid extending around the globe. Further, Shambhala still exists within a framework that awaits reactivation.

The Teutonic Knights of Europe, in touch with Sufism, were almost certainly aware of a primary center of initiation in the heart of Asia. But whether Aristeas of Proconnesus had any knowledge of Shambhala as he searched for Apollo's northern station we do not know, nor whether Plato had likewise through his intimacy with the Pythagoreans. Yet it may well be so, for the East drew Greek mystics irresistibly. Pythagoras is said to have made a journey to Hindustan in his search for wisdom, and Philostratus has recorded the journey Apollonius of Tyana made to a region beyond the Trans-Himalayas which could only have been Tibet, in a search for the land the Greek sage called the Abode of the Gods.

But unlike their foremost philosophers, the ordinary run of Athenians of Plato's day were bounded by very small horizons. Pious and conservative, their spiritual aspirations were centered on the Elysian Fields in the western sea, where the blessed dead lived with the gods; a mythic place that Homer located among the Nordic Cimbrian tribes. There, says the sea-god Proteus in the *Odyssey*, "is Rhadamathus of the fair hair, where life is easiest for men. No snow is there, nor yet great storm, nor any rain; but always Ocean sendeth forth the breeze of the shrill West to blow cool on men."[1] In that idyllic land, so Athenians believed, sang the daughters of the Goddess of Night, and there Atlas the Heaven-Bearer supported the essential wheeling of the cosmic order. Plato's stark and ill-omened tale of Atlantis, therefore, with its echoes of this northern Elysium, was not at all in harmony with the poetic religious mood of the Athenians, who no doubt found little appeal in a story of divine glory overthrown, of a splendid island-kingdom in the Western ocean founded by gods who became corrupt and were destroyed for it.

In the Athens of the fifth century B.C., religious freedom was heavily circumscribed. Plato's celebrated but eccentric mentor, Socrates, had recently been executed by enforced suicide for neglect of the gods and for religious doctrines that were thought to endanger the morality of Athens' youth. His death effectively demonstrated that there were religious as well as political topics on which it was wise not to speak too freely, and so Plato's historically bald and circumstantial account of Atlantis and its tragic end, stripped of nearly all mythic embellishments, won little popular support.

Yet despite wide contemporary scepticism, some Greeks of erudition found it plausible. Plato himself seems to have believed in its historical veracity, for in the *Timaeus* dialogues he has Critias twice declare it was something that really happened; and he has Socrates too accept it on that understanding. As one recent researcher, the geoarchaeologist Eberhard Zanggar says, this is certainly *prima facie* evidence for what Plato really believed. The story of Atlantis passed down through Platonic and Neo-Platonic ranks and inspired a search for the lost kingdom that has ever since occupied generations of scholars and occultists. Countless attempts have been made to explain, date and locate it, and thousands of books have been written on the subject since Ignatius Donnelly sensationally popularized it at the beginning of the century by locating the remains of the sunken kingdom in the Azores—an armchair theory, however, which was later disproved by geological research in the Atlantic Ocean.[2]

Edgar Cayce clairvoyantly sited Atlantis near the Bahamas; Robert Graves has suggested Tunisia or Nigeria; others Crete, Ceylon, Britain or ancient Tartessos on the Iberian coast. Others again have placed it in even more exotic lands ranging from the Crimea to Australia, and have in each case supported their arguments with seemingly faultless logic. Zanggar has identified it with ancient Troy, doing so as persuasively as has Jurgen Spanuth in his location of it on a sunken ridge now lying beneath the North Sea between Heligoland and the Eiderstadt on the Schleswig-Holstein mainland.

Spanuth, an Austrian who became pastor of Bordelum on the North Sea coast of Germany, conducted numerous excavations in the area of Heligoland. As a consequence, he believes that until c. 1200 B.C. this was the sacred center of a Germanic culture area that grew rich on amber, a substance found in great quantities in the nearby river Eider; but that after that date Northern Europe sank into barbarism and the memory of its golden age was lost.[3] Zanggar, on the other hand, bases his theory on extensive excavations conducted in Tiryns in the eastern Mediterranean that convinced him that Atlantis was really a retelling of the Trojan War. Both writers have their critics; and since the most zealous research covering every part of the world has failed to uncover indisputable evidence connecting these two sites or any others with Atlantis, many people are now inclined to regard the lost sanctuary, like Shambhala, as an exploded myth, a nostalgic chimera.

However, there are others who join Spanuth in asserting that Atlantis lay in the North Sea and that the Atlanteans and the Hyperboreans were one and the same race, thus arriving independently at the same conclusion as Blavatsky and Guénon. Pytheas of Massilia, a learned geographer of the fourth century B.C. who explored the Atlantic Sea extensively as well as the Cronian Sea (as the North Sea was then called), was of this opinion.[4] His observations and astronomical measurements, unique in his day, and his account of his travels in the Baltic region provoked centuries of disbelief and argument among Greek scholars, especially as he also called Basiliea/Electris by the name of Scheria, Homer's name for the royal island of the Phaeacians, the race Odysseus visited in the Cronian Sea, and who also claimed to be descended from Poseidon.[5]

Olaf Rudbeck, a Swedish professor of medicine and a distinguished botanist of the seventeenth century, was another who believed that the Atlanteans, the Hyperboreans and the Phaeacians were one and the same race; and after studying Sweden's history he came to the conclusion that the Atlantean/Hyperborean/Phaeacian kingdom had lain in his own Scandinavian country.[6]

But far more perplexing than its location is the question of Atlantis's age when it sank. It was obvious to Greek historians that Plato's Bronze Age Atlantis (c. 3000 B.C.–1200 B.C.) could not be the Atlantis that disappeared beneath the sea nine thousand years before Solon's visit to Egypt, for at that remote time neither Greeks nor Egyptians existed. Quick to note the anachronism, Eudoxus of Cnidos in the fourth century B.C. proposed the solution. The Egyptians, he explained, reckoned a month as a year, so that in their calendar nine thousand years converted to something like six hundred and ninety years.[7] His solution, however, is unlikely to be correct, though it has been adopted by countless baffled researchers over the centuries, some of whom had their own axe to grind. Thus Eusebius of Caesarea, a fourth-century Christian chronicler, was primarily concerned to make Egyptian chronology conform to biblical and especially Roman Christian views of history. Hence he declared in regard to the ancient Egyptian calendar: "The 'year' I take . . . to be a lunar one consisting of thirty days: what we now call a month the Egyptians used to style 'a year.'"[8]

But S. R. K. Glanville, an Egyptologist whose work has been quoted by such researchers as Hapgood, Bauval and Gilbert, disputes this popular solution. He has shown conclusively that the ancient Egyptians had a double calendar which he described as "the most scientific combination of calendars that has yet been used by man,"[9] in which both the lunar and solar cycles are combined, and that may have been in use as early as the fifth millennium, in the predynastic age. More recently, Bauval and Gilbert have offered compelling evidence that the Egyptians arrived at their calendrical system through long observation of the stellar precession of the equinoxes, and say that although it is not known exactly when their solar calendar was developed it is generally accepted that it was well before 2500 B.C.

"In the calendar system used by the Egyptians," these authors amplify, "the year was divided into 12 months each having three *decans* of 10 days, thus 30 days in the month and 36 *decans* in a year. This gives a year of 360 days to which 5 extra epagomenal days were added; these were called 'the five days upon the year.'"[10] It is therefore clear that the Egyptians were as well aware as the Babylonians, with whose advanced astronomy they were closely in touch, that the year was a solar phenomenon and not to be confused with the lunar monthly one; and accordingly the information received by Solon as to Atlantis's great age must be regarded as reliable, at least to the best knowledge of the Egyptian priesthood.

And this is the conclusion reached by Lewis Spence, a Scottish anthropologist who, as a result of his study of the Atlantis narrative, suggested the city was actually a Cro-Magnon settlement of the Ice Age which sank beneath the sea twelve thousand years ago, precisely as reported by Solon. For one thing, the manner of the Atlantean bull hunt as described by Plato indicates the immense antiquity of the religion in which tribal chiefs, who were also priests, hunted the wild aurochs for sacrifice armed only with clubs and nooses, the oldest weapons of mankind, in a time long before animals were hunted for domestication. Noting such telling details among others, Spence advanced the view in 1924 that the Atlanteans were Cro-Magnon people of the Aurignacian culture period and that Plato's literary Bronze Age version of Atlantis with its great metropolis, its sophisticated arts, its chariots and use of metals, was based on far older folk legends from prehistory.[11]

Spence's opinion was that during the last Ice Age there had been two large islands in the Atlantic, one being Atlantis and the other Antillia, a name from which the islands of the Antilles in the West Indies are supposed to be derived. Although Atlantis was eventually submerged under the rising seas, Antillia survived in fragmented form, but not before both gave birth to a Palaeolithic culture that spread into America on one hand and western Europe on the other. Spence's Atlanteans gave their superior culture to the Eurasian continent and were the shaman cave artists of Spain and France. In support of Spence's theory, the Caribs and the tribes of Hispaniola have long had a tradition that many of the islands of the Antilles, a well-known earthquake zone, were once connected by a single landmass, but that a great cataclysm had submerged the connections and left only the island fragments known at present. For the sea level, says Zanggar, "began to rise abruptly c. 13,000 years ago; 5000 years later it had completed most of its 120-metre increase and the extensive coastal plains had largely been drowned."[12]

Spence's hypothesis is unsatisfactory on its own, but when we combine it with Guénon's statement that through the ages Wisdom centers have been established as subsidiaries of the primary center, more or less superseding it though in a strictly hierarchical fashion, it is feasible to suppose there have been several Atlantises and that with the vast spans of time involved the Egyptian records may well have included elisions and inaccuracies concerning them. The first Atlantis settlement could have been built near the Antilles, as Spence suggests, and have disappeared forever under the rising seas at the end of the last Ice Age, though it is something we shall never know for certain. But if so, then the Atlantis of which the Saitian priests spoke is most likely to have been a sanctuary rebuilt elsewhere, a secondary or tertiary center which began as a Neolithic settlement and expanded and rose to great prominence and power as described, and which met its end in some general disaster of which history has a known and legible record.

The most likely such event is the invasion of the Mediterranean lands by the northern federation of the Sea Peoples: an invasion which threatened Egypt but did not overcome it, thanks to the military aid of a number of other similarly threatened nations, including Athens. This great attack by sea and land by skilled seafarers from the north was more or less contemporaneous with the devastation of Mycenaean Greece, possibly by major flooding,[13] as well as with the mysterious global disaster at the end of the thirteenth century B.C. that ruined many other lands and their great cities and empires. The last Atlantis may well have perished at that time.

REACTIVATING THE ANCIENT POWER GRID

Everything that has been written about Atlantis suggests a basic historical reality, however distorted by time and confused reportage. It also suggests, as has been said, a close connection with Shambhala; and in fact the legend of Atlantis has converged with that of Shambhala and the Altai region in a number of different contexts. Guénon, for instance, applies similar archetypal designations to both Atlantis and Shambhala. In India, he says, Shambhala is called "the white isle" and the "abode of the blessed," after the original polar "white isle." But in Celtic tradition the "white isle," the "isle of the Saints" and the "isle of the Blessed" are names also applied to a terrestrial paradise in the West that is sometimes located in Ireland, Britain or Heligoland, and which refers to Atlantis.[14]

In 1776 Jacob Bryant, a noted student of philology and an expert in Homeric Troy, published an encyclopedia of ancient mythology in which he claimed the Trojans were descended from a very old Atlantean race that had settled across the whole of Eurasia. As a result of his philological researches, he determined that traces of the culture were to be found from Western Africa to the Indus. Thus he unwittingly confirmed the Atlantean connection with Central Asia and Shambhala.[15]

On many counts we are justified in assuming that the knowledge of a great web of spiritual powerhouses that once illumined the pagan world, linking East to West, was preserved throughout the millennia in the circuits of Europe's initiatic underworld and erupted every so often in these curious ways, impelling the Jesuits to seek the mysterious Asian kingdom of Prester John and the Russian Old Believers the blessed land of Belovodye to the east. There is little doubt, for instance, that an extremely ancient thread of esoteric knowledge preserved through the ages provided the basis for the religious mystique which we know inspired the Teutonic Knights of Bornholm in their "drive to the East" in order to spread the message of Christianity.

On one hand they were strongly influenced by the Sufi tradition the Saracens brought with them to the Holy Land during the Crusades, and on the other by the old Celtic Mysteries of Europe. The Teutonic Knights' chief area of operations was the Baltic region and Germany, where the heterodox proclivities of the Holy Roman Emperor Frederick II had saturated the Prussian court in the esoteric erudition of the Arabs, alchemical and mystical, as well as in the arboreal Druidic lore of northern Europe, passed down from a pre-Celtic age. But beneath these seemingly very different traditions was a single substratum of ancient wisdom that had been borne into Europe by millennia of migratory waves from Central Asia—of which the Celtic people had been the last of many—telling of a great power center there and of the secret knowledge of a long-forgotten Megalithic people.

Some esoteric societies have always been aware of this gnostic substratum beneath the orthodox veneer of history. Thus the Templars, whose order was founded in Palestine in 1118, were known to have believed secretly in the unity of all blood-lines, all races and all religions, and to have practiced spiritual techniques and rituals that bear many points of resemblance to ones from Asia, such as the Tibetan Dzog Chen cult of the Severed Heads.[16] So it is by no means impossible that the medieval knightly orders of Europe, ambitious to extend the domain of Christendom, were aware of and even had certain covert connections with the initiatic center in High Asia for their own religious purposes.

Tomas believes so. He points out that in 1184 Wolfram von Eschanbach, a troubadour and Knight Templar who summarized the Holy Grail legends in the romance *Titurel*, hinted at a spiritual link between the Holy Grail and Asia and described the Grail as a stone—*"und dieser Stein ist Gral gennant"* (and this stone is called grail). Was Eschenbach, Tomas asks, speaking of Shambhala and the Chintamani Stone? In the meistersinger's tale, the hero Parsifal carries the sacred cup or stone to Asia, to the kingdom of Titurel, a priest-king who bears a strong resemblance to the Phantom Emperor of Asia whom Christians called Prester John, and who, like Titurel, lived for about five hundred years.

Like Shambhala, the mythical kingdom of Prester John was a country full of marvels. It was said to lie in the Gobi Desert and to possess a Fountain of Eternal Youth from which all the inhabitants could drink, thus banishing sickness and old age. Only the purest souls could live in Prester John's land, where crime, poverty and injustice were unknown. A magic mirror enabled the king to observe everything that happened in the world; flying dragons carried men for long distances through the air, and a magic ring could make them invisible. A huge tower rose in the middle of the city and there a wonderful magical stone was guarded day and night. Tomas regards all these legendary ideas, from which Eschenbach drew so much of his material, as hinting at the real existence of an Asiatic world center of initiation and as furnishing elements of the Templars' secret gnostic doctrines.[17]

In *The Messianic Legacy*, the journalists Michael Baigent, Richard Leigh and Henry Lincoln trace the grandiose neo-occultist fantasies of the Nazi

Party back to this richly religious and learned period of German history, whose esoteric ideas the Nazis subverted to their own ends. They were fascinated by the Central Asian mythos and the Secret Doctrine which, according to some sources, was revealed to Hitler by General Karl Haushofer, an initiate in an important Buddhist secret society in Japan, and who became a kind of magician-adviser to Hitler. Haushofer's esoteric theories concerning Shambhala as a great magical power base from which the Nazi elite could draw, among other things, a knowledge of astral projection and thought control formed the inner framework of Himmler's SS.

Baigent, Leigh and Lincoln suggest that Himmler was equally interested in the *exotica* of pagan nature worship. The town surrounding his castle-headquarters in Wewelsburg, though never finished, was to be built as a troy town, and he spoke of it as a power-center similar to Stonehenge, discoursing also on geomancy, ley lines, earth magic and the like. Himmler conceived of the SS as an occult order like the Knights Templar, "and saw it, quite specifically, as a reconstituted Deutschritter—a modern equivalent of the white-mantled knights with black crosses who, 700 years before, had spearheaded an earlier Germanic Drang nach Osten (drive to the East) into Russia."[18]

On the grounds of what we now know, it is clear that from the great pool of arcane knowledge made available to them by the Crusades, the Templars and their offshoot orders learned something of the ancient power-grid still girdling the earth and were able to reconstruct it, and that in their drive eastward they may have been seeking its Asiatic hub in order to link it up with their own vaunting religious enterprise: the uniting of Europe under the banner of the universal Christ. The traveler Earnest Von Salomon says the Basques, whose history goes back to the Ice Ages, have a tradition that in prehistoric times the Pyrenees and the Atlas mountains in Morocco were part of a vast western hegemony ruled by the gods, and that it perished in a great natural disaster just as Plato reported.[19] But Plato also indicated it was part of an even greater worldwide empire ruled by the God of gods, Zeus himself; and so it may have been the establishment of this greater Eurasian hegemony the Templars ultimately had in mind, and which—in a spirit stripped of all such religious idealism—drove the Nazis on to their suicidal eastern alliances and invasions.

217

The knightly orders' great western enterprise failed, but the vision lived on and wove its seductive thread through the revolutionary esoteric discourse of later Renaissance and Reformation circles. The early seventeenth century saw the publication of Francis Bacon's posthumous work *New Atlantis* in which he set forth his utopia. It was an allegorical account embodying his conception of the ideal religious and scientific society, the perfect social state already foreshadowed by the medieval Initiate Orders and later by the Rosicrucians.[20]

Atlantis Not a Utopian Society

Bacon modeled his ideal New Atlantis on Plato's Atlantis, as the name implies. It was a land unknown to the world, where brotherly love and an advanced state of scientific knowledge reigned, and in which, in a great college of wisdom called Solomon's House, an order of priest-scientists studied those arts and sciences that would most benefit humanity. Filled with a deeply pious Hermetic-Cabalistic mysticism, the inhabitants of New Atlantis, observes Frances Yates, were therefore returned to the state of Adam in Paradise before the Fall, and lived in the presence of divine powers and beings angelic rather than magical.

But in reality Atlantis was not utopian. It was not constituted as a perfect society, even at its inception, and its inhabitants were not in a state of primordial grace. It was not a paradisial kingdom like Shambhala, but was, as Plato tells us, morally and spiritually flawed. If there were any living model for Bacon's New Atlantis it would have to have been the community of adepts in High Asia; for it was Shambhala, not Atlantis, that was aureoled by the authentic glow of sanctity, enlightenment, transcendence.

Guénon says that geographical symbolism is such that on the Heaven-Earth axis *yang*, the East, is always Heaven, and *yin*, the West, is always Earth; and this invariable relationship determines seniority. "Traditional doctrines will always view the East," he says, "as the 'luminous side' (*yang*) and the West as the 'dark side' (*yin*) . . . and the side that has preeminence will always, invariably, be the East."[21] Atlantis and Shambhala bore out this occult principle: the latter was the senior station.

While Atlantis was subject to the vagaries of nature and human history,

Shambhala is not. "This region is 'the supreme country,'" Guénon stresses, "which has become inaccessible to ordinary humanity and is beyond the reach of those cataclysms which upset the human world at the end of certain cyclic periods. . . . It is the 'white mountain,' 'the mountain of the sun' as it is also called, never submerged by any flood."[22] Shambhala alone embodies the celestial qualities of benevolence, enlightenment and eternal purity that Bacon strove to symbolize in his New Atlantis, while the original Atlantis, however illustrious in its time, never transcended the limitations of a mere earthly imperium, subject like all earthly societies to the laws of generation, decay and death.

From our knowledge of Neolithic and early Bronze Age society in general and our Atlantean/Hyperborean literature in particular, we can form a fairly comprehensive picture of the Atlantean Wisdom center; and it is one with which we are only too familiar. However well it began, it evolved into a hieratic city-state governed by a monarchy that was a law unto itself; rich, well armed and concerned with territory, trade and raw political power, and dominated and indeed shaped by a supremely powerful religious autocracy that functioned in the background, ostensibly serving the State, but which nevertheless held kings and nations to ransom. As a great quasi-religious power, Atlantis was in fact a prototype of all western societies to come, implicitly determining the form even of our own present culture, whose late-come secularism imperfectly conceals its hoary traditional roots.

In its postglacial career Atlantis became the center of a dualistic religion that worshiped the Magna Mater and her spouse, the god of the World Pillar, in his various phallic guises; the principle of unity lost its force, and that of dualism, which the British mystic and Cabalist Dion Fortune has called a "fundamental heresy," became increasingly entrenched. It has imposed its polarizing pattern on all subsequent cultures.

In an earlier Paleolithic society the Supreme Being was worshipped as embodying both male and female forces and all they represented, as we can intuit from the little Paleolithic figurines of the Great Mother, in which the female principle is given in the rounded egg-shaped body with its birth-giving contours, while the male principle resides in the pillar-like neck and head. But in Neolithic cultures the originally androgynous Goddess separated into male and female elements and divine pairs appear, god and goddess together. "The discovery of agriculture," says Eliade, "above all brings about radical changes in the divine hierarchy: it is the Great Goddesses, the Divine Mothers and their spouses the Divine Males, who then thrust their way into the foreground . . . "[23] The Supreme Being is fractured and becomes dual.

By the time the literate civilizations arose this process of breakdown had inevitably brought in its train a loss of cohesion in the collective psyche, a fracturing and decentralization that split in two its perception of reality; and this deterioration modified in its turn the principles of social and institutional organization. Atlantis, it seems, shared in this universal lowering of psychic health. Seduced perhaps by the vast natural wealth of its domain, perhaps also by the adoption of the barbarous values and practices of surrounding races, it became increasingly exoteric, revealing itself as the headquarters of a highly ritualized, visible and well-funded religious institution such as we would recognize today in any one of our Semitic religions, whose monistic claims are sadly at variance with their dualistic philosophies.

In the Pillar faith as it comes down to us, with its costly temples, professional priesthoods, figurative theology and anthropomorphic gods; its proselytizing missionaries; its vast quasi-political empire, commercial interests and linkage to State law; its wealth, its moral coerciveness and its monolithic style, we recognize the foundations not of Utopia, but of an early facsimile of our own anguished Western society torn by conflicting forces and ideals. The same unresolved dilemma of the warfare between spirit and matter, male and female, sacred and profane, confronts us across the ages. From Thebes to the Vatican the agricultural heresy lives on, dividing and polarizing.

In its heyday the Atlantean Pillar religion must have been a powerful developmental force in society, creating stable monarchies and liberating an unparalleled creativity in the arts and sciences, such that to this day the early Bronze Age is associated in the Western mind with a legendary golden age. But in reality towards the end of its life, when degeneration set in in the immensely wealthy temples of the Goddess, such a monolithic faith must have lain heavily on a world ready for change, its massive inertia as well as its illicit encroachment on every aspect of life, its practice of human sacrifice, its erotic and sacrificial excesses and its waning spiritual content a burden to the awakening Iron Age spirit. Although ultimately forced to give way to the new patri-archal imperatives, it cast a long shadow across the future. The crude concret-ization of the divine and the yoking of religion to State law undoubtedly af-fected the future course of Western religion, as did the dualistic theology.

The latter in particular contributed to the West's excessive polarization of good and evil, leading to enormous tensions on the moral plane. "The instructed and enlightened expositors of all religions," writes Dion Fortune, "regard dualism as a heresy; it is only ignorant adherents of a faith who believe in the conflict between light and darkness, spirit and matter . . . who make the mistake of classing one of a pair of contending forces as good and the other as evil; to do so is to fall into the fundamental heresy of dualism."[24] We cannot redeem evil, she says, by waging war on it, but only by "absorbing and harmo-nizing it" in a spirit of peace. Having failed this task, the West's malaise is a moral one that has led inevitably to a century of hate-filled and xenophobic religio-nationalistic wars, whose seeds were sown long ago in the first shrines to pairs of male and female deities.

HOW SHOULD WISDOM GOVERN?

Atlantis and Shambhala offer sharply contrasting models of religious government, engendering profound questions about the nature of institution-al religion and its proper role in society. In the past these questions have rarely been addressed, but one well-known author and student of the Institute of General Semantics has not been so reticent. In her book *Insights for the Age of Aquarius* Gina Cerminara argues that we should remove religion from its sac-rosanct niche where it has lain for so long, dust it off and subject it to the same critical examination we would give to any other area of knowledge.[25] And in view of the worldwide religious warfare that has became endemic to our times—Christians against Muslims, Muslims against Hindus, Protestants against Cath-olics, Hindus against Sikhs and Buddhists, Jews against Muslims, Muslims against Muslims—such an enquiry is perhaps long overdue.

It may be that first we shall have to explore such issues as the difference between dogma and spiritual knowledge, the delusional roots of the quest for religious supremacy and the lessons we can learn from religious history. But ultimately we shall have to ask ourselves the fundamental questions: How should religion be instituted, according to what principles and in what form? How should it enter into the body politic. How should it relate to the social and moral norms of the day: what are its legitimate parameters?

These were the concerns that engaged the attention of the esoteric schools of ancient Greece and prompted Plato to his renowned studies of the role of religion in good government. His fellow initiates were well aware of the climate of ideological repression: Pythagoras, who had sought to place an advisory panel of initiates above institutions of government, was with all his followers murdered; and Socrates, as we know, was sentenced to death for impiety towards the gods. Although making great advances in the natural sciences, Dorian Greece was in the sunset of its life, exhausted by the Peloponnesian wars, spiritually hide-bound and impoverished and turning increasingly to material goals of power and authority: goals that encouraged the growth of xenophobia and ruthlessly depreciated the rights of women and slaves. The initiatic schools saw this moral decline as related to the rise of State religion.

It is generally believed that Plato used the Atlantis tale as an historical vehicle for his cosmological and scientific ideas, intending, as Zanggar says, "to provide a coherent, scientific account of the past . . . and award [him] an opportunity to present it in the light of his own doctrines."[26] But these doctrines included his ever-present concern for the State's need of higher disinterested guidance, as proposed by Pythagoras. It is therefore altogether likely that in the story of Atlantis Plato was illustrating this need for a truly wise and altruistic initiate or body of initiates, above self-interest, to monitor the course of the collective, lest religion, originally beneficent, become mere superstition and turn its destructive tyrannical aspect towards society, with tragic results.

The broad canvas of the *Timaeus and Critias* covers the process of degeneration and death in every aspect of life—in the human body, in the soil erosion of the land, in the human soul—and seems to correlate these with the same process in religious institutions. Like his mentor Socrates, Plato had scant time for mythology, which he regarded as the invention of poets fit only for the popular imagination, and we may wonder whether he was drawing parallels between the spiritual decadence of Atlantis, with its progress from high principles to superstition, repression and violence, and the Athenian State cult, and issuing a warning.

The conclusion of his narrative suggests it. At that point there is a recall of the preamble contained in the *Timaeus*, and the reader is again reminded that the Atlantean god-kings were by no means above the law, but merely one family within a greater brotherhood of gods who now convened to pass judgement on an erring member for its "pursuit of unbridled ambition and power." For many generations, the story of the Atlantean kings continues,

> so long as the divine element in their nature survived, they obeyed the laws and loved the divine to which they were akin. . . . But when the divine element in them became weakened by frequent admixture with mortal stock, and their human traits became predominant, they ceased to be able to carry their prosperity with moderation. . . . To the perceptive eye the depth of their degeneration was clear enough . . . but to those whose judgement of true happiness is defective they seemed to be at the height of their fame and fortune. And the god of gods, Zeus, who reigns by law, and whose eye can see such things, when he perceived the wretched state of this admirable stock decided to punish them and reduce them to order by discipline.

> He accordingly summoned all the gods to his own most glorious abode, which stands at the centre of the universe and looks out over the whole realm of change, and when they had assembled addressed them as follows . . .[27]

And here the tale abruptly ends, to the perplexity of generations of readers. Several theories have been put forward to explain this strange termination of the narrative in mid-flight; but none has been really satisfactory. But it would not be too far-fetched to speculate on one that has not been suggested to date: that Plato the initiate, the intimate of the Pythagorean and Egyptian esoteric schools, either realized for himself or perhaps received instructions from above that it would be prudent to discontinue any further publication of such sensitive material.

Plato knew the gods were initiate culture-bearers and, like ourselves, capable of making mistakes, but at the time of writing that was by no means common knowledge: for most Greeks it would have constituted heresy. Were it disclosed in the public domain that the gods were capable of turning their occult powers against humankind and doing evil, even taking up arms against the nursling races they had sworn to cherish and instigating terrible natural disasters that threatened the human race (as Plato's story suggests), it would have destroyed faith and attacked the very root of Greek religious feeling, as well as perhaps endangering Plato's life.

Moreover, the whole tenor of the Atlantis story was leading inevitably to those agonizing questions Gilgamesh had asked of his own soul in a similar case, when confronted by the moral ambiguity of his flood-bringing Sumerian gods. If the gods out of their magnanimity had benefited humanity by mixing their divine blood with that of mortals, how could they become evil? And if the gods could become evil, what of the religion they had brought with them? Could it too become outworn, corrupt, open to divine judgment? Could Olympus be overthrown? And if so, what of the moral categories? Were good and evil relative, uncertain, perhaps ultimately void? Can we be surprised that, contemplating the opening up of an endless vista of such moral questions, and remembering Socrates' fate, on this topic Plato's voice fell silent?

In any case, he had already made his point. We of the modern world no longer value the myth of gods, and it is not of the least real importance where Atlantis lay geographically, nor how or when it came to its apocalyptic end. But it is important—and increasingly important in a world destroying itself by religious acrimony—that we give due regard to the methodological differences between Atlantis and Shambhala as centers of spiritual government. Plato enables us to do this.

The lesson he teaches is that the methods of the Atlanteans failed because fundamentally they were motivated by self-interest, however benignly disposed towards those they governed. They manipulated the world by the world's tools of wealth and political power, believing that the end justifies the means, and they were imbued with a militant will to survive, to protect Atlantean boundaries at whatever cost, to be the best and to live forever. They believed, and no doubt sincerely, that the Pillar religion was best for humanity, but without reference to the rhythms of history whose cosmic rule it is the task of religion to discern, rightly interpret and obey, regardless of immediate self-interest. Such egoistic methods and motives were bound to fail, to lead only to strife and to the destruction of the very institution they were designed to protect, as they have done ever since.

But when we consider Shambhala's very different methods, we are hampered by the fact that its very existence is still a matter of conjecture, its operations invisible. Nevertheless, that too may be considered part of its method of government: for that very reason Shambhala has been enabled to survive the millennia in its original primordial role, uncorrupted, unshadowed by the traumas of history. It is an integral part of our culture to assume that authority, to be effective, must wear the visible insignia of office, must be manifestly enforceable through some displayed system of command, some moral or judicial legislation or, at its simplest, through the tyranny of sheer muscle-power. But there is another kind of authority that proceeds from the *vajra* body and its hidden instruments of will; and this, backed by the divine will, is the true authority, which is rarely visible.

The use of this invisible power is the cornerstone of the doctrine of alternative forms of government first formulated by Pythagoras and enshrined in Western mysticism by the sixteenth-century English magus and mathematician John Dee in his famous *Monas Hieroglyphica*. The *Monas Hieroglyphica*, says Frances Yates, "the influence of which we have traced behind the Rosicrucian manifesto, opens with a diagram of the Pythagorean Y, and applies this to two possible ways which a ruler may take: one the broad way of 'tyrants,' the other the straight and narrow way of the 'adepti' or inspired mystics."[28]

Shambhala takes the second way. Nonaligned to any one faith, without a church or congregation, without fiat or encyclical, without regnal power or insignia of office, without territorial claims, without moral or military coercion, without a commercial empire or visible place of government, and with an impartially cherishing love for every race and religion on earth, it has endured successfully to the present day precisely because its authority is invisible and has never been available to attack. And it has achieved this impregnability by following the way of Tao, the Heavenly Way that yields to conquer, of which the *Tao Te Ching* declares: "The Tao never does; yet through it all things are done."[29]

This nondual way does not mean Shambhala is inactive, but that it acts on the rest of the world in the role of a catalyst, a hidden alchemical reagent that interacts with history yet is never changed by it; that remains at the unmotivated center, intervening and regulating as the need arises, but indirectly, without being trapped in its own machinery. By reflecting "the actionless activity of Heaven" which is at the root of all religions and indeed of all earthly affairs, it remains uncommitted to any and for that reason is at rest, at perfect peace, acting yet actionless. "To be concentrated in non-action—that is the Way of Heaven," says Chuang Tzu.[30]

Shambhala is presented to us as the channel for the transmission of the axial grace and power of Heaven that falls on all religions and cultures without discrimination and which therefore does not need to proselytize or to make itself known, to pass laws or punish unbelievers. It is like the Chinese emperors of old who strove to be passive instruments of the cosmic powers. According to Chuang Tzu:

> The rulers of old abstained from any action of their own and allowed Heaven to govern everything through them. At the pinnacle of the universe the Principle exerts its influence over Heaven and Earth, which then act as transmitters of this influence to every being. In the world of men this influence becomes sound government, which brings all talents and abilities to fruition. . . . Accordingly, the rulers of old wanted nothing and the world was filled with abundance; they did not act, and everything was modified in accordance with the norm; they remained sunk deep in meditation, and the people kept themselves in perfect order. As the ancient saying sums it up: Everything prospers for whoever unites himself to Unity, and even the genii submit to whoever has no self-interest.[31]

THE ALTERNATIVE SCIENCE

In the surrounding folklore Shambhala's technology has always been extolled as magical, its science as a form of supernatural sorcery; but whether it really is so depends on one's angle of vision. Esoteric tradition emphasizes the advanced scientific knowledge of those who live in Shambhala and claims that if their technology appears to be miraculous it is only because we do not understand the principles on which it rests. People who say they have visited the hidden kingdom, either literally or in vision or dream, report seeing technical achievements there that far surpass those of our modern science. They relate the wonders they have seen to the many legends concerning a vast network of caves and underground tunnels that extend beneath the mountain ranges and are said to have been carved out in a remote time.

"Only a high technology," says Andrew Tomas, "with a powerful energy at its disposal, could have constructed a network of tunnels which, according to some reports, are hundreds of kilometres long."[1] Cars of strange design flash along their length and they are illumined by a brilliant artificial light "which affords growth to the grains and vegetables and long life without disease to the people,"[2] Ossendowsky declares. Many marvels are supposed to have been seen in this underground world: museums, libraries, stores of jewels and other priceless artefacts, as well as technological inventions thousands of years before their time.

How have they been guarded for so long from profane view? Travelers have seen in the deserts and snow fields of High Asia men whom the natives of the region refer to as the Azaras, the guardians of the sacred land who are able to repel intruders by the power of their mental vibrations. Nicholas Roerich conjectures: "When they suddenly appear amidst the desert one begins to think—where was the long waterless journey started, how was it made? But long, long caverns without end have been found."[3] He also reported seeing great flashes and pillars of light in the darkness of the desert nights, hundreds of miles from any habitation or other source of illumination, where electricity was unknown and the Aurora Borealis did not occur.

Air travel is another recurring theme in the legends of Shambhala. Interstellar travel was attributed to its inhabitants long before the development of modern technological and astronomical knowledge. According to ancient Chinese lore, the aircraft and space vehicles of the Immortals journey among the stars, observing the habitats of other races and kingdoms. Andrew Tomas says there is a well-known Tibetan legend that the Chintamani Stone, whose inner radiation is said to be mightier than radium, was brought to earth on the back of a winged horse or Lung-ta, which he believes may be a metaphor for a space vehicle. Lung-ta was supposed to be able to traverse the whole universe as a messenger of the gods, and tales of Tibetan kings and saints making flights on it over enormous distances circulated in Tibet for centuries.

Tomas draws attention too to one of Nicholas Roerich's paintings, which is in the form of a cryptogram and is called "Rigden Jyepo, Ruler of Shambhala." Within its rocky mountainous landscape is a cavern in which a fiery Buddha-like figure stands giving orders to mounted messengers grouped before him. Viewed from a certain angle, Roerich's bearded profile can be seen in the contours of the mountains in the upper left-hand corner, and in the center of the composition is the outline of a rocket or fuselage of a wingless aircraft aimed at the sky. Is the cryptogram saying, asks Tomas, that Roerich has flown in this vehicle?[4]

Another Shambhalic legend declares that the most advanced residents wear bodies that neither age nor die; some, the "mind-born," create a visible but artificial body out of elementary atomic matter that appears solid and real; others remain invisible and join the People of the Fire Mist who live in the heart of the sun. They can travel at will through the universe, become heavier and denser or lighter and more ethereal at will, move at great speeds, appear in two places at once and materialize or disappear as they wish. The Buddhist explorer Alexandra David-Neel alludes in her memoirs to lamas who suddenly became invisible or, on the contrary, seemed to appear suddenly out of nowhere.

And then there are the stories of feats of superhuman control of the mental forces, in which crowds of people are induced to mass-hallucinate whole landscapes, towns or armies for considerable lengths of time. It is said that in the past Masters used to come unexpectedly out of Shambhala to teach certain lamas such things. A Chinese surgeon who wrote in the *Shanghai Times* about his journey with a Nepalese yogi to an Inner Asian center of advanced yoga told of the many scientific wonders he found there, and of complex experiments in will power and telepathy conducted over immense distances. Ernest Scott reports similar extrasensory studies being undertaken in the Sarmoun monastery, a Sufi training center in Afghanistan.[5]

It is hard to say what credence we can place on these sometimes bizarre legends and rumors. What, for instance, are we to make of the ordinary *siddhis* known to Tibetan yogis as categorized by Tsultrim Allione, an American who became a Buddhist nun initiated and trained in a Katmandu monastery? According to Allione, these *siddhis* include:

> the power to pass through walls, to transform stones into gold, to walk on water without sinking, to enter fire without getting burned, to melt snow with one's body in extreme cold, to travel to a far distant cosmos in a few seconds, to fly in the sky and walk through rocks and mountains, extraordinary abilities to read minds and know the future, and the development of all the senses far beyond their ordinary capacities. One can also radiate beams of light from the body and stand in sunlight without casting a shadow, make one's body vanish and other so-called miracles.[6]

Philo Judaeus, the Jewish philosopher of the first century of the common era, said that the Mysteries unveiled the secret operations of Nature. His disclosure gains greater meaning when juxtaposed with Allione's revelations of the miracles made possible by means of Tibetan Buddhist meditative techniques. Confronted by such supernatural enigmas, she says:

> We must surrender our Western frame of reference which limits our ideas of what is possible and what is impossible, and understand that, at higher levels of spiritual development, the material world can be manipulated by the consciousness, and many things become possible. . . . I ask the readers to put aside their ideas of the limits of mind and body, and open themselves to further possibilities.[7]

What seems to come of the further exploration Allione recommends is the realization that whatever science underlies the above manifestations, it is not simply a more advanced extension of modern science, but is based on a fundamentally different model of reality, involving the knowledge of a psychophysical energy world of which we have as yet little cognizance. The nearest approach to it, though more apparent than real, is being made at the leading edge of theoretical science with its new Unified Field Theory, regarded by some scientists as a more enlightened version of the traditional cosmology of Eastern yoga. This it is not; yet it does reflect it as in shadow-play.

The modern cosmological version entails the idea of formative fields contained hierarchically within ever-larger such fields and ultimately within one primal unified field, the latter of which is seen as a state of space that, with energy, constitutes the basis of all physical reality. It is the ordering principle of the whole universe. Superficially this holistic and organismic picture is not dissimilar to that of the ancient Hermetic-Cabalistic system in which the cosmos is made up of a hierarchy of planes or worlds of increasingly refined matter, the whole contained within the infinite universal being of the Ain Soph, the ultimate Source. But the similarity is misleading. It has induced in us the largely unwarranted feeling that a return is being made in our postmechanistic era to a traditional and more valid way of thought.

However desirable that might be, a closer examination of the discourse of modern evolutionary physics reveals the gulf that exists, albeit covertly, between contemporary and traditional views of Nature. In the latter case, *consciousness*, intelligent and goal-seeking, is the ordering principle underlying all phenomena: in the former case, there is much discussion of the way in which evolutionary physics is putting spontaneity, creativity and purpose back into the Newtonian universe, but without specifying any vital principle that could bring such an outcome about. In evolutionary physics, says Sheldrake, the universe is a unified whole, an organism in which one universal formative principle determines its entire course of development. But what is this formative principle? So far it eludes definition. Science does not know what it is. Science has no name for it, and worse still, no qualifying framework by which to arrive at one.

In the case of developmental biology, it is fully acknowledged that there must be a formative influence other than DNA involved in the building of the differently shaped limbs and organs of the body, since the DNA genes are identically programmed throughout every cell of the body, and yet differentiation occurs. But what is this formative influence? Every mechanistic explanation offered to date, says Sheldrake, peters out in vague statements about "complex spatio-temporal patterns of physico-chemical interaction not yet understood." As he points out, "This is not a solution, but just another way of stating the problem."[8] In 1984 Sydney Brenner said at a conference of developmental biologists:

> At the beginning it was said that the answer to the understanding of development was going to come from a knowledge of the molecular mechanism of gene control. I doubt whether anyone believes that any more. The molecular mechanisms look boringly simple, and they don't tell us what we want to know. We have to try to discover the principles of organization.[9]

Nevertheless, despite the difficulties, physicists believe it is only a matter of time before the nature of the organizing principle is understood. Already, they say, it is taking the place in modern physics of the concept of *soul* that played such an important part in the natural philosophies of antiquity. Ancient philosophers believed all things were organized from within by psychoid factors, immaterial souls or *entelechies*, as Aristotle called them, and these entelechies were in essence the creative agents of God, the Great Architect Himself. Today, says Sheldrake, a new way of thinking has developed in which a hierarchy of morphic fields has replaced the old vitalist idea of souls. In the science of magnetism and electricity, electromagnetic fields have replaced souls. By a comparable step, biological morphic fields have replaced entelechies in biology. And at the highest level of organization the universal gravitational field has replaced the old idea of the World Soul.[10] Thus self-organization, he assures us, is once again being put back into nature.

But is it? Modern scientific theory departs from esoteric tradition in one central and absolutely crucial respect: *consciousness* is excluded from its field of operations. While esoteric tradition imputes to souls or entelechies those psychospiritual attributes of consciousness and mind and purpose that it regards as definitive of all organizing activity, modern physicists assume no such attributes in the morphic energy fields supposed to replace them. On the contrary, mechanistic assumptions have been retained, and the energy-fields of science, far from usurping the psychoid function of souls, continue to be regarded as unconscious, mindless, purposeless arenas for an organizing principle that has, as a consequence, no rationale for existing or basis for definition.

The late Gregory Bateson, whose revolutionary work on the nature of knowledge was summed up in his book, *Steps to an Ecology of Mind*, was one of the few modern thinkers to endorse the traditional unitive viewpoint. He stated, in the words of Fritjof Capra, that "the organizing activity of a living system is mental activity, and all of its interactions with its environment are mental interactions. . . . Mind and life [are] inseparably connected, with mind— or, more accurately, mental process—being immanent in matter at all levels of life."[11]

Bateson placed life and consciousness at the center of his worldview. But current field theory is in general still dominated by the Cartesian matter-mind dichotomy that seeks to exclude mind from a mechanical material universe, and no unitive philosophy has so far unseated this heresy. Undermined by an implicit dualism that is rarely admitted, the unitary trend of field theory, whether in physics or biology, has in fact little of the explanatory value so often ascribed to it. It is still exerting its intolerable pressure on the fractured world model that is hastening the decline of our present technological civilization, and is likely to continue doing so until science dismantles one of its most fundamental and deeply cherished assumptions: the irreducible opposition of mind and matter.

This step has already been taken in the inner brotherhoods, where there are many indications of a secret alternative science based on a unitive principle that transcends and annuls the polarity of mind and matter. This unitive principle can be found in the exploits of Zen and Sufi masters no less than in those of Tibetan yogis, all of them pointing to a superb mastery of unknown laws of nature; yet it should be stressed that their mystical and supernatural overtones mask a perfectly practical vision of the universe that can be applied in all manner of technological and academic areas seemingly remote from the spiritual. What is required to grasp this unitive vision is an acknowledgment that spirit and matter are one, and that consciousness and intelligence pervade every atom of the universe. This is what all the great sages recommend; it is the key to the adept's incredible expertise. And, although it is difficult for us to imagine today, it is also the key to our own science of the future.

The disempowering limitation of the new evolutionary physics is that its hidden agenda erodes the very principle it is trying to find; that is, a universal goal-seeking formative principle, essentially holistic, intelligent and purposive, at work within nature. For as scientists point out, nature's developmental mechanisms—electromagnetic, chemical or molecular—as observed by them, are only the raw material of form on which some unknown organizing principle must impose its creative influence; but what that mysterious agency is has not been identified and is likely to remain obscure in the present scientific climate.

In fact the only known formative agent with all the philosophically required properties is the one proposed by Indian Tantra: kundalini shakti—or rather, kundalini in its universal form as Maha-kundali, Mother of Space and Time—the primal energy of the universe. It alone manifests the intelligent and goal-directed bonding power demanded of a truly creative principle in the universe. But kundalini does not inspire confidence in scientists for two compelling reasons: first, it is tainted by subjectivity, and to admit subjectivity with its intuitive animistic values into the realm of science would be to replace certainties by probabilities, with highly unwelcome consequences. And second, the kundalini concept fits only into a nondual framework and would therefore seriously jeopardize the consistency and stability of the whole of Western technological science, whose massive edifice relies solely on the underpinning of a dualistic philosophy. Thus the two reasons are fundamentally one: to save the present system. In the service of such a pressing exigency scientists are therefore continually driven, albeit unconsciously, to abort their own vision of a primal unity.

UNITIVE ENERGY IS INCREASING IN THE UNIVERSE

Heisenberg, the physicist who formulated the Unified Field Theory, said in an interview with the historian William Irwin Thompson that he believed the great age of the physical sciences was over. The ecological limit on the growth of civilization was only the outward sign of the fact that the human spirit could grow no further in the material dimension it had been exploring since the Renaissance. The post-Renaissance scientific era was reaching its limit, and the path to the spiritual order must now be found.[12]

As though in response to this need, Shambhala appears to be already generating the intellectual climate needed to arrive at a new and less destructive type of technology based on genuinely unitive rather than dualistic principles. There is evidence that a wave of primal energy is now flooding the world to a degree unprecedented in history and will in time revolutionize our old attitudes whether we will it or no, bringing us much closer to a comprehension of the alternative science of the Masters. Because of this new development, we shall have an increasing range of opportunities to witness the working of kundalini at first hand, to observe directly its miraculous formative powers and to understand the role it plays in the building of the universe. In the following chapter we shall see that these opportunities may already be occurring, leading us to the very threshold of new scientific principles like those Gregory Bateson formulated.

John Bennett is one who believes the Directorate is preparing us for the next stage of our evolution through this influx of a new energy, which he calls the higher cosmic impulse of love. The evolutionary process that has culminated in man has been achieved by making available to the earth a succession of energies, each of a higher frequency than the one before; and in that process we have needed to master constructive, vital, automatic, sensitive, conscious and creative energies in turn. These have given rise to the entire evolutionary progression from molecule to human being. We are now on the threshold of the next one: unitive energy.[13]

The traditional Sufi ideas Bennett is putting forward are substantially the same as those of René Guénon's that have already been reviewed. They tell us that the earth's chakric system operates in the service of evolution in precisely the same way as does the human chakric system. The chakras are like valves which open during initiation to permit the irradiation into the bodily apparatus of energies from higher psychospiritual levels. These new energies have a permanently transformative effect on every aspect of the individual system, physical, psychic and spiritual, sometimes acting suddenly with the effect of an evolutionary mutation. In the same manner, new energies erupt into the world from time to time from the spiritual order that subtends the physical universe, effecting, through the World Axis, radical transformations in the earth and all its life forms, frequently in the form of sudden great mutations.

The sequence of becoming by which this process is effected over vast spans of time, and the ordered emergence of energies into our universe, from the lowest constructive energy to the highest unitive energy, is one of the great metaphysical mysteries that preoccupy Sufi philosophers. Professor E. H. Palmer, a foremost authority on Sufi mysticism for more than a hundred years, said that its whole basis is the idea of a circle—from Godhead back to Godhead—the tracing of which journey covers the entire creation from molecule to perfected man. Only at the end of his journey does the traveler realize that it was a mirage; all is complete at the beginning; perfection is always present and the highest energy is one with the lowest.

As man sprang from the Intelligence which originated the Universe . . . the Sufis proceed to consider his existence as a circle meeting in the Intelligence which reveals the Godhead. This circle they divide into twin arcs; the former called Descent includes every stage, from the first scintillation from the original intelligence to the full development of man's reasoning powers; the latter arc, called Ascent includes every stage, from his first use of reason for its true purpose to his final reabsorption into the Divine Intelligence. This is what is meant when they speak of the Origin and Return of Man.[14]

In the service of this great event, Bennett believes that for the past forty thousand years or more, humanity has been painfully engaged in the struggle to assimilate creativity into its psyche—a power on which the strength of the ego is founded. But now the new unitive principle, coming from a far higher energetic level than any previously, is challenging us to an even greater engagement with evolutionary growth. As has been said, it is thought of as an attractive bonding principle that can manifest in many different ways according to the plane on which it operates: on the emotional plane as love, on the mental plane as synthesis, on the physical plane as magnetism. Scott calls it objective love to distinguish it from "its precognitive echo in sexual or polar love,"[15] but it has a more universal breadth of meaning than Scott's term implies. In Hindu-Buddhism it is called the love/wisdom energy of the Christ and the Buddha. Initiates believes that no energy lower than this divine level is capable of overpowering the potentially destructive force of the dualistic mind or of taking us successfully into the next phase of our evolution.

Scott, who with four companions was given permission to visit the Sarmoun monastery in Afghanistan—a Sufi training center the exact location of which has always remained tantalizingly vague—glimpsed the operation of this unitive principle in all the supernatural phenomena he witnessed in the monastery, and realized that a few people in every generation, the mystics and geniuses, receive the coming energy in advance of the species as a whole. He is convinced that the energy of objective love—that is, of kundalini—is the basis for the whole of the dervish tradition and that it is woven secretly into the history of esoteric philosophy through the ages, receiving formulation by those who understand it with greater or lesser degrees of success. Thus the thirteenth-century Christian saint Raymond Lully, son of a Spanish Templar and companion of Arabian philosophers, was one who sought to frame the universal principle in mathematical-cybernetic formulae which are recognized as the forerunner of the computer.

In his book *The Medieval World*, Friedrich Heer describes Lully's cybernetic machine in the following way:

> It took the form of what can only be described as a computing engine which linked up the basic principles or "ground words" of all knowledge by a mechanism consisting of concentric circles segmented by radii and of geometric symbols. It seems to have been what might be called a cybernetic machine prepared to unravel every problem, every science, even faith itself. Here in rudimentary fashion were anticipated the great universal formulae of Einstein and Heisenberg which have provided man with the mathematical keys to the problems of matter, light, energy and fundamental laws of the cosmos. . . . A miracle machine or, as later scoffers were to say, a wind machine. . . . Leibnitz was, however, not among the mockers. Lully's vision came too close to his own dream of finding a universal scientifically viable language which would enlighten all men impartially, the prerequisite of universal peace.[16]

But philosophers like Lully and Leibnitz were before their time. It is only in the twentieth century that a new psychospiritual energy has made itself unmistakably felt in the world at large and made possible, for the first time, the beginnings of true enlightenment, not for a few isolated mystics or esoteric schools, but for the whole race. This is an event of enormous importance. Only now can we hope to look forward to a civilization based on the Vedantic concept of a living cosmos governed by one universal energy from which all lower energies flow, and which manifests in the phenomenal world, as Guénon says, as kundalini shakti.

The Light That Shines Beyond the World

There is a kind of higher knowledge, a gnosis, that cannot be acquired from either organized religion or the current sciences. It is transmitted purely through the activation of the heart chakra, leading to an expansion of consciousness that illumines and transforms the faculty of perception that resides there, and opens up the possibility of acquiring a science that is, in brief, the knowledge of Reality itself.

This higher knowledge, which flows from a realm of light that interpenetrates the phenomenal world and yet lies beyond it, reveals a hyperphysical Light beyond light in which we all live and move and have our being, and from which each individual *vajra* body or light-body is built, the template of the physical frame. By virtue of this ineffable Light beyond light each of us is connected through his or her energy centers to the web of inner life of the universe; to the light-body of Nature and its multitude of forms, to the light-body of the earth, the light-bodies of other suns and planets, and ultimately to the light-body of the universe. The adept who is fully conscious of this vital light-world beyond the physical one can move into it and interact creatively with a light-field that has its own laws and purposes and that is formative of all the physical phenomena lying within it. In this way he becomes the master of the physical plane and of those beyond it and controls matter, life, time and destiny.

All spiritual traditions the world over speak of the living Light. The sense of the secret Light doctrine they all share lies in an allegory from the 24th Surah, verse 35, of the Koran:

Allah is the Light of the heavens and earth. The similitude of His light is as a niche wherein is a lamp. The lamp is in a glass which is as it were a shining star. This lamp is kindled from a blessed tree, an olive neither of the East nor the West, whose oil would almost glow forth of itself though no fire touched it. Light upon light, Allah guideth unto his light whom He will. And Allah speaks to mankind in allegories, for Allah is the Knower of all things.

Now the tree is a symbol for *baraka*, the Muslim spiritual blessing that, although often used loosely in Islamic and Sufic parlance, has the specific technical meaning of an initiation that awakens the *lataif* or chakric centers of the human "tree" of the nervous system. And the "oil" of the tree that renders the initiation effective is a term commonly used by Buddhists as a symbol for kundalini. Thus Lama Yeshe, a tantric Buddhist of the Vajrayana school, says that this body of ours "for all its suffering nature, contains the most valuable of natural resources: kundalini gold, kundalini oil!"[17] Therefore the Koranic passage quoted above is in effect referring to the human being's inner bodies and their awakening; to the light-body that shines "like a star" within the "niche" of the gross physical system, and within the light-body, as in an impregnable inner citadel, to the ever-burning glory of the lamp of the spirit.

This divine lamp, says the Koran, this Light within light, once discovered, will lead the individual, if Allah wills, to supreme enlightenment. Moreover, the blessed tree that is "neither of the East nor the West," belonging as it does to all peoples and all ideologies, points analogously beyond the individual system to the universal, to the World Axis, the spinal cord of the universe. At the pinnacle of that tree dwells the divine Cosmic Presence, the supreme Initiator and giver of *baraka* to the whole of the planet. His Light is a spiritual light; it shines throughout the world and yet comes from beyond it, from an energic realm beyond space-time that we are able to apprehend only by a radical spiritual awakening.

The psychospiritual techniques practiced by initiates in the Shambhalic region all testify to the sovereignty of this Light. In psychic terms it is a magnetic energy that augments the creative drive and neutralizes its potential destructiveness by the power of synthesis and centralization. Without it the creative order flies apart, dying almost as soon as it is born, as we see of the countless ephemeral cultures and their works in the course of history. The infusion of unitive energy pacifies, slows down the wheel of time and brings to the instability and impermanence of the creative act its quietus. The difference between the golden age of a Sattva Yuga and the dark age of a Kali Yuga is precisely the presence or absence of this radiant force that alone imbues human works with durable strength, authority and long life. Scott alludes to it in his quotation of a beautiful passage of Sufi poetry called "Shirin and Farhad," taken from a work by Sir William Jones on the philosophy of the dervishes, in which the unitive energy manifests as magnetism:

There is a strong propensity which dances through every atom, and attracts the minutest particle to some peculiar object: search this universe from its base to its summit, from fire to air, from water to earth, from all below the moon to all above the celestial sphere, and thou wilt not find a corpuscle destitute of that natural attractability; the very point of the first thread in this apparently tangled skein is no other than such a principle of attraction, and all principles beside are void of real basis; from such a propensity arises every motion perceived in heavenly or in terrestrial bodies; it is a disposition to be attracted which taught hard steel to rush from its place and rivet itself on the magnet; it is the same disposition which impels the light straw to attach itself firmly to amber; it is this quality which gives every substance in nature a tendency toward another, and an inclination forcibly directed to a determinate point.[18]

This is the power that unites the Tibetan Buddhist yogi to nature in so many of his practices. By recourse to his light-body he gains access to the energies of the elemental world that reside in the planetary light-body and is able to survive the harsh Tibetan winters without attaching himself to the amenities of a monastery, employing techniques that heat and nourish the physical body where neither fuel nor food is available over several months. In place of material food he can extract essences from rock minerals, water, tree saps and even air in order to sustain physical life, and also practice *tummo*, by which the body generates sufficient heat to stay comfortably alive in subzero temperatures.

The yogi draws on the same unitive energy in the Dzog Chen practice of Yang-Ti, a yogic technique which Allione says "aims at the dissolution of the physical and mental world into the body of light or the rainbow body." When the yogi, at the threshold of death, takes the rainbow body, he leaves nothing of his physical body behind except the hair and the fingernails. This translation into light is conducted in a windowless place in perfect darkness over several months, using techniques of meditation and Hatha yoga that activate the internal vision and space that is to be externalized as a sphere of luminosity holding all the potentialities of consciousness. "The practice of the dark," says Allione, "shows clearly the nonduality of internal and external space because of the manifestation of light from the mind in complete external darkness."[19] In that darkness the yogi can see as clearly as we could see with the aid of a good lamp.

The practice is an example par excellence of the power a highly developed consciousness has over matter. Once matter is understood to be energy crystallized in a pattern whose components can be broken up and reorganized by the laser beam of a highly concentrated mind, or that can be transferred to a field of finer light-vibrations by the same means, the practice of Yang-Ti can be better understood.

Over a number of months the yogi prepares for death by causing all the energized transformable cells of his body to be transformed into their essence, which is light; they are gradually absorbed into the immortal *vajra* body and are seen no more in the physical world. His physical body grows smaller and smaller until it is no bigger than that of a child. Finally he takes on "the everlasting robe of glory" visible only to clairvoyant eyes and is seen by his disciples to fly up into the sky and disappear in a rainbow as he joins a host of other light-beings in the spiritual world, leaving nothing of himself on earth.[20] He becomes one of those beings of light of which the philosopher Plotinus spoke, who became visible in the Mystery initiations and who move invisibly in our earthly world on their errands of mercy, the Bodhisattvas of the higher regions.[21]

Yang-Ti seems to have been not uncommon among Tibetan holy men and women; many reports of it occur in the recent translations of their biographies and autobiographies made in Dharamsala, India for western publication. The practice does not of course define the science of Shambhala, but it points us towards its underlying principles and possibilities. It tells us that inner and outer space are interchangeable; that what is subjective, like the experience of vision, can be objectified; physical light can be created from consciousness, and by the same token matter can be converted into a form of hyperphysical light. What is reality? Where do we find an absolute referent? In Yang-Ti all the things we think of as absolutes are instead negotiable; all resolve themselves into interchangeable states of consciousness.

Modern quantum theory comes near to the unitive insights of Yang-Ti; it is aware, for instance, that energy and matter are interchangeable. But the third factor, that of consciousness, has been excluded from its discourse lest it contaminate the objective purity of the methods science assumes are essential to the success of its empirical experiments. But what does "objective" mean when subject and object are closely related? What does "empirical" mean when the function of observation itself is in question? Is there any value in rigorously excluding subjectivity when such a state is an integral part of the field of study? And above all, how far is an answer to these questions dependent on an understanding of the organizing powers, propensities and existential limitations of the human mind? This is an area that has never been explored outside of the initiatic schools but which is fundamental to the higher technology associated with Shambhala.

The adept knows that the individual mind is only one functioning element in the mind of Gaia; that ultimately his smallest action entails the activity of the whole universe, and his work depends in the last analysis on the play of all the forces that exist and the cooperation of all beings if it is to succeed. For the purposes of their work, therefore, Allione says that Tibetan Buddhist Masters can unite themselves to the intelligences of the nonhuman kingdoms that share the earth with us but which are normally invisible, unknown, and can draw on their nonhuman culture to aid them in their enterprises.

In such a case the yogi, working in his light-body, can transcend the boundaries of his own mental-egoic identity, though without destroying it, in the interests of an inter-kingdom liaison. Thus Guru Padma Sambhava is said to have created his termas with the help of the *dakinis*, the nature-beings who are personifications of a feminine spiritual force whose name means literally "sky-dancer" or one who moves in the sky. The dakini is also called a wisdom deity, a nonhuman being composed of elemental energy who normally manifests in the fairy kingdom but who, when interacting with humans, may take human form. She embodies feminine wisdom, the creative force in human beings, dynamic, blissful, wise. "She springs out of the cosmic cervix, the triangular source of dharmas," says Allione, "burning with unbearable bliss, energy in an unconditioned state. . . She may appear as a human being, or as a goddess—either peaceful or wrathful—or she may be perceived as the general play of energy in the phenomenal world."[22]

Nature-beings like the dakini generally ensoul natural phenomena like rivers or trees or mountains, or man-made phenomena like shrines, ships or temples if properly consecrated. But the human mind potentiated by kundalini awakening may interact with the dakini principle when it is ensouled in any one of a number of anthropoid forms more familiar to humans, such as deities or wise inner teachers.[23] But these forms are, as Dion Fortune says, made by the imagination of men themselves.

> Wherever man comes in touch with the astral, whether as psychic or magician, he always anthropomorphoses, and creates forms in his own likeness to represent to himself the elusive subtle forces [of other forms of evolution than the human] that he is endeavouring to contact, understand and harness to his will. He is a true child of the Great Mother, and carries his natural propensities for organizing and form-making to whatever plane he is able to exalt consciousness.[24]

This imaginal ability casts its equivocal and deceptive spell over the contours of our own world, but extends also to the whole of the unseen world that teems about us: from troll to angel, man himself conjures its forms in his own image, according to his own subjective conditioning. But, says Dion Fortune, "the intelligences of other forms of evolution than ours, if they come into touch with human life, can . . . make use of these forms, just as a man puts on a diving-suit and descends into another element." Then the alien intelligence will ensoul the form and, if willing, work with the initiate in enterprises of mutual benefit.[25, 26]

According to Tibetan annals, it was in this manner that Padma Sambhava was able to preserve his termas for hundreds of years, hiding them as he did in the dakini language. This language, Allione tells us, consists of letters or symbols which have no set translation, and the ability to understand them is reserved for the very few—"those who are in contact with the energy field of the dakini."[27] This highly symbolic cipher is so condensed that many volumes of teachings could be compressed in a few letters, yet later could expand into a lengthy text: a process reminiscent, curiously enough, of the modern storage and retrieval function of the microchip. Thus Padma Sambhava's consort, Yeshe Tsogyel, who lived during the first wave of Buddhism in Tibet in the seventh century and was credited with being the incarnation of a great dakini, was able to hide many of the Guru's texts by putting them into a dakini cipher. In this way a whole teaching could be condensed into a single symbol, so it is said, and hidden in the earth, a tree or water until the destined terton could, at the appointed time, translate the text.

Besides the secret signs of the dakinis there is another half-concealed language called "the twilight language." It deciphers termas known as "mind-treasures" which are received from birds, from all kinds of light and from heavenly space, wherein letters may be seen to form which the terton can read and translate into the language of ordinary beings. Bernbaum says that many of the more secret Kalachakric teachings are couched in the twilight language. Once again, it is an actual cipher that can only be understood by a revelation granted to those in touch with the wisdom deities. But the understanding of the dakini language does not come, as we might expect, from the dark abyss of the unconscious nor from the heights of the intuitive mind, but directly from the world of the Bodhisattvas, the subtle spiritual realm beyond the astral and therefore altogether beyond the bounds of sensory awareness or of the mental-emotional psyche. Tibetans believe that it is because Shambhala, as the only Pure Land on earth, is uniquely in touch with that Light-world that the Masters can continue by means of termas and other such devices to intervene in history to keep truth alive.

THE SIGN OF SHAMBHALA:
UNIDENTIFIED FLYING OBJECTS

So far we have considered only meditational techniques; but what technology produced the shining spheroid oval Roerich and his party saw speeding high across the cloudless Inner Asian skies, suddenly changing direction, in 1927? Of all the strange manifestations attributed to Shambhala this is the most mysterious, the most inexplicable. Even allowing for an hallucinatory factor, eminently possible in anything connected with Shambhala, the purely material aeronautical basis of the phenomenon, witnessed through three pairs of binoculars and familiar to the lamas present, is undeniable. It is only in the twentieth century that we can fully appreciate how mysterious this is, and can ask ourselves whether the same Shambhalic technology is responsible for the flying saucers that have been seen by millions of people in every part of the world. If so, how and where was it developed, and how long ago? What are its principles? And how has it escaped detection? We can answer none of these questions.

The lamas told Roerich that the flying object he saw was the signature of Shambhala and the sign of its blessing. When it flies overhead one may know that august powers are at hand to succor struggling humanity and to help in enterprises of humanitarian value. As to the energy that empowers its flight, it is the primal energy, "this fine imponderable matter which is scattered everywhere and which is within our use at any moment"[28]—the same energy that Tomas has called "the intelligent force in the core of the atom."[29] Whether the sign of Shambhala is psychophysical rather than purely physical in the sense that we normally understand the term is something we do not yet know. But not only are stories of strange aircraft traditionally associated with Shambhala, more than one sighting of UFOs have been reliably reported in the region. In 1933 the British mountaineer Frank Smythe, on reaching an altitude of 26,000 feet on Mount Everest, saw to his amazement two aircraft hovering far above him. One had squat wings, the other a kind of beak, and both were surrounded by a radiant pulsating aura.

Up until recently the unidentified flying object was generally the mass target of either credulous cultist fascination or disbelief and scorn. But the number of hardened skeptics in the population is rapidly waning as trained enquiry by scientists and academics, plus the sheer overwhelming weight of reliable observers, is tending to support the authenticity of the phenomenon—although its interpretation is another matter. It has been almost universally assumed that the UFO, if given any credence at all, must be a spacecraft manned by extraterrestrial beings, especially since their craft appears to be capable of moving in and out of visibility, passing through material barriers and executing maneuvers that defy gravity and mass and are impossible for the human frame to withstand. But as more facts become known and their study has moved onto a more sophisticated level of research, different options are being considered.

Dr. Kenneth Ring, professor of psychology at the University of Connecticut, has conducted an exhaustive survey of the subject. In his book *The Omega Project*, Ring, like other academics, has come to the conclusion that the UFO seems to be a psychophysical event that somehow has its origin in humanity itself, coming from an unknown *terrestrial* source; and that it may be the outward manifestation of a major evolutionary advance in human consciousness. While some researchers do not go as far as that, and a few believe that flying saucers are simply a natural phenomenon—such as "earth-lights," the electro-magnetic effects of tectonic stress in the earth which are known to cause peculiar psychic and hallucinatory effects in some susceptible people— in all cases the world of science fiction is being abandoned.

Dr. Jacques Vallee, a computer expert trained in astrophysics, is one of the most prominent investigators of UFO phenomena. According to Vallee:

> It is curious to observe that even scientifically trained researchers who accept the idea of multiple universes, or the few ufologists who understand the idea that space-time could be folded to allow almost instantaneous travel from one point of our universe to another, still cling emotionally to the notion that any nonhuman form of consciousness is necessarily from outer space.[30]

In the light of thousands of personal accounts of close encounters and abductions involving UFOs, and the extraordinary consistency and sincerity of these accounts, strong arguments are now being marshaled against this assumption of extraterrestrial visitation in favor of an unknown earth-agency that is manipulating the popular mind in such a way as to create a global metamorphosis of consciousness. Like the near-death experience, which is equally ubiquitous, the UFO experience with its strong psychic and paranormal overtones has features that are increasingly being interpreted as a form of spiritual awakening or initiation, although with puzzlingly physical elements.

It has been observed by modern researchers that, although these unknown aerial objects are physical enough to be tracked by radar and witnessed by hundreds of people at the same time, in many cases of close encounter a psychic dimension is present, indicative of trance, altered states of consciousness, time loss, hazy reportage, etc., which throws the objectivity of the experience into doubt. Many witnesses report leaving normal reality behind and moving as though within a lucid dream—as though ordinary space-time physics no longer applies—until they are returned to the normal world with the sense of a break in time. But in fact this is an accurate description of any out-of-the-body experience in which the physical body is left behind in an entranced sleep while the inner body, carrying the egoic consciousness with it, moves elsewhere for a time, often unaware that the physical body is not involved in its adventures.

An unusually clear example of such an experience has been recounted by a woman in Wollongong, Australia. She says she woke up in the middle of the night to see through the roof a round aircraft, silent and without lights, hovering directly over her house. A chain, which was dangling from it over her bed, was made of some kind of energy in the form of links, and was making a horrible screeching noise. She decided to go up it out of curiosity, but on arriving in the cabin of the aircraft, now lighted, was so nauseated by the nerve-wracking noise of the energy chain that she returned to her bed and went back to sleep. She says that just at the last she was aware that, although awake and with her eyes open throughout, her physical body had somehow never left her bed.

On the other hand, some people seem to be well aware of the psycho-physical nature of their encounter and state frankly that it has been a deeply personal initiatory experience resulting in physical healings, psychic gifts or a radical change in spiritual direction. Such an experience involving a UFO was recounted by L. C. W., whom we met in Chapter 6. She writes:

> I left my bed and joined K. We walked across fields to the waiting aircraft. Men and women were coming to it from all directions. The pilot—a tall, fair, young man in a blue uniform—welcomed each of us with a package of food for the journey. We took off and I was taken up to the mother-ship; but K. told me the next day he was taken elsewhere, to a planet with golden cities on it. The mother-ship was huge. I was led through dark passages by a fiery cross moving before me until I came to the control-room in the nose of the ship. The walls were transparent and beyond them one could see all the glittering stars of deep space. In the middle of the room was a round chart-table of polished silver, with the signs of the zodiac engraved round its edge. I particularly noticed the Pythagorean Y [the sign of choice between good and evil].

> There were men attending to the navigation. I asked one of them what was the purpose of the ship. What were they doing? He said they transmitted messages to the stars and received messages back. Three months after this experience I joined a spiritual movement that changed my life and was welcomed to it by the man I had spoken to in the airship.

Clearly this event cannot be taken literally, yet it was no ordinary dream. For example, L. C. W. says that the next day K. reported an identical experience on the same night, joining her to walk across the fields to the aircraft, and corroborating every detail of the event, even to the seating arrangements on the plane, until they parted company at some point during the journey to proceed to different destinations according to their disparate temperaments. Many researchers now deem it highly probable that UFO witnesses, especially those involved in close encounters and abductions, are reporting events that have a genuinely objective basis but which are perceived imaginally, as dreams are, through the lens of a subjective and entranced consciousness, and in terms that are according to their own unconscious prejudices, expectations, neuroses and level of intellectual or psychospiritual development.

Reading their experiences in that light casts doubt on all the simplistic extraterrestrial interpretations of flying saucers. Summing up the new awareness of a need for a much deeper exploration of the subject, John Spencer of the British UFO Research Association says that "there has been a tendency in recent years to recognize the possibility that the UFO phenomenon represents an unknown agent of our own earth's environment and as such the term alien can now often be found referring to entities where the meaning is 'alien to the human race' (but not necessarily alien to the Earth)."[31]

This is a strange statement to make unless an occult perspective is being envisaged, and such seems to be the case. Jacques Vallee concludes that "if there is a form of life and consciousness that operates on properties of space-time we have not yet discovered, then it does not have to be extraterrestrial. It could certainly come from another solar system in our galaxy, or from another galaxy. But it could also coexist with us and remain undetected."[32]

This is precisely the proposition esoteric teachings put forward regarding Shambhala, and brings us back to Roerich's report of a flying aerial object seen over Central Asia which the lamas with him called the sign of Shambhala. Their familiarity with the phenomenon suggests that Shambhala may well be the missing factor in the UFO equation. Indeed Geoffrey Ashe has expressed surprise that UFO researchers have not taken keener note of Roerich's sighting and the significance of the lamas' comments on it. "Here perhaps," he says, "is the key to the notorious UFO mania of recent years. . . . It is linked with Shambhala and the Ancient Wisdom territory."[33]

The World Axis is the one place on earth where world lines intersect, where space-time is without normal boundaries, and where spiritual adepts who can date their hidden society to Cro-Magnon times have had at least forty thousand years in which to experiment with metal alloys, ultimate energy, aerodynamics and multidimensional space. According to the wealth of legends collated by a galaxy of eminent explorers and authors on this subject, Shambhala's adepts constitute the one earthly agency known to be able to manipulate the consciousness of others in just such ways as are described by UFO witnesses; to be able to alter our reality perceptions at just such a deep level, to induce just such deep trance and hypnotic states and to objectify, in just such dramatic ways as UFO abductees describe, the contents of the human unconscious such as fear, awe, hostility and lust.

The same literary accounts refer to the extraordinary ability of these masters to create material forms that can cross and recross at will the threshold of visibility, and to enjoin the participation in their projects of elemental life-forms who, like the dakinis, may temporarily mirror us in human guise yet remain as intrinsically alien in their nature and purposes as if they had come from another star. If such accounts are to be believed, all the various powers ascribed to flying saucers—high-level manipulation of consciousness, control of matter-creation, access to a higher-order universe and unknown energies, interaction with nonhuman intelligences and other transcendental abilities—are not so much evidence of the invasion of an alien extraterrestrial science as the working out of our own human destiny at its leading scientific edge. It is our own higher intellect embodied in Shambhala that is writing its signature in the skies.

I would suggest that in the UFO we are gaining a foretaste of the future, and one that apprises us that our physical sciences are not the only path possible nor the ultimate in achievement. Beyond them lies the vastly greater realm of synergistic life-energy fields that subtend the physical, and it is this higher Shambhalic ground that is going to offer us alternative technological paths of far greater potential than those we know today.

A Sign for the New Millennium

The abnormal, all-engulfing stress that characterizes the twentieth century has led Mircea Eliade to reflect on the way in which a primitive society would view our own today, as presenting the anguishing conditions of a tribal initiation, but one enlarged to the collective scale. It would liken the situation of the modern world, says Eliade, to that

> of a man swallowed by a monster . . . or wandering in a labyrinth which itself is the symbol of the Infernal. . . . And yet, in the eyes of the primitive, this terrible experience is indispensable to the birth of the new man. No initiation is possible without the ritual of an agony, a death and a resurrection. . . . The anguish of the modern world is the sign of an imminent death, but of a death that is necessary and redemptive, for it will be followed by a resurrection and the possibility of attaining a new mode of being, that of maturity and responsibility.[1]

This millennial theme of apocalypse and world initiation has recurred with increasing frequency as the century draws to its close, and is now insistent. But its note was first struck with a supernatural timbre at the beginning of the century at Fatima in Portugal. As is well known, the Virgin Mary is believed to have appeared there in a shining globe of light to three children with a warning to the world of catastrophes to come, but also offering the spiritual means, through prayer, of resolving the impending evil.

On October 13, 1917, when the "Lady of the Rosary" had promised to send a miracle that would convince the world of her reality, seventy thousand people gathered to honor her. They witnessed the clouds parting and a great silvery disc seemed to cover the sun like a lambent eclipse, making it possible to view it with the naked eye without harm. For about ten minutes the orb seemed to spin like a Catherine wheel, to pulse, to send forth prismatic rays, changing color through the whole spectrum; and twice it plunged earthwards in sharp zigzagging maneuvers, to the terror of all those watching it. Others in the area saw the extraordinary solar spectacle from their homes.

Over the ensuing decades, similar solar phenomena at shrines of the Virgin Mary have been seen by many thousands of the faithful at Hriushiw and Hoshiv in the Ukraine, Medjugorje in Herzegovina, Svata Hora in Bohemia, Czestochowa in Poland, Garabandal in Spain and Walsingham in England. In almost all cases an appearance of the Virgin Mother accompanies the solar dance. Frequently she seems to be enclosed in a globe of fiery silver light that oscillates to and fro before settling in one place; and at Hoshiv the appearance was preceded by radiant celestial spheres which, according to the watching crowds, could be seen from many miles away and were mistaken by some for aerial nuclear weapons.[2] At Walsingham, a place of Catholic pilgrimage for about a thousand years, much the same phenomena as at Fatima were seen in 1988 in the skies above a small medieval chapel called the Slipper Chapel.

Two independent witnesses, one a Catholic scientist attending a conference next door to the chapel, and another a pilgrim, reported seeing a number of "small red suns" revolving around the sun, which had a brilliant light shining behind it and appeared to rotate against the background of a brilliant white disc. The pilgrim added that she saw circles of constantly changing colors coming out of the sun, approaching the earth and returning.[3] The startling affinity between some of these solar phenomena and the aerial visitations of UFOs has been noted with interest by many people and has strengthened the growing belief that the twentieth century is, besides all else, a century of supernatural intervention on a grand scale.

Yet the aerial display Nicholas Roerich was to call the sign of Shambhala only ten years after Fatima is not new to the twentieth century; it has long been a part of history, although never before on the present scale. It has appeared sporadically in the annals of past civilizations as a strange visitation seen in the sky in times of great tribulation, extreme social crisis and transition from one cultural phase to another; as a portent, a forewarning, perhaps as a benediction, perhaps to give strength and courage.

Most frequently it has been associated with luminosity, with silvery, moonlike or fiery radiance, sometimes with rainbow-colored lights; all of which suggests that whatever the source, it is one that, like Shambhala, knows how to utilize the secrets of primal energy. It appeared as floating "circles of fire" in c. 1500 B.C. during the disastrous Hyksos invasions of ancient Egypt, "shining in the sky more than the brightness of the sun";[4] the Hebrew prophet Ezekiel, captive in Babylon, saw the aerial visitation come out of a fiery whirlwind "as it were a wheel within a wheel";[5] the Indian Ramayana war epic speaks of it as a heavenly car "golden in shape and radiance";[6] and it appeared in the sky over Cloera, Ireland, in the ominous thirteenth century that saw the rise of the Inquisition and the death of the Irish golden age of learning. Shambhala's prophetic sign appeared over Tübingen, Germany on October 5, 1577, when the amazed burghers saw descending from the clouds in great numbers whirling shapes that "resembled tall, wide hats in a variety of colours."[7]

At the time of these celestial visitations, Egypt, India, Israel and Ireland were all at a fateful turning point in their cultures, poised at the end of a golden age or already entering a period of apocalyptic catastrophe that would change their destiny; and this was also the case in Reformation Europe. In the 16th century Germany was the center of a brilliant efflorescence of post-Renaissance learning, and Tübingen, the university city of Württemberg, had become the breeding ground for liberal new ideas centering on the need for new social and political principles, for religious reform and scientific exploration. Tübingen was the cradle of the Rosicrucian ferment, the great cultural reforming movement that was already incubating when the shower of flying hats over the city provided Europe with a nine days' wonder that was recorded for posterity in numerous illustrations of the time.

The miraculous aerial display occurred only a couple of years after the great English mathematician and magus John Dee had toured Germany with tidings of a higher knowledge to be gained through number, geometry and revelation, "through which the adept believed he could achieve both a profound insight into nature and a vision of a divine world beyond nature."[8] Dee profoundly influenced the learned men of his day, and as a result Johann Valentin Andreae, a Lutheran pastor and mystic of Württemberg, while still a student at the Tübingen University, wrote the first of his Rosicrucian works, *The Chemical Wedding* in the early seventeenth century.[9]

Although it has now been forgotten, this was a major turning point in European history. Beginning though it did in a mystical Hermetic-Cabalistic framework and doomed to be short-lived, the intellectual revolution that ensued in Lutheran Germany nevertheless paved the way for the modern scientific age, and consequently had the utmost significance for Europe for centuries to come, and indeed for the whole course of our cultural evolution. It is therefore extremely tempting to interpret the celestial spectacle that took place over Tübingen at that precise period as a benedictory salute such as the Lords of Shambhala gave to Roerich's cultural mission in 1927, and as coming from the same source.

We may ask ourselves whether the flotilla of strange aircraft was Shambhala's way of giving the city a preview of the technological marvels to come in the new age; or whether it was a visible form of *baraka*, transmitting powerful higher energies for the purpose of creating an energetic field over Württemberg that would illumine the trained intellects of the day, shake them free of old dogmas and inspire them to radically new ideas and visions. Or was it as well an omen of disaster, warning them of the imminence of the Thirty Years' War that would crush the Rosicrucian movement and delay Europe's mystical and intellectual awakening?

Today we are again at an historical turning point, and not only for Europe but for the whole of the world. Tübingen is like a preview in miniature of the twentieth-century crisis with its relentless pressure of change, its clash of evolutionary and counter-evolutionary forces, its technological revolution, its omens of apocalypse, its sense of initiation and judgment, transformation and death. Once again enigmatic portents are writing their messages in our skies. Once again it seems Shambhala is giving *baraka* as it did over Tübingen and Babylon and Egypt, its numinous sign in the heavens generating a field of higher energies around the earth that is subliminally affecting the whole race. Like that other heavenly harbinger of the twentieth century, the epiphanies of the Virgin Mary, it is the sign and portent of the new millennium, its mission now being to warn, strengthen and prepare us for the great transformation ahead.

THE SPIRITUALIZING OF HUMANITY

The signs of the times are directing our attention more and more forcibly to the remarkable metamorphosis taking place at the growing tip of society, at its evolutionary cutting edge, a metamorphosis which is similar to the Tübingen awakening but on a global scale. It is happening in China, Russia, Europe and America. Professor Ring refers to it as the spiritualizing of humanity, which he attributes to contact with a higher transcendental order presently unknown to us. The change overtaking society is perhaps best summarized as a secularization of the divine, a process that is taking place at a number of levels and which has many different facets. In fact we may note that it is the kind of process characteristic of Shambhala's wide-ranging nonpartisan activities, which work without favor wherever the sap is rising, in whatever way is best suited to current conditions.

One of the most notable features of the trend Ring cites is the proliferation of individuals all over the world who have inborn gifts of clairvoyance, psychokinesis, spiritual healing powers, telepathy and other spontaneous psychic talents that owe little if anything to the formal training procedures necessary in the past. Accompanying this trend is a massive opening up to the world of religio-occult secrets that have always in the past been guarded behind the closed doors of esoteric fraternities, and also the usurpation by secular scholars of the teaching province traditionally reserved to theologians.

Perhaps of even greater significance is the ability of an increasing number of highly educated psychics in the West, often of the professional class, to channel the spiritual teachings of discarnate beings in the metaphysical terms appropriate to the intellectual level of a highly literate, informed and generally freethinking society. We have only to think of *A Course in Miracles*, the *Seth* and *Lazaris* books, the Findhorn material and many other channellings of like quality to realize that despite the specifically religious terminology often borrowed in the course of transmission, they are essentially eclectic and esoteric in tone and aimed at an intellectual rather than a religious audience. We are probably seeing here an absolutely new development more appropriate to pre-cultic shamanism than to the institutional religions that have generally shaped the style of such communications in the past, and more suited to the secular seeker than to the devout.

We are also witnessing in every part of the world, though perhaps primarily in America, a growing number of people, usually young women of no known religious or spiritualistic allegiances, the innate ability to read the dynamic energy-field or auric field surrounding others' bodies and to diagnose and heal the psychosomatic illnesses that first manifest in these fields. This sensitivity to what one physician has called "an extremely complex biomagnetic energy field that operates outside the confines of the nervous system"[10] Barbara Ann Brennan calls Higher Sense Perception, which she claims is possible for all of us. "Modern science," she says, "tells us that we are moving out of the world of static solid form into a world of dynamic energy fields. Our old world of solid concrete objects is surrounded and permeated with a fluid world of radiating energy, constantly moving, constantly changing like the seas," and fully accessible to us because we are a part of it.[11]

Even more astonishing than this inborn possession of Higher Sense Perception is the ability of such spiritual healers to collaborate closely and consciously by a form of channelling with spirit guides who train, advise and assist them in their healing work. Again, Brennan believes this is possible for all of us in time. "We are all guided by spiritual teachers," she says, "who speak to us in our dreams, through our intuition, and eventually, if we listen, they speak to us directly, perhaps through writing at first, then through sound, voice, or concepts."[12] It may be noted that this creative collaboration with the spirit world is the *sine qua non* of the shaman's experience, without which he cannot receive initiation from the ancestors or learn the secrets of his trade; and its spontaneous appearance in the modern world is so new and impressive a development that some researchers are arguing for the birth of a new race possessing an innate shamanic consciousness.

Besides an awakening of psychism, a new secular idealism is spreading which is again characteristic of nature-loving shamanism. Those individuals in particular who have been exposed to unusual psychic encounters, such as near-death or UFO experiences, report a subsequent awakening of concern, often for the first time, for ecological and green issues, the equitable distribution of wealth, reconciliation between religions and other reformist ideas not dissimilar to those Utopian ones that revolutionized the vanguard of European thought in the early seventeenth century and which also stimulated an interest in nature.

Now let us note that wherever we find shamanism in its quintessential manifestations—as in the Siberian medicine man—there we also find the World Tree, the creative psychic powers of kundalini and the mythology of Shambhala: we find, in short, this complex of causal elements always indissolubly entwined together. Wherever one is, there the others invariably appear. And so when Ring discerns in the shamanic trend presently sweeping society a primary source that he identifies with a higher order, perhaps humanity's higher Self or higher Mind, its association with Shambhala acquires an irresistible logic. The Connecticut psychologist does not take such a step himself, but his studies of kundalini phenomena in the near-death and UFO experiences provide a firm basis for it.

In the Omega research project, Ring associates the postulated higher order with the mysterious power to awaken and transform consciousness which we have found to be invariably consequent on contact with Shambhala. He claims that in the majority of the hundreds of cases studied there have been deep and permanent changes, unaltered even after thirty years, following extraordinary psychic encounters with this higher order, and that without exception they are symptomatic of the kundalini arousal customary in the training of a shaman. Despite a multitude of superficial differences, the archetypal structure of the experience is the same as the initiation of the shaman: an involuntary descent into ordeal, an initiatory journey and a psychospiritual rebirth. Again, this is precisely the hallmark of the Shambhalic experience.

Like that of the shaman, the near-death and UFO experiences involve a snatching away to an alternate reality, a meeting with mysterious beings who have mind-controlling powers and then the return to the everyday world with new values and in many cases new psychic gifts. This higher-order experience has significant parallels with the kind of psychophysical transformation that

Gopi Krishna reported after the awakening of his kundalini that led to a refining of character, a heightening of intellectual performance, a greatly expanded and clarified worldview and the development of mystical faculties stemming from an increased sensitivity of the body and the intuition. Of course, the same kind of "deep sea change" underlies the ability to live in two worlds at once that is traditionally imputed to the inhabitants of Shambhala.

Gallup Polls conducted in the last couple of decades show that about eight million people in the United States alone have had near-death experiences and up to *nineteen million* have witnessed UFOs—many of them having experienced close encounters with them as well.[13] These findings have reinforced Kenneth Ring's belief that by means of mind-transforming experiences of such a kind modern humanity is on the way to becoming *shamanized*—that is to say, to becoming a traveler in other worlds, a voyager on supraconscious planes like the prototypic shaman. And he sees the actual mechanism at the heart of this process as a collective awakening of kundalini in which this latent organizing force, once released into the physiological system of each person, transforms the nervous system and hastens racial evolution. He says in summary:

> Our findings reveal increases in a variety of physical sensitivities, suggestions of mutually consistent differences in physiological functioning, alterations of neurological and brain states, as well as a miscellany of unusual psycho-energetic, psychological and paranormal experiences. . . . We are experiencing the first bursts of a new self-renewing power for the healing of the earth with millenial energies that have been liberated through direct contact with the transcendental order. . . . I would argue that the findings from the Omega Project suggest that we could be in the beginning stages of a major shift in levels of consciousness that will eventually lead to humanity's being able to live in two worlds at once. . . . This is of course precisely what the shaman in traditional cultures is trained to do . . . and is what I mean by the shamanizing of humanity.[14]

The gist of serious speculative research like that undertaken by Dr. Ring[15] is that there is a permanent cabal with transcendental powers hidden within the body of the race that represents its higher Mind or higher Self throughout history, and that functions as the lever precipitating the species along its evolutionary path by opening significantly large numbers of people to an irradiation of higher energies. Thus, says Ring, "the prophetic function is being democratized; ordinary men and women in increasing numbers are having bestowed upon them profound soul-opening experiences that carry the charge of prophetic revelation."[16] They are the mystical carriers of a message of renewal to the planet as a whole. His view goes a long way towards supporting the thesis that I have put forward throughout this book: that Shambhala, and Shambhala alone, is the hidden evolutionary agency that over the course of history has been driving the race onward towards its spiritual destiny.

As already mentioned, some researchers have suggested that a widespread activation of the kundalini energy by near-death and/or UFO experiences, supplementing meditational practices, is creating a new and higher type of humanity out of the old, one that will presently crowd out the species now populating the earth, perhaps as Cro-Magnon man once crowded out the inferior Neanderthal stock. John White, for example, the author and editor of numerous works on evolving consciousness, believes our present species with its reasoning and self-conscious powers will be superseded by a more advanced one that embodies the noetic higher mind. In a journal of essays on the subject, he writes:

> Higher human development—evolution—has been accelerating in the last few centuries. The pace of change is now unprecedented for our species, and what is to come is, I believe, a new species. We are witnessing the final phase of *Homo sapiens* and the simultaneous emergence, still quite tentative because of the nuclear and environmental threats to life, of what I have named *Homo noeticus,* a more advanced form of humanity.[17]

Professor Ring too is prepared to consider such a possibility, although in a more cautious spirit. And in *Return from Death*, a work concerned solely with near-death experiences, the psychologist Margot Grey is another who postulates a coming evolutionary mutation within the human race. She says:

> It would seem that similar physiological mechanisms are operating in both the near-death experience and kundalini phenomena and that they are both aspects of the same evolutionary force. Taken together, these spectacular instances of transformation add up to a surprisingly large and increasing percentage of the population and might therefore be expected to have a growing influence on the collective awareness of the rest of the species. . . . It would appear that a new breed of mankind may be about to be born, and that in order for this to happen our consciousness and biological structure are undergoing a radical transformation.[18]

The general implications of ideas like the above are enormous. We can no longer unquestioningly assume that we are at the end of our evolutionary journey as a race, nor that we are capable as yet of understanding its true meaning or *modus operandi*. A whole range of questions must now engage our attention. Is there an unexplored relationship between religion and evolution? Between spiritual initiation and genetic change? Does the shaman's physiological and genetic programming result, as we suspect, in a higher order of complexity than that of his fellowmen? And is he at a higher spiritual level than has been achieved as yet by the race as a whole?

These are questions to which we still have only the most tentative answers. But some leading exponents of spiritual psychology are in agreement that the evolution of the few has always been far in advance of the many, and that the level of spiritual consciousness reached by the Siberian shaman perhaps fifty thousand years ago is only now becoming a possibility for the race as a whole. The consensus among them is that the shaman's way of kundalini arousal marks the entrance to the true spiritual path; above him are higher states, but his is the beginning of a genuine religious awareness of which the bulk of humanity is not yet capable. What we have hitherto thought of as religion may be only a preparation for it.

Joseph Campbell was of the opinion that for the great majority of human beings life consists of three egoistic drives, either innate or acquired by social conditioning: pleasure, power and the laws of the collective moral order. These three passions drive the engine, so to speak, of the pres piritual state and connect each community to its separate and mutually conflicting religio-ethnic context. But the shaman embodies a fourth principle unmotivated by ego; a principle that alone offers divine release into mysticism, wisdom and the knowledge of God; one that is universal, transcending all local religions, cults and philosophies of life and conflicting with none. "The Way of Suffering of the shaman," says Campbell, "is the earliest example we know of a lifetime devoted to the fourth end. . . "[19] that is, to the pursuit of self-transformation that is the true meaning of religion.

In *Up From Eden*, the metapsychologist Ken Wilber reaches a similar conclusion. Humanity, he believes, is still moving up the great Chain of Being from the lowest rung of prehuman, matter-dominated consciousness towards the highest rung, the superconsciousness of soul and spirit. Its present level is the mental-egoic stage midway on the Chain; a rational, self-reflexive, uniquely human condition that is bounded by purely personal horizons at which we have arrived from an earlier prepersonal stage that was rooted in a dreamlike immersion in nature, the animal body and the subconscious. At present we stand as a species on the threshold of the next stage, that of transpersonal soul, and are preparing to enter into the expanded consciousness of the shaman.

Like Campbell, Wilber sees the shaman as the first truly spiritual figure to tread the path of transcendence, even though he is not the ultimate in spiritual development. Above him in the racial womb is the saint, then the sage, and lastly the avatar, who is free of all earthly conditions whatsoever. Yet the spiritual potential of the shamanic level, low though it is on the scale of transcendence, is incalculably greater than that of the mental-egoic level at which humanity presently functions. Its appropriate developmental technique is Kundalini yoga, its characteristic path the awakening of the inner senses. Wilber consequently refers to the shamanic path in tantric terms and describes it as the way of trance, "of bodily ecstasy, of swooning in release, and as being usually accompanied by psychosomatic changes of a dramatic and overt variety (*kriyas*)—all of which results at its peak in certain psychic intuitions and powers."[20] Wilber is convinced that this is the class of religious experience to which humanity is now beginning to aspire, though at a higher level than was possible for the shamans of earlier societies; and for that reason he calls the coming age the Kundalini Age.

The above are just some of the many voices raised in support of the idea that the race is being inundated by a new energy that is moving it onto a higher evolutionary level and therefore closer to the religious territory of the shaman, the World Axis and the Masters—in other words, to Shambhala. It is an immense evolutionary step, greater than any the species is accustomed to, involving a 180-degree turn in a new direction, beyond mind, beyond the physical world, and impossible of achievement without help. As the plant grows by heliotropism, so humanity grows by an inner compulsion towards the Light that draws it to itself. Unconscious of the process though we may be, I believe Shambhala governs this spiritual tropism, drawing us soulward as though by the pull of an interior lodestone. It is our sun; under its burning lens that refracts divinity the metamorphosis becomes possible.

A Search for Love and Purity

Shambhala's magnetic power is the power of love—the same power that "taught hard steel to rush from its place and rivet itself on the magnet";[21] but operating at a higher level. All the legends about Shambhala emphasize this point. Its inhabitants live in harmony with each other, even though their lives are a thousand years long; in Shambhala—as in the Sumerian myth of the paradise called Dilmun, where "the raven utters no cry, the lion kills not, the wolf snatches not the lamb, unknown is the grain-devouring boar"—all the kingdoms live at peace with one another.[22] And this love and peace and purity are, moreover, incorruptible, which is why Shambhala is called the only Pure Land on earth.

Because of these qualities, says Bernbaum, Shambhala stirs a deep yearning and spiritual intuition within us. Because it is hidden, because only those can enter it who will never despoil it, it cannot be corrupted by the external world. "This gives Shambhala," he says, a special quality that sets it apart from other idyllic places, which although remote are nevertheless accessible and vulnerable to exploitation. . . . It is difficult to imagine Shambhala ever turning into a resort for wealthy tourists. In our minds the kingdom lies far beyond the reach of anyone who might use it in such a way. The powerful appeal of Shambhala reflects a yearning we have for some pure and uncorrupted place that neither we nor others can ever defile.[23]

But where does it come from, this inextinguishable longing for what is incorruptible, this nostalgia for purity which is shared by everyone, even the most degenerate? One has only to recall Hitler's obsession with the myth of Germanic racial purity, or the chauvinism of the Godfathers, notorious for their protection of the purity of their womenfolk, to sense that in all cases it springs from an intimation of spiritual incompleteness, from the longing of the soul that knows it is not yet perfected. The Buddhist idea that Shambhala symbolizes what we have not yet attained, the diamond mind of enlightenment that shines in the inner heart, may be applied with equal validity to religious ideals in general; Shambhala signifies all our unrealized religious aspirations, by whatever name we give them.

And from those unrealized longings comes an exhalation of pure love, for whatever deity we worship it is an image of the unknown and unrealized Self. We are fascinated, magnetized and helplessly in love with the divine Being who is not yet manifest within us, who lives still in the unrealized depths of the collective psyche, and we displace our longing onto the ever-radiant image of Shambhala. Shambhala signifies our liberation and joyful release into a more completely evolved state, and so moves us to a yearning love that is never satisfied, though we do not know its source.

For if humanity is irradiated in the course of its evolution by a succession of increasingly empowering energies, it is also subjected to a succession of prisons, since each energy—sensitive, conscious, rational, creative—can give to the race as a whole only the functional freedom inherent in that particular energy and those below it. Each level is more spacious than the ones below it, which it includes; yet at each one there is a ceiling, a set of limitations in which every individual born must share to some degree, however much he may yearn for greater scope. Some will be aware of this evolutionary strait-jacketing, others not, since the magical ring-pass-not that marks their boundaries of action is by its nature invisible; but all will unconsciously prefigure their release from it in dreams of paradise.

We can see this process reflected in history. Early Palaeolithic man, being without self-consciousness, was confined to the most brutal and vegetative mode of life; unknown to himself, his social instincts slumbered, his intelligence burned dimly. Later he became self-conscious and reasoning; yet without creativity his culture was static, his social order remained primitive, his stone tools unchanged for countless thousands of years; inventive intelligence remained latent, although he did not suspect it. Now creative man has been freed to invent, trade, make philosophies, civilizations and wars; yet without unitive energy he is in danger of destroying himself. He is immured in anxiety; everything he essays ends in warfare; everything he values dies. He is nailed to the cross of the opposites.

Without unitive energy modern man is a creature of intensely egoistic suffering; unknowingly he is without love; the higher religious faculties slumber. At this point in his evolution he is a sensitive, self-conscious, intelligent and creative being, but he is not yet a moral being in the true sense of the word.

To express love in sustained action requires an act of will stronger than the deeply entrenched self-interested passions that have hitherto driven him, and for that his will-power is in general not yet sufficiently developed. He lacks the shining arrow of will, the *vajra*-bolt that is forged only in the fire of kundalini and which belongs only to those who, like the shaman, have advanced beyond him on the Ladder of Being; and therefore he lacks the *dynamis* of genuine altruism.

Another way of putting our situation as a species is that, as Wilber suggests, we have become amnesiacs, relegating our higher faculties to the unconscious, and each energy in turn is a key that further unlocks the memory of our essential nature as pure lovingkind Spirit, as eternal and transcendent Being. But however it is expressed, this fundamentally Sufi view of unfolding evolution is linked to the belief that the search for the unitive principle is now the key signature of our society, the one motif common to every aspect of our suffering and struggling global civilization, and in that sense a search for Shambhala.

Some Sufi writers claim that the search began a long time ago, because the unitive energy frequency was first given to the race at the Crucifixion two thousand years ago, but was not understood and was rejected. Man, says Bennett, "has used his creativity to dominate rather than serve nature. Two thousand five hundred years ago the lust for power was threatening to poison the race and the Great Revelation was set in motion to prepare man for the coming of the higher cosmic impulse of love."[24] He believes the Hidden Directorate's preparations for the event were continuous from the time of Zoroaster, about 500 B.C., and were implemented through the Chaldaean magi and the Essenes.

The Directorate knew that only when the descending Holy Spirit was able to enter into the psychosomatic body itself, into the last citadel of matter where kundalini lay dormant, could the energy of love be born in humanity. Only then, by the opening up of the body itself to the action of soul and spirit—the central meaning of the Christian mystery—could humankind be fully divinized. But before this challenge the Church failed in courage and the plans of the Directorate could not be fully implemented. What was intended has still not come about.

Ernest Scott, referring to the range of energies required for evolution, stresses the difficulties of the operation:

> The action of these energies suggests that each new, higher frequency is applied while life is still struggling to come to terms with the one before. . . . Seen against the progression of energies along the evolutionary process, it may be supposed that unitive energy would lie far in the future. Man has not yet accommodated to consciousness, much less to creativity. Yet it seems that in the appearance of Jesus on earth unitive energy *was* transmitted to man and we have to speculate that this happened before man was ready for it.[25]

The transmission of the energy of love demanded a corresponding birth of wisdom in the new religion, an approach to nondual doctrines such as the Hermetic-Cabalistic and Gnostic philosophies of Alexandria offered; and early Christians did in fact embrace them for a time. But the Church rejected the esoteric path, Scott continues, and as a consequence the liberating vision of a new heaven and a new earth that John of Patmos prophesied was not able to materialize, and the Christ is still not actualized within us. To that extent Christianity is a religion that has failed.

Nevertheless, the action that the Hidden Directorate is said to have begun twenty-five hundred years ago seems now, at the end of the second millennium, to be accelerating strongly in every part of the world. A new drive towards unity is expressing itself among nations, economies, sciences, ethnic groups, technologies and religions, as well as in the new tantric sects and schools of meditation, combating with mounting force the countervailing currents of separatism and division. The struggle for freedom is clearly only beginning. Yet if that struggle is a flight from lovelessness, can it succeed without a reformation of the lovelessness that lies at the very root of our worldview, in our definition of the physical world?

The Search for a New World Model

That there is a very close relationship between the evolution of a race and its model of the world is a metaphysical truism. The early Christians intuited it and the Buddha implied it in his doctrine of the simultaneous arising and interconnectedness of everything that exists. The essence of his teachings in this regard, as David Ling points out in his study of the Buddha's life, is that a civilization comes into being with its own paradigms or it is not born at all; a civilization and its religion, social and political structures, arts and ethics, definition of humankind and cosmic philosophy arise together and perish together, for each constituent is not more than a contingent reflection of the whole.[26] Consequently, the current notion that one's personal development is a private affair that has nothing to do with the prevailing worldview, that it can be independent of the collectivity and its model of the cosmos, is invalid. On the contrary, the kind of world we collectively agree to profoundly affects our evolutionary possibilities.

Thus, although a few intellectuals knew better, medieval European man in the mass was imprisoned by his conception of a flat earth, a conception whose inadequacy exactly mirrored the social and religious squalor in which he lived; and nothing but its destruction and reconstitution in a more enlightened geography released him into a relatively wholesome existence. Moreover, the further adoption of a heliocentric cosmography released him still more. In the same way we ourselves are imprisoned by the inadequate picture of the world on which our contemporary culture is based, and can only be freed from it by the same kind of conceptual revolution that ended the Middle Ages.

As long as the planet is conceived of as a purely physical unsouled body, albeit a spherical one, meaninglessly rotating in an unconscious, loveless physical universe; as long as we have no coherent theory of a current of compassionate and intelligent life-energy at the heart of everything that exists—the earth and the universe no less than ourselves—it seems likely that we are consigning ourselves to death and the earth to continuing degradation. Unless the whole cosmic configuration that provides our cultural background is reconstituted so as to accommodate a crucial new factor—that is, the axial reality of unitive energy; and not as a mere abstraction, but as a viable structural component of the geography of our world—we will be unable to cross the next threshold in our evolutionary journey. *As long as we cannot recognize Gaia as a spiritual being we cannot recognize our own spirituality, for we are bound together.* If we reject the ecological reforms demanded by the unitive vision we will fail to realize our own human potential.

The outcome depends on whether the eye of the shaman opens within the racial psyche, revealing once again Gaia's centralized chakric structure. If that happens, the full power of the unitive force—of terrestrial kundalini—will become available to the race: world religions will unify and draw nearer to science; a conscious communion with higher guiding Powers will become possible, and both the earth and humanity, inextricably linked, will be able to enter onto a much faster process of spiritualization. The vision of an earth empowered by a conscious, intelligent and loving energy at its heart, an energy to which every human being has access, would most surely revolutionize our species' evolutionary course beyond anything we can imagine today.

"THE KING OF SHAMBHALA WILL CHANGE HIS RESIDENCE"

For those raised in the esoteric traditions of Central Asia these themes of transcendence are woven into the magic of Shambhala. Shambhala is the very apotheosis of the principle of unity that inheres in diversity; it is our destination, our gravitational Center, the alpha and omega of all religions, all souls, all collective works of transcendence on this planet. It draws us irresistibly to itself to be spiritualized like the shaman; it is the wordless call that summons us back to the divine heart of the race, to a sense of the ineffable Oneness of living beings. A lama told Roerich that now that calling could be heard. "The great stirring has begun! A new cosmic energy is manifesting in the world. . . . Kalagiya, kalagiya, kalagiya. Come to Shambhala!"[27]

Shambhala has had many locations, many names, many forms; over the ages it has been known as a taboo region of Palaeolithic magic, a vast Megalithic sanctuary, a sacred kingdom, an underground Wisdom center, a modern complex of ashrams and training-schools. It has sometimes been accessible to the outside world, sometimes hidden; but no one knows what its real nature is, and Tibetans say no one can reach it except those whose karma is ripe. Shambhala seems to have drawn about itself a cordon of invisibility that no ordinary force can breach, yet it can always be found by the soul's radar.

As for its destiny, the Kalachakric texts say that one day the reign of the King of Shambhala will extend over the whole earth, which will become like a garden; a new Wisdom age will dawn and humanity will make rapid spiritual progress. The enemies of Shambhala will be defeated and those barbarians who invade its sacred territory will be destroyed; yet that destruction will be their salvation. For Shambhala's high vibrations will purify them, and their souls will become as pellucid as crystal, so that after death on the battlefield they will be reborn into a Pure Land or else liberated beyond any earthly paradise into Nirvana.

Nearer to hand, Scott, as a result of his researches into Sufism in Afghanistan, has suggested that that region may no longer be tenable for Shambhala's purposes. He believes it possible that the *baraka* of Central Asian Sufi communities like the Sarmouni may have already been withdrawn because their teaching activities are now concentrated elsewhere. And even as early as 1928, when the forces were gathering that would soon destroy the Tibetan theocracy, the Nyingmapa lamas told Roerich that at one time the Great Ones were sometimes seen walking in the market-places, but now were seen no more. Their ashrams near Shigatze had been closed down, for what reason was not known; but possibly, it was intimated, in order to withdraw deeper into the refuge of Shambhala's central territory; perhaps into some of the forbidden valleys where—so it was said—etheric towns and parklands had been glimpsed. "My old teacher," said a lama, "told me much of the wisdom of the Azaras. We know several places where these Great Ones dwelt, but for the moment these places are deserted."[28]

It would appear that the twentieth century has been as critical a period for the hidden kingdom as it has been for the rest of the world. The brutal technology of the outside world is now rampant at its very borders. Tibet's forests, as vast as those of the Amazon, have been cut down, its wildlife massacred, its plateaus and rivers polluted with nuclear waste: Chinese nuclear tests are being conducted in the heart of the Lob Nor territory, thousands of Buddhist monasteries have been destroyed, and the spiritual culture of this whole enormous region laid waste. In all this intrusive devastation there is danger for the entire race. What lies ahead for Central Asia—for Shambhala? A Chinese lama told Andrew Tomas that after the wars of Shambhala—of which we may already be seeing the beginning—"the King of Shambhala will change his Residence and the Perfect Age will dawn anew."[29]

This means that, regardless of the vicissitudes of the moment, Shambhala will live on, an indestructible power. And indeed its benign star is rising, although still hidden below the horizon. Its credibility has probably never been so severely tested as in this age of high technology, dense population and intensive exploration; and yet in another sense we have never been more open to transcendental ideas, to the possibility of dimensions unseen, of higher-order beings and energies and presences celestial, of guidance from above. At this time, on the threshold of a new millennium, there are many lamas and others by the thousand who have visited Shambhala in dreams and visions and who can testify that it persists as a font of limitless creative force and continues to exercise its sacred function as it has in the past.

For acknowledged or not by the outside world, there can be no doubt that the idea of a hidden spiritual center in Asia has worked subterraneously but with a powerful creativity in the consciousness of generations of leading thinkers in both the East and the West. In the West especially, the rumor of Shambhala's existence has coincided with an extraordinary explosion of cultural activity. From the time that the two seventeenth-century Dutch Jesuits, Fathers Cacella and Cabral, reported the fact of the kingdom and the extent of its boundaries in High Asia, a shaft of light, piercing the darkness of European thought, has expanded and brightened like the dawn, inspiring world exploration and showing us the immensity of our new horizons. Indirectly, unrecognized, it has urged us forward in countless ways and kept alive the image of transcendence. And now at the end of the twentieth century, at the very height of millennial anxiety, Shambhala is sending out its wordless reassurance that all will be well. The Way is open. Kalagiya, kalagiya! We may not recognize the calling or understand it, but the soul hears and responds.

Notes

Chapter One: The Quest for Shambhala

1 Eliade, Mircea. *The Myth of the Eternal Return*, Princeton University Press, Princeton, 1974, p. 17.

2 Cited by William Irwin Thompson in *Passages About Earth*, Rider, London, 1974, pp. 89-90.

3 Garje K'am-trul Rinpoche. *A Geography and History of Shambhala*, Library of Tibetan Works and Archives, Dharamsala, 1974.

4 Bernbaum, Edwin. *The Way To Shambhala*, J. P. Tarcher, Los Angeles, 1989, p. 8.

5 Eliade, op. cit., p. 18.

6 Ossendowski, Ferdinand. *Beasts, Men and Gods*, Edward Arnold, London, 1976, p. 300.

7 Tomas, Andrew. *Shambhala: Oasis of Light*, Sphere Books, London, 1976, p. 32.

8 Ibid., p. 32.

9 Scott, Ernest. *The People of the Secret*, Octagon Press, London, 1985, pp. 173-74. Scott is unclear here. He seems to identify Shambhala with the ancient city of Shams-i-Balkh in Afghanistan that was destroyed by Genghis Khan, but elsewhere indicates that Shambhala is still active.

10 Evans-Wentz, W.Y., ed. and trans. *The Tibetan Book of the Dead*, Oxford University Press, London, 1960, p. 3.

11 Quoted by Tomas, op. cit., p. 32.

12 Ibid., p. 32.

13 Blavatsky, Helena. *The Secret Doctrine*, Theosophical Publishing House Wheaton, Ill., 1993

14 Tomas, op. cit., pp. 61-3.

15 Roerich, Nicholas. *Shambhala*, Inner Traditions International, Rochester, Vt., 1990, p. 7.

16 Ibid., p. 297.

17 Tomas, op. cit., p. 11.

18 Ibid., p. 29.

19 Guénon, René. *The Lord of the World*, Coombe Springs Press, U.K., 1983, pp. 65-6.

20 The Armenian spiritual teacher George Gurdjieff spoke of a honeycomb of cav-

erns under the Syr Darya as having harbored secret schools of mysticism for thousands of years; and, according to Roerich, Central Asians everywhere refer to the Agharti (meaning concealed, secret) as a people of great wisdom and virtue who withdrew long ago into an underground kingdom. *Shambhala*, Nicholas Roerich, p. 213.

21   Alder, Vera Stanley. *The Initiation of the World*, Rider, London, 1960.

22   Yates, Frances A. *The Rosicrucian Enlightenment*, ARK Paperbacks, London, 1986.

23   Pauwels, Louis and Bergier, Jacques. *The Morning of the Magicians*, R. Myers, trans., Mayflower, 1971, pp. 193-9.

24   Ravenscroft, Trevor. *The Spear of Destiny*, Corgi Books, London, 1974, pp. 254-57.

25   Bernbaum, op. cit., p. 34.

26   Tomas, op. cit., p. 29.

CHAPTER TWO: THE MANDALIC MIRROR

1   Conze, Edward. *A Short History of Buddhism*, Unwin, London, 1986, p. 76.

2   Schuré, Edouard. *The Great Initiates*, Harper & Row, New York, 1961, pp. 189-90.

3   Bernbaum, Edwin. *The Way to Shambhala*, J. P. Tarcher, Los Angeles, 1989, p. 8.

4   Ngawang Sopa. *The Collected Works*, New Delhi, 1975.

5   Bernbaum, op. cit., p. 125.

6   Ibid., p. 122.

7   Ibid., pp. 6-11.

8   Ibid., pp. 12-24.

9   Ibid., p. 12.

10   Brennan, Barbara Ann. *Hands of Light*, Bantam, New York, 1988, p. 43.

11   Avalon, Arthur. *The Serpent Power*, Dover, New York, 1974.

12   According to the tantric system described by Sir John Woodroffe (as Arthur Avalon), the *anahata* chakra has twelve rather than eight petals, as some lamas claim, but includes a small subsidiary lotus of eight petals situated just below it. "There," says the Sanskrit text, "are the Kalpa tree, the jewelled altar surmounted by an awning and decorated by flags and the like, which is the place of mental worship." *The Serpent Power*, Arthur Avalon, Dover, New York, 1974, p. 383.

13   From the Mundaka Upanishad, Swami Prabhavananda and F. Manchester, trans. *The Upanishads: Breath of the Eternal*, Mentor, New York, 1957.

14 Avalon, op. cit., p. 110.

15 Eliade, Mircea. *The Myth of the Eternal Return*, Princeton University Press, Princeton, N.J., 1974, p. 16.

16 Bernbaum, op. cit., pp. 141-42.

17 Ibid., p. 144.

18 Ibid., pp. 168-74.

19 Steiger, Brad. *The Gods of Aquarius*, W. H. Allen, London, 1977, p. 146.

20 Brennan, Martin. *The Stars and Stones*, Thames & Hudson, London, 1983, p. 53.

21 Roerich, Nicholas. *Shambhala*, Inner Traditions International, Rochester, Vt., 1990, pp. 32-3.

Chapter Three: A Wreath of Religions

1 Hedin, Sven. *My Life As An Explorer*, A. Huebsch, trans., Garden City Publishing Co., New York, 1925, p. 188.

2 Ossendowski, Ferdinand. *Beasts, Men and Gods*, Edward Arnold, London, 1924, p. 300.

3 Ibid., p. 302.

4 Bernbaum, Edwin. *The Way to Shambhala*, J. P. Tarcher, Los Angeles, 1989, p. 1.

5 Roerich, Nicholas. *Shambhala*, Inner Traditions International, Rochester, Vt., 1990, p. 13.

6 Allione, Tsultrim. *Women of Wisdom*, Routledge & Kegan Paul, London, 1986, p. 43.

7 Bernbaum, op. cit., p. 66.

8 Ashe, Geoffrey. *The Ancient Wisdom*, Sphere Books, London, 1979, p. 144. This material appears by permission of the Peters, Fraser and Dunlop Group, Ltd.

9 The Mahabharata 6.8., adapted from *The Mahabharata of Krishna-Dwaipayna Vyasa*, Pratap Chandra Roy, trans., Datta Bose, Calcutta, 1925.

10 Tomas, Andrew. *Shambhala: Oasis of Light*, Sphere Books, London, 1976, pp. 25-6.

11 Trans. in Homer H. Dubs, "An Ancient Chinese Mystery Cult," *Harvard Theological Review* 35, no. 4, 1942, p. 231.

12 Snelling, John. *The Sacred Mountain*, East-West Publications, London, 1983.

13 Govinda, Lama Anagarika. "Pilgrims and Monasteries in the Himalayas,"

Crystal Mirror, vol. IV, Dharma Publishing, Berkeley, Calif., 1975, pp. 245-46.

14 Ali, S. K. *The Geography of the Puranas*, New Delhi, 1966.

15 Tomas, op. cit., p. 38.

16 Eckartshausen, K. von. *The Cloud Upon the Sanctuary*, London, 1919.

17 Tomas, op.cit., pp. 22-3.

18 Gesar is the eleventh-century hero-king of Kham, Tibet whom the Nyingmapa lamas regard as an incarnation of their founder, the Indian saint and missionary Padma Sambhava. The belief is widespread that Gesar waits in an underground kingdom to be reborn in Shambhala as the saviour and avatar Rudra Cakrin, and that from thence he will ride forth at the head of a great horde of warriors at the end of the age in order to deliver the world from the demonic power of the barbarians. Gradually the heroic figure of Gesar has merged with that of Maitreya, the fifth and future Buddha, providing the basis for a popular apocalyptic movement that has spread throughout most of Central Asia. *The Way to Shambhala*, Bernbaum, op. cit., p. 81.

19 Hoffman, Helmut. "Kalachakra Studies 1, Manicheism, Christianity and Islam in the Kalachakra Tantra," *Central Asiatic Journal* 13, no. i, 1969, p. 44.

20 Bauer, Wolfgang. *China and the Search for Happiness*, M. Shaw, trans., Seabury Press, New York, 1976, p. 87.

21 Bernbaum, op. cit., p. 46.

22 King, Peter. *Afghanistan: Cockpit of High Asia*, Geoffrey Bles, London, 1960: quoted by Ernest Scott, *The People of the Secret*, Octagon Press, London, 1983, p. 168.

23 Ibid., p. 168.

24 Ibid., p. 252.

25 Michell, John. *The Earth Spirit*, Thames & Hudson, London, 1975, p. 7.

26 Ibid., note 37.

27 Ibid., note 42.

28 Lincoln, Henry. *The Holy Place*, Jonathon Cape, London, 1991, p. 17.

29 Ibid., p. 155.

30 Michell, op. cit., p. 147.

31 Bauval and Gilbert contend that the fourteen or so pyramids built along the Nile during the Egyptian Pyramid Age (c. 2686-2181 B.C.) correlate exactly with the star group along the Milky Way that makes up the Orion constellation, which ancient Egyptians believed was the starry body of the risen god Osiris. The two researchers insist too that the three Giza pyramids (two large

and one small) are specifically aligned to the three stars of Orion's Belt, and that furthermore, the shafts that have been found to extend from the King's and the Queen's Chambers in the great Giza pyramid built by Cheops are not air shafts, as thought by most Egyptologists, but are astronomical alignments, pointing at the time of building to Sirius, to the largest star of Orion's Belt and to the then-pole star, Alpha Draconis in Ursa Minor. According to Bauval and Gilbert, the Cheops pyramid is therefore the key par excellence to the Egyptian religious and astronomical beliefs centred on the Osiris Mysteries. *The Orion Mystery,* Robert Bauval and Adrian Gilbert, Mandarin Paperbacks, London, 1994, pp. 126-28.

32   Scott, op. cit., p. 171.

33   Campbell, Joseph. *The Hero With a Thousand Faces,* Fontana Press, London, 1993, p. 385.

CHAPTER FOUR: THE COSMIC MOUNTAIN

1   Campbell, Joseph. *The Hero With a Thousand Faces,* Fontana Press, London, 1993, p. 3.

2   Some mystics say that in former times humans could apprehend all nine of the inner worlds; thus the prophetess of the Icelandic Edda says of the World Tree, Yggdrasil:

> Nine worlds I knew,
> The nine of the Tree,
> With its mighty roots,
> Under the mould.

But in modern times, because the range of human consciousness has shrunk, they say only seven of the worlds can be perceived and so our cosmological overview has been adjusted downward. (Unpublished Javanese teachings.)

3   Baring, Anne and Cashford, Jules. *The Myth of the Goddess,* Penguin, Harmonds-worth, 1993, p. 250.

4   *The Mahabharata,* M.N. Dutt, trans., 3 vols., H. C. Dass, Calcutta, 1895-1901.

5   Eliade, Mircea. *The Myth of the Eternal Return,* Princeton University Press, Princeton, N.J., 1974, p. 14.

6   Ibid., p. 15.

7   Guénon, René. *The Lord of the World,* Coombe Springs Press, U.K., 1983, p. 50.

8   Ashe, Geoffrey. *The Ancient Wisdom,* Sphere Books, London, 1979, pp. 134-35.

9   Kisa'l, fol. 15. Cited by A. J. Wensinck in *The Ideas of the Western Semites Concerning the Navel of the Earth*, Amsterdam, 1916.

10   Ashe, op. cit., p. 94.

11   Ibid., p.100.

12   Guthrie, W. K. C. *The Greeks and Their Gods*, Methuen, London, 1950, p. 73, n. 2, and pp. 193-96.

13   In the Rig Veda the stars of Ursa Major, the Great Bear, are called Saptarshi, the Seven Sages. "Their homes were in the sky, and from there they made periodic descents on Meru," says Geoffrey Ashe. In other words, Hindus especially associated this constellation with the wisdom of Shambhala and believed it emanated from the Great Bear. But Ashe points out that in the ancient Altaic Bear cult the bear was regarded as a divine figure, a healer and spiritual guide, and represented the shaman himself. Ashe, op. cit., pp. 125 and 167.

14   Ibid., p. 166.

15   Lissner, Ivar. *Man, God and Magic*, Jonathan Cape, London, 1977.

16   Ashe, op. cit., p. 148.

17   Yeshe, Lama Thubten. *An Introduction to Tantra*, Wisdom Publications, London, 1987, p. 111.

18   Balfour, Mark. *The Sign of the Serpent*, Prism Press, Dorset, U.K., 1990, p. 24.

19   Motoyama, Hiroshi and Brown, Rande. *Science and Evolution of Consciousness*, Autumn Press, Mass., 1978, p. 139.

20   Ibid., p. 140.

21   Guénon, op. cit., p. 48.

22   Drower, Lady. *Angel Peacock*, London, 1941.

23   Crossingham, Lesley. "The Medicine Wheel and the Star People," *The Whole Person* 4, no. 5, October 1992, p. 15.

24   Spangler, David. *The Iona Report*, Findhorn, Forres, Scotland, 1972, p. 1.

25   Ibid.

CHAPTER FIVE: A TRAFFICWAY OF ANGELS

1   Prjevalsky, N. M. *Mongolia*, London, 1876, quoted by Andrew Tomas in *Shambhala: Oasis of Light*, Sphere Books, London, 1976, pp. 32-3.

2   Ashe, Geoffrey. *The Ancient Wisdom*, Sphere Books, London, 1979, p. 168.

3   Ibid., p. 171.

4   Ibid.

5 Ibid.

6 Godwin, Joscelyn. *Mystery Religions in the Ancient World*, Thames & Hudson, London, 1981, p. 79.

7 Schonfield, Hugh. *The Essene Odyssey*, Element Books, Wiltshire, U.K., 1984, p. 7.

8 Originally the High God of the whole of the Near East, El or a variant such as Eloah, Elyon, Allah, etc., was the nameless and ineffable One who reigned high over the proliferating pantheon of local gods. "Elohim is the plural of Elo," says Fabre d'Olivet, "a name given to the Supreme Being by the Hebrews and Chaldeans, and itself derived from the root El, which depicts elevation, strength and expansive power, and which means in a universal sense, God." *The Hebraic Tongue Restored*, Fabre d'Olivet, tr. Redfield, Putnam's, New York, 1921, quoted by Edouard Schuré in *The Great Initiates,* Harper & Row, New York, 1961, p. 514.

9 "Son of the Sun" and its equivalent, "Son of God," were titles bestowed on the highest initiatic rank in the temples of antiquity. "In the language of the temples," says Schuré, "'son of woman' designated the lower stage of initiation, woman meaning here, nature. Above these were 'sons of men' or initiates of spirit and soul, the 'sons of gods' or initiates of cosmogonic science, and 'Sons of God' or initiates of the supreme science." *The Great Initiates*, Edouard Schuré, p. 520.

10 In Abraham's time the Supreme Being, the righteous and loving One called El, had been long forgotten in favor of a multitude of lower local manifestations of divinity. Jacob, therefore, like Abraham and his son Isaac, was initiated into a Solar religion that reinstated the worship of the Supreme Being and downgraded the local desert deities, hitherto the only objects of worship among the Semitic nomads of Palestine. Judaism was thus founded on a religious revolution that was undoubtedly the work of the incoming Indo-Aryan prophets, as Guénon notes. His interpretation of Hebrew history consorts with Prof. T. J. Meek's linguistic analysis of the Old Testament texts, from which he concludes that an interplay of Hurrian (Indo-Aryan) and Semitic factors can be found in the building of biblical myth and narrative. *Hebrew Origins*, T. J. Meek, Harper & Row, New York, 1960. Cited by Joseph Campbell in *The Masks of God:* vol. 3, Penguin, Harmondsworth, 1984, pp. 120-21.

11 Guénon, René. *The Lord of the World*, Coombe Springs Press, U.K., 1983, pp. 39-41.

12 Ibid., p. 42.

13 Ibid., p. 43.

14 Ibid.

15 Ibid., p. 44.

16 Thomas, Lewis. *Lives of a Cell: Notes of a Biology Watcher,* Viking Press, New York, 1974. Quoted by James Lovelock in *The Ages of Gaia,* Oxford University Press, 1988, prelude.

17 Valentinus, Vasilius, quoted by John Michell in *Earth Spirit,* Thames & Hudson, London, 1975, p. 4.

18 Michell, *Earth Spirit,* p. 145.

19 Cobbett, William. *History of the Protestant "Reformation" in England and Ireland,* London, 1824.

20 Michell, op. cit., p. 10-22.

21 Sheldrake, Rupert. *The Rebirth of Nature,* Bantam Books, New York and London, 1991, p. 37.

22 Michell, op. cit., p. 22.

23 Dong, Paul. *The Four Major Mysteries of Mainland China,* Prentice-Hall Inc., New Jersey, 1984.

24 Watson, Lyall. *Gifts of Unknown Things,* Hodder & Stoughton, London, 1976, p. 112.

25 Ibid., p. 115.

26 Lovelock, James. *The Ages of Gaia,* W. W. Norton, New York, 1988.

27 Cited by Sheldrake, op. cit., pp. 124-30.

28 Quoted by Roger Lewin in *Complexity: Life at the Edge of Chaos,* Macmillan, New York, 1992, pp. 115-16.

29 Overbye, Dennis. "The Shadow Universe," from *Discover,* May 1985.

30 Sheldrake, op. cit., p. 75.

31 Ibid., p. 74.

32 Ibid.

33 Krishna, Gopi. *Kundalini,* Shambhala Publications, Berkeley, 1971, p. 88.

CHAPTER SIX: THE PERFECTION OF THE SHORTEST PATH

1 The new Shakti schools such as Mahikari, Subud, Sumarah and others are not always recognized as such, because they employ a modified form of kundalini awakening rather than the classical kind that awakens kundalini in the mu-

ladhara chakra at the base of the spine. An Indian Sufi told Irina Tweedie: "By our system it [kundalini] is awakened gently . . . we awaken the 'King', the heart chakra, and leave it to the 'King' to awaken all the other chakras." By this method man's natural state of purity is regained not by meditation or ascetic disciplines, or by any abstraction of the senses, but in full consciousness; ideally by a spontaneous union with the pure consciousness of the guru. Variations on this method, which awaken kundalini in the higher centers, seem to have widely supplanted the traditional technique and are offering a spiritual revolution to the modern world. See *The Chasm of Fire*, Irina Tweedie, Element Books, Dorset, U. K., 1984, p. 27.

2   Quoted by Andrew Harvey in *Hidden Journey*, Henry Holt, New York, 1991, p. 109.

3   Mother Meera. *Answers*, Meeramma, New York, 1991, p. 12.

4   Michell, John. *The View Over Atlantis*, Sphere Books, London, 1975, p. 71.

5   Wilson, Colin. *The Quest for Wilhelm Reich*, Granada, London, 1982.

6   Ostrander, Sheila and Schroeder, Lynne. *PSI: Psychic Discoveries Behind the Iron Curtain*, Sphere Books, London, 1973, p. 372.

7   Ibid., p. 368.

8   Ibid., p. 372.

9   Ibid.

10   Brennan, Barbara Ann. *Hands of Light*, Bantam Books, New York, 1988, p. 40.

11   Ibid.

12   *The Tantratattva of Siva-candra Vidyarnava Battacarya*, tr. A. Avalon, London-Madras, 1914.

13   *Devi-Bhagavata, Hymns to the Goddess*, tr. A. Avalon, London, 1913.

14   Harshe, R. G. "Mount Meru: The Homeland of the Aryans," *Vishveshvarananda Indological Journal* 2, 1964, p. 140.

15   Evans-Wentz, W. Y. "Introduction" to the *Tibetan Book of the Dead*, ed. W.Y. Evans-Wentz, Oxford University Press, London-Oxford, 1960, pp. 61-6.

16   Ibid., p. 62.

17   See the Cosmic Mandala in *Easy Death* by Heart-Master Da. The Heart-Master's diagram is from an imminent rather than a transcendent perspective, but

metaphysically the inner and outer viewpoints are interchangeable. In the first case, the center of the mandala is the radiant white light of Transcendental Being lying at the core of the blue mental realm; in the second case the center is black, the black of pure potentiality, and lies at the core of the innermost red planes. See *Easy Death*, Heart-Master Da, The Dawn Horse Press, San Rafael, Calif., 1987, p. 250.

18   Bennett, J. G. *The Masters of Wisdom*, Turnstone Books, London, 1977, p. 153.

19   Roerich, Nicholas. *Shambhala*, Inner Traditions International, Rochester, Vt., 1990, p. 31.

20   The whole question of the hierarchical meaning of the symbols, of ritual orientation and of the values involved in the Heaven-Earth axis, for which there is not space in this book, is discussed at length by René Guénon in *The Great Triad*, P. Kingsley, trans., Quinta Essentia, Cambridge, 1991.

21   Alder, Vera Stanley. *From the Mundane to the Magnificent*, Rider, London, 1988, pp. 174 and 193.

22   Guénon, op. cit., pp. 18-48.

23   Zanggar, Eberhard. *The Flood from Heaven*, Sidgwick & Jackson, London, 1992, pp. 107-8.

24   Hoeller, Stephan. *Jung and the Lost Gospels*, Quest Books, The Theosophical Publishing House, Wheaton, Ill., 1990, p. 225.

25   Lissner, Ivar. *Man, God and Magic*, Jonathan Cape, London, 1977

26   Eliade, Mircea. *Myths, Dreams and Mysteries*, Harper & Row, New York, 1975, p. 65.

CHAPTER SEVEN:
THE KALACHAKRA: PROPHECIES OF SHAMBHALA

1   Tomas, Andrew. *Shambhala: Oasis of Light*, Sphere Books, London, 1976, p. 34.

2   There is disagreement between the Dalai Lama and the Chinese government over the identity of the Panchen Lama's successor, as the boy approved by His Holiness has been replaced by one chosen by Chinese officials. If the wrong person is elected as the new incarnation or true spiritual re-embodiment of the Panchen Lama, there could be serious consequences for the continuing trans-

mission of the Kalachakric tradition in China.

3   Tomas, op. cit., p. 73.

4   Roerich, Nicholas. *Shambhala*, Inner Traditions International, Vermont, 1990, p. 28.

5   Quoted by Tomas, Andrew. *Shambhala: Oasis of Light*, Sphere Books, London, 1976, p. 72.

6   Roerich, op. cit., p. 28.

7   Bernbaum, Edwin. *The Way to Shambhala*, J. P. Tarcher, Los Angeles, 1989, p. 123.

8   Ibid., p. 124.

9   Tomas, op. cit., p. 71.

10   Ibid., p. 156.

11   Scott, Ernest. *The People of the Secret*, Octagon Press, U.K., 1984.

12   Campbell, Joseph. *The Masks of God*, vol. 2. Penguin, Harmondsworth, 1985, p. 118.

13   Sellars, J. B. *The Death of the Gods in Ancient Egypt*, Penguin, Harmondsworth, 1992, p. 199.

14   A fuller description of the cosmic clock can be found in the sect's main book for Westerners, *Mahikari*, and in other Mahikari literature. According to Shinto Buddhist belief, the cosmic clock is the basis of the chrysanthemum emblem of the Japanese royal family. *Mahikari*, Dr. Andris Tebecis, Yoko Shuppansha, Tokyo, 1982.

15   Capra, Fritjof. *The Turning Point*, Bantam Books, London, 1982, p. 363.

16   Ibid., p. 14.

17   Part of a conversation held with Stanislav Grof and recorded by Fritjof Capra and quoted in his book *Uncommon Wisdom*, Fontana, London, 1989, p. 126.

18   Avalon, Arthur (Sir John Woodroffe). *The Serpent Power*, Dover, New York, 1974, p. 19.

19   Eliade, Mircea. *The Myth of the Eternal Return*, Princeton University Press, Princeton, N.J., 1974, p. 114.

20   *The Vishnu Purana, a System of Hindu Mythology and Tradition*, F. Hall, ed., H. H. Wilson, trans., Trubner, London, 1868, 4:225-27.

21   The white (or blue) steed is regarded as the special sign of Kalki, distinguishing him from the other nine preceding incarnations of Vishnu and symbolizing the purified desire-body. Bernbaum, op. cit., p. 84.

22   *The Vishnu Purana.*

23 Ossendowski, Ferdinand. *Beasts, Men and Gods*, Edward Arnold, London, 1921, pp. 313-14.

24 The four-spoked diagram of the *muladhara* chakra is found in Arthur Avalon's *The Serpent Power*, p. 355.

25 Guénon, René. *The Lord of the World*, Coombe Springs Press, U.K., 1983, p. 62.

26 Bernbaum, op. cit., p. 80.

CHAPTER EIGHT: THE HIDDEN DIRECTORATE

1 Bennett, John G. *Gurdjieff: Making a New World*, Turnstone Books, London, 1973, p. 25.

2 Ibid., p. 75.

3 Guénon, René. *The Lord of the World*, Coombe Springs Press, U.K., 1983, p. 18.

4 d'Alveydre, Saint-Yves. *Mission de l'Inde*, 1910, 2nd. ed. 1949, quoted by René Guénon, ibid., p. 23.

5 Ibid., p. 5.

6 Ravenscroft, Trevor and Wallace-Murphy, T. *The Mark of the Beast*, Sphere Books, U.K., 1990, p. 60.

7 Schonfield, Hugh. *The Essene Odyssey*, Element Books, Dorset, U.K., 1984.

8 Many religious historians believe modern Rosicrucians should not be confused with the seventeenth-century brotherhood of the same name, with which they do not seem to have any known connection. *The People of the Secret*, Ernest Scott, Octagon Press, U.K., 1985, p. 176.

9 Yates, Frances A. *The Rosicrucian Enlightenment*, ARK Publications, London, 1986, p. 232.

10 Bennett, op, cit., pp. 29-50.

11 Sheldrake, Rupert. *The Rebirth of Nature*, Bantam Books, New York and London, 1991, p. 37.

12 Scott, op. cit., pp. 250-57.

13 Bennett, op. cit., p. 52.

14 Ibid., p. 53.

15 Bennett has said of the cultural achievements of the Ice Age: "On the one hand we find surpassing genius in the guidance of human progress and in the introduction of new techniques. As against this, we are forced also to take into account the primitive conditions of ordinary existence as shown in the cave-settlements of western Europe and the primitive dwellings in Asia. . . . We find the

masterpieces of cave-painting within a few miles of primitive settlements which can be identified as contemporaneous . . . . These cave-dwellers lived on what we should now regard as a level of primitive savagery. The discrepancy in the levels of culture simultaneously present can be accounted for only if we ascribe the cave-paintings to the work of groups of creative men living in a quite differ ent manner from the surrounding primitive tribes." *The Dramatic Universe*, vol. IV, John G. Bennett, Hodder & Stoughton, London, 1961, p. 250.

16   Hapgood, Charles. *Maps of the Ancient Sea-Kings*, Chiltern Books, Philadelphia, 1966, p. 193.

17   Ibid.

18   Bennett, op. cit.

19   Shushud, Hasan L. Article published in the *Journal of Systematics* 6, no. 4, 1969. Quoted by Ernest Scott, op. cit., p. 260.

20   Owen, Walter. *More Things in Heaven*, London, 1947, quoted by Andrew Tomas in *Shambhala: Oasis of Light*, Sphere Books, London, 1976, p. 21.

21   Herodotus, *The Histories*, A. de Selincourt, trans., Penguin, Harmondsworth, 1954.

22   The Ousir were probably the gods of the Capsian race, a people who hunted in the Sahara during the last Ice Age and who, around 10,000 B.C., began to domesticate animals. Later they inscribed planetary symbols on their rocks and practised sun worship, so they clearly possessed astronomical knowledge. They migrated westward to the Nile valley as well as to more northerly parts of the world. *The Masks of God*, vol. 1, Joseph Campbell, Penguin, Harmondsworth, 1984, pp. 379-83.

23   *The Gospel of the Egyptians*, The Nag Hammadi Library, New York, 1977, p. 195.

24   Hoeller, Stephan. *Jung and the Lost Gospels*, The Theosophical Publishing House, Wheaton, Ill., 1990, p. 226.

25   Ibid., p. 31.

26   Josephus. *The Antiquities of the Jews*, The Loeb Classical Library, 9 vols., Heinemann, London.

27   Schuré, Edouard. *The Great Initiates*, Harper & Row, New York, 1961, p. 323.

28   Ibid.

29   Scott, op. cit., p. 217.

30   Ibid., p. 246.

31   Guénon, op. cit., p. 5.

CHAPTER NINE:
SHAMBHALA: THE GARDEN OF THE TREE OF LIFE

1   The Hindus' *amrita*, the nectar of immortality, is also milked from the trees in the abode of the Siddhas, Siddhaloka (which is another name for Shambhala); and Guénon points out that in Christianity, trees producing incorruptible gum or resin have long been taken as emblems of the Christ. *The Lord of the World*, René Guénon, Coombe Springs Press, U.K., 1983, p. 22.

2   Baring, Anne and Cashford, Jules. *The Myth of the Goddess*, Penguin, Harmondsworth, 1993, p. 563.

3   Ibid., p. 488.

4   Scott, Ernest. *The People of the Secret*, Octagon Press, London, 1985, p. 74.

5   Ibid., p. 75.

6   Baring and Cashford, op. cit., p. 497.

7   The runic script is thought by some to have developed from the Greek alphabet, but others find evidence of a much earlier pre-Runic script that may even go back to the end of the Ice Age. The basic runic stave is of twenty-four letters, every letter having both a magical and a mystical meaning. *The Masks of God*, vol. 3, Joseph Campbell, Penguin, Harmondsworth, 1985, pp. 481-2; and *Atlantis of the North*, Jurgen Spanuth, Sidgwick & Jackson, London, 1979, pp. 80-1.

8   *The Poetic Edda*. Hovamol 139, 140, 142, Bellows, trans.,The American-Scandinavian Foundation, New York, 1923, pp. 60-61.

9   Hauer, W. *Arkunden und Gestalten der Germanischdeutschen Glaubensgeschichte*, Stuttgart, 1940, p. 92.

10   Yggdrasil means "the horse of Ygg," that is, of Odin; and like Maitreya's white horse, is therefore a cosmic power the god rides and which serves him faithfully and obediently. *The Masks of God*. vol. 1, Joseph Campbell, Penguin, Harmondsworth, 1984, p. 121.

11   Campbell, op. cit., vol. 3, p. 488.

12   Bellows, op. cit., Voluspa 2, 46, 47.

13   Bellows, op. cit., Voluspa 57, 59, 62, pp. 24–25.

14   Evans, Sir A. J. *The Palace of Minos*, vol. II, MacMillan, London, 1921-35, quoted by Joseph Campbell, op. cit., p. 50.

15   Plutarch. Fragment 178, Loeb Edition, quoted by Joscelyn Godwin, *Mystery Religions in the Ancient World*, Thames & Hudson, London, 1981, p. 36.

16   Baring and Cashford, op. cit., p. 23.

17   Lissner, Ivar. *Man, God and Magic,* Jonathan Cape, London, 1977, cited by Joseph Campbell, *The Masks of God.* vol. 2, Penguin, Harmondsworth, 1984, p. 256.

18   Schuré, Edouard. *The Great Initiates,* Harper & Row, New York, 1974, Notes: pp. 515-16.

19   Budge, E. A. Wallis. *The Gods of the Egyptians,* vol. 2, London, 1902, pp. 202-3.

20   Hauer, op. cit., p. 175.

21   Budge, op. cit., vol.1, p. 154.

22   An was originally the Sumerian god of the heavens, but his place as chief of the gods was later usurped by Enlil. *The Sirius Mystery,* Robert K. G. Temple, Sidgwick & Jackson, London, 1976, p. 133.

23   From an Egyptian New Kingdom hymn quoted by Rundle Clark, R. T. *Myth and Symbol in Ancient Egypt,* Thames & Hudson, London, 1978, p. 103.

24   Plutarch. *Isis and Osiris,* in Moralia, Book 5, F. C. Babbit, trans., William Heinemann, Loeb Classical Library, 1969, pp. 31-49.

25   Ksenofontov, G.V. *Schamanengeschichten aus Siberien,* A. Friedrich and G. Buddress, trans., Otto Wilhelm Barth-Verlag, Munich, 1955, pp. 211-12.

26   Plutarch, op. cit., pp. 31-49.

27   Baring and Cashford, op. cit., p. 232.

28   Isis is often shown crowned with the moon enclosed in two horns, the usual interpretation of this being that these are the horns of the sacred bull or cow almost universally revered in antiquity. However, the more likely meaning of this symbol is that the two horns represent the two streams of psychospiritual energy that customarily emerge from the head of enlightened beings and which can be seen clairvoyantly and even photographed on occasion. For instance, in ancient illustrations these diverging streams of energy always adorn the heads of dragons, which are traditionally regarded as clairvoyant beings. The bull may have been chosen for worship purely because, possessing horns, he was believed to possess clairvoyance like the dragon. This hypothesis is supported by the vision Apuleius had of Isis, in which two vipers emerged on either side of her head. "Just above her brow shone a round disc, like a mirror, or like the bright face of the moon . . . vipers rising from the left-hand and right-hand partings of her hair supported this disc, with ears of corn bristling beside them." The moon on the head of the goddess, then, if Apuleius's spiritual vision is correct, symbol-

izes the mirror of suprasensible intuition or clairvoyance arising from the action of an awakened kundalini. Apuleius, *The Golden Ass*, Robert Graves, trans., Penguin, Harmondsworth, 1950, pp. 227-28.

CHAPTER TEN: WHERE IS THE WORLD AXIS?

1   The practice of sacral regicide in which the god-king was ritually slain at the end of a certain set period (often seven or twelve years) spread from the fifth millennium onward over large areas of the world from Africa to Indonesia, and survived in a few backward communities until quite recent times. It is believed to have begun in Anatolia in the wake of an invasion from the East of nomadic steppe people, Aryan-speakers whose society was hierarchical and warlike. *The Masks of God*, vol. 1, Joseph Campbell, Penguin, Harmondsworth, 1984, pp. 166-68. Also *The Myth of the Goddess*, Anne Baring and Jules Cashford, Penguin, Harmondsworth, 1991, pp. 79-82.

2   Eisler, R., Leipzig, 1928, quoted by Jurgen Spanuth, *Atlantis of the North*, Sidgwick & Jackson, London, 1979, p. 92.

3   Ibid. p. 101.

4   Wirth, W. *Die Volute, Symbol einer kultischen Weltordnunsidee*, Antios, y.5, Stuttgart, 1966, p. 427.

5   Of the two trees in the center of Eden—the Tree of Knowledge and the Tree of Life—the latter, writes Joseph Campbell, "has became inaccessible to man through a deliberate act of God, whereas in other mythologies, both of Europe and the Orient, the Tree of Knowledge is itself the Tree of Immortal Life, and moreover, still accessible to man." The Tree in its various forms is frequently thus divided into two, representing the two modalities of knowledge and life-power, and not only in Judaism but in mythologies around the world. *The Masks of God*, vol. 3, Joseph Campbell, Penguin, Harmondsworth, 1984, p. 106.

6   Ravenscroft, Trevor and Wallace-Murphy, T. *The Mark of the Beast*, Sphere Books, U.K., 1990, p. 67.

7   Ibid, p. 64.

8   Baring and Cashford, op. cit., pp. 341-43.

9   Lurker, Manfred. Quoted in *The Gods and Symbols of Ancient Egypt, An Illustrated Dictionary*, Thames & Hudson, London, 1980, p. 47.

10   Baring and Cashford, op. cit., p. 243.

11   Faulkner, R.O. *The Ancient Egyptian Pyramid Texts*, Clarendon Press, Oxford,

1969, quoted by Spanuth, op. cit., p. 28.

12 On the Rosetta Stone the word Haunebu is translated as Hellenikos, or Greek; but the Stone dates from 40 B.C., when Greeks had long forgotten their northern provenance. *Atlantis of the North*, Jurgen Spanuth, p. 28.

13 Apollodorus of Athens. *The Library*, Sir James Frazer, trans., Loeb Classical Library, London, 1921, quoted by Spanuth, op. cit., pp. 99-100.

14 Virgil. *The Aeneid*, W. J. Jackson Knight, trans., Penguin, Harmondsworth, 1956, 6.797.

15 Spanuth, op. cit., p. 30.

16 Guénon, René. *The Great Triad*, Quinta Essentia, Cambridge, 1991, p. 120.

17 Pliny. *Natural History*, with English tr., Loeb Classical Library, London, 1938-62, quoted by Spanuth, op. cit., p. 253.

18 Guénon, René. *The Lord of the World*, Coombe Springs Press, U.K., 1983, p. 60.

19 Here a Platonic concept of reality as being composed of a series of increasingly comprehensive energy fields is invoked, the highest of which contain the unchanging essential archetypes of form. *Motion* increases with the gradual descent to the physical level. Barbara Ann Brennan, confining herself to a human rather than a planetary context, brilliantly describes and illustrates these various levels of energetic activity, which are also worlds filled with living beings, and so demonstrates that her clairvoyance entirely supports Guénon's Neoplatonic scheme of the universe. See *Hands of Light*, Barbara Ann Brennan, Bantam Books, New York, 1987, Ch. 7.

20 Guénon, op. cit., p. 9.

21 Chuang Tzu, quoted by Guénon, *The Great Triad*, p. 133.

22 Bohm, David. *Wholeness and the Implicate Order*, Routledge & Kegan Paul, London, 1980, p. 192.

23 We know that the magnetic pole has an enormous range of wander, but the movement of the North Pole (beyond a few feet) is still debated by scientists. However, the case for pole shift, involving sudden catastrophic events in the earth's evolution, is extremely strong. Despite the objections of many mainstream scientists, evidence from historical records, celestial charts, ancient maps, calendars, sundials and water clocks, classical and sacred literature from East and West alike and mythological oral traditions from all parts of the world, as well as persuasive evidence from geology, archaeology and astronomy, attest to the viability of the concept on all criteria. It is one that has the support of a long

occult tradition from at least the time of Pythagoras. See *The Great Initiates,* Edouard Schuré, Harper & Row, New York, 1961, p. 325.

24   From the "Homeric Hymn to Gaia," Jules Cashford, trans., *Harvest: Journal for Jungian Studies,* vol, 34, 1988-9, pp. 155-60.

25   Hesiod, quoted in Riane Eisler, *The Chalice and the Blade: Our History, Our Future,* Harper & Row, San Francisco, 1987, p. 108.

26   Baring and Cashford, op. cit., p. 305.

CHAPTER ELEVEN:
ATLANTIS AND THE HYPERBOREANS:
SEEDBEDS OF CIVILIZATION

1   The initiatic triangle traditionally symbolizes the three ruling aspects or functions of the supreme head of the Hierarchy: those of pontiff, king and legislator; or again these can be expressed as "spirit," "soul" and "body." René Guénon, *The Lord of the World,* Coombe Springs Press, U.K., 1983, pp. 18-21.

2   Pindar. *Pythian Odes,* E. Snell, ed., R. Lattimore, trans., Chicago, 1947.

3   Ashe, Geoffrey. *The Ancient Wisdom,* Sphere Books, London, 1979, p. 101.

4   Hesiod [Works]. R. Lattimore, trans., University of Michigan Press, Ann Arbor, 1959, pp. 172-3.

5   Bennett, J. G. *The Masters of Wisdom,* Turnstone Books, U.K., 1977, p. 49.

6   Campbell, Joseph. *The Masks of God,* vol. 1, Penguin, Harmondsworth, 1984, p. 374.

7   Ibid., p. 19.

8   Meillet, A. and Cohen, Marcel. *Les Langues du Monde,* H. Champion, Paris, 1952, p. 6.

9   Baring, Anne and Cashford, Jules. *The Myth of the Goddess,* Penguin, Harmondsworth, 1991, p. 25.

10   Mitra, Sisirkumar. *The Dawn Eternal,* Sri Aurobindo Ashram, Madras State, 1954, pp. 168-76.

11   The white race whom the ancient Egyptians called the Tamahu were of northern Cro-Magnon stock. They built a megalithic culture in northern Africa. The nineteenth-century French researchers Ferand and Latourneux said of the prodigious megalithic works of Brittany, Spain and northern Africa that the builders were the dolmen people "who came from the shores of the Baltic, wandered through England, France and the Iberian peninsula, until finally as the blond

and blue-eyed Libyans and the northern people of the Tamahu, they troubled the borders of Egypt." Jurgen Spanuth, *Atlantis of the North*, Sidgwick & Jackson, 1979, pp. 123-24, citing E. Krause, *Tuiskoland*, Glogau, 1891, p. 69.

12 Spanuth, op. cit., p. 69.

13 Baring and Cashford, op. cit., p.20.

14 Michell, John. *The View Over Atlantis*, Sphere Books, London, 1975, p. 117.

15 Diodorus Siculus. *The Library of History*, text with English tr. by C.H. Oldfather et al., Loeb Classical Library, London, 1936-67, 2.47.

16 Bernbaum, Edwin. *The Way to Shambhala*, J. P. Tarcher, Los Angeles, 1989, p. 92.

17 Ibid.

18 Apollonius of Rhodes. *Argonautica*, tr. as *The Voyage of Argo*, E. V. Rieu, trans., Penguin, Harmondsworth, 1971.

19 Ashe, Geoffrey. *Atlantis*, Thames & Hudson, London, 1992, p. 5.

20 Donnelly, Ignatius. *Atlantis: The Antediluvian World*, Sidgwick & Jackson, London, 1979, quoted by Geoffrey Ashe, op. cit., p. 9.

21 Plato. *Timaeus and Critias*, Desmond Lee, trans., Penguin, Harmondsworth, 1983, p. 140.

22 Ibid., p. 137.

23 Ibid., p. 37.

24 Zanggar, Eberhard. *The Flood from Heaven*, Sidgwick & Jackson, London, 1992, p. 114.

25 Frankfort, Henri. *Cylinder Seals*, MacMillan, London, 1939, pp. 75-77.

26 In the *hieros gamos* the king was initiated with all due temple ceremony by sexual union with the high priestess, who represented the Great Goddess. By this method of kundalini-awakening he too became divine and so fit to rule as a god-king. Thus each reign "descended from heaven." This is the best-known and earliest form of the practice, which goes back to Neolithic times, generally dated between 10,000 B.C. and 8000 B.C. Thus Poseidon, whose name means spouse— i.e. spouse of the Great Goddess—would actually have been a "mortal" divinized by his union with the Magna Mater. Later, however, patriarchal norms among the Hellenes demanded a reversal of the gender roles, and we find the god-kings of Atlantis—as portrayed by Plato—spiritually impregnating "mortal" women. *The Myth of the Goddess*, Anne Baring and Jules Cashford, op. cit., pp. 46-105.

27 Spanuth, op. cit., p. 116.

28 Hesiod, op. cit.

29 Plato, op. cit., pp. 131-32.

30 Ibid. pp. 143-44.

31 An archaeologist, Rhys Carpenter, first advanced the theory that a global climatic change had occurred around 1200 B.C. In corroboration, a Swedish ocean-
ographer obtained drill-cores from the Mediterranean seabed for analysis in
1947, as a consequence of which it was found that the temperature of the sea
had begun to rise c. 5000 B.C. to reach its maximum somewhere around 1000
B.C. But at that point a series of volcanic eruptions occurred which were the
most violent for the past ten thousand years, after which the temperature of the
seas fell to its lowest level in seven thousand years. A wealth of ancient records
attest to this sudden drop in temperature worldwide between 1200 and 1000
B.C., accompanied by other symptoms indicative of a devastating global catastrophe. *Atlantis of the North*, Spanuth, op. cit., p. 150.

32 Schuré, Edouard. *The Great Initiates*, Harper & Row, New York, 1961, Notes:
p. 515.

33 Guthrie argues Apollo's Siberian origin on the grounds of his devotees' powers
of shape-shifting, astral traveling and thaumaturgy of various kinds, which have
no parallel in Greek religion but are similar to those of Siberian shamans and
medicine men. But even more convincing is the fact that Apollo's sister Artemis, the Greek goddess of the hunt, is related in Greek star-mythology to Ursa
Major, the Great Bear constellation of the polar regions. Called the Bear-Moth-
er who traditionally led Greek girls in a round bear-dance identical to that performed by Siberian shamans, her cultic roots are pre-Hellenic, going back to our
earliest totemic ancestors and the prehistoric animal cults, and can be traced
back along the north littoral to Russia and from thence to the great Bear cult of
Central Asia and Siberia. *The Greeks and Their Gods*, W. K. C. Guthrie, Methuen, London, 1950. See also *The Ancient Wisdom*, Geoffrey Ashe, pp. 128-33.

34 Plato, op. cit., p. 145.

35 McKie, Euan. *The Megalith-Builders*, Phaidon-Oxford, U.K., 1977.

CHAPTER TWELVE: THE PYTHAGOREAN "Y"

1 Homer. *The Odyssey*, IV, 563, S. H. Butcher and A. Lang, trans., as cited by Sir
Arthur Evans, *Journal of Hellenic Studies*, vol. III, pp. 155-56.

2 Bore samples brought back from the Azores in 1968 by an American research

ship show that for the last two hundred million years there has been no habitable land there. The islands that form the Mid-Atlantic Ridge are not the mountain peaks of a sunken continent, but the highest points of masses of volcanic rock bursting out of the earth's interior through a cleft in the African and European continental plates. *Atlantis of the North*, Jurgen Spanuth, Sidgwick & Jackson, London, 1979, p. 249.

3   Until the end of the thirteenth century B.C. Scandinavia was warmer than at present, with deciduous forests up to the Arctic Circle, a rich wheat- and vine growing agriculture and a dense population. Folklore repeatedly tells of the extraordinary wealth and ease of living of the people of the amber trade, and of their richly decorated temples, ornaments of gold, ploughs of silver and drains and canals of copper. However, northern Europe and Scandinavia sank into relative poverty and barbarism after an extreme climatic drop around 1200 B.C., when the amber trade ceased. The paradisial conditions never returned. There is archaeological evidence of terrible fires and floods in the bogs of Holland, North Germany and Scandinavia during the period around 1200 B.C. Spanuth, op. cit., pp. 68-69 and 107.

4   Pytheas of Massilia. Fragments preserved in various Greek and Latin authors, collected by D. Stichtenoth, Weimar, 1959, and cited by Spanuth, op. cit., pp. 250-54.

5   Homer, cited by Spanuth, op. cit., pp. 217-24.

6   Rudbeck, Olof. *Atlantica,* Uppsala, Sweden, published over the years 1657 to 1698.

7   *Eudoxus of Cnidos.* F. Lassere, ed., Berlin, 1966, cited by Spanuth, op. cit., p. 21.

8   A. G. Gilbert, ed., *The Hermetica*, Solos Press, 1992.

9   S. R. K. Glanville, ed., *The Legacy of Egypt*, The Clarendon Press, Oxford, 1957, quoted by Charles Hapgood, *Maps of the Ancient Sea Kings*, Chilton Books, Philadelphia 1966, p. 197.

10   Bauval, R. and Gilbert, A. *The Orion Mystery*, Mandarin Books, London, 1994, p. 263.

11   Spence, Lewis. *The History of Atlantis*, Rider, London, 1926; University Books, New Hyde Park, N.Y., 1968. Cited by Geoffrey Ashe, *Atlantis*, Thames & Hudson, London, 1992, p. 21.

12   Zanggar, Eberhard. *The Flood from Heaven*, Sidgwick & Jackson, London, 1992, p. 66.

13 In the cataclysms at the end of the thirteenth century B.C., says Spanuth, "The Mycenaean culture of the Greek mainland, the Minoan culture on Crete and Thera, the Hittite on Asia Minor, Syria with its great capital city of Ugarit, Palestine, with its strongly fortified city of Jericho, were all destroyed, and everywhere only a few survivors remained. Archaeological evidence proves it. Of 320 settlements in Greece in the thirteenth century, only forty were still inhabited in the twelfth. The population had shrunk to a hundredth of what it had been only a century before." *Atlantis of the North*, Jurgen Spanuth, p. 161.

14 Guénon, René. *The Lord of the World*, Coombe Springs Press, U.K., 1984, p. 58.

15 Bryant, Jacob. *A New System or An Analysis of Ancient Mythology*, T. Payne, P. Elmsly, B. White and J. Walter, publishers, London, 1776.

16 In the Tibetan cult of the Severed Heads the Khatvanga staff carried by a certain deity bears three heads, one below the other. The top one is a dry skull and represents the Dharmakaya, the causal body of enlightenment. The next is a head that has been severed for several days; it represents the Sambhogakaya, the subtle body of sainthood; and below that again is a freshly severed head representing the Nirmanakaya, the manifested body of enlightened enjoyment, which is the visible body of the Buddha. In Templar accounts reference is made to three highly revered heads and an early Grand Master of the Order had three heads depicted on his shield. In Sufism there is also a practice called Making a Head. *Women of Wisdom*, Tsultrim Allione, Routledge & Kegan Paul, Arkana, London, 1986, pp. 34-35.

17 Tomas, Andrew. *Shambhala: Oasis of Light*, Sphere Books, London, 1976, p. 100.

18 Baigent, Michael, et al. *The Messianic Legacy*, Corgi Books, London, 1987, p. 201.

19 Muck, Otto. *The Secret of Atlantis*, F. Bradley, trans., Fontana Collins, London, 1979, pp. 151-52.

20 Yates, Frances A. *The Rosicrucian Enlightenment*, Routledge & Kegan Paul, ARK Ed., London, 1986, pp. 125-29.

21 Guénon, René. *The Great Triad*, Quint Essentia, Cambridge, 1991, p. 53.

22 Guénon, René. *The Lord of the World*, p. 58.

23 Eliade, Mircea. *Myths, Dreams and Mysteries*, Harper Torchbooks, New York, 1975 pp. 138-39.

24 Fortune, Dion. *The Mystical Qabalah*, The Aquarian Press, London, 1987, p. 300.

25   Cerminara, Gina. *Insights for the Age of Aquarius*, The Theosophical Publishing House, Wheaton, Ill., 1985, pp. 1-13.

26   Zanggar, op. cit., p. 56.

27   Plato. *Timaeus and Critias*, Desmond Lee, trans., Penguin, Harmondsworth, 1983, p. 145.

28   Yates, op. cit., p. 58.

29   Waley, Arthur. *The Way and the Power*, MacMillan: George Allen & Unwin, London, 1949.

30   Chuang Tzu, quoted by René Guénon in *The Great Triad*, p. 127.

31   Ibid., p. 127.

CHAPTER THIRTEEN: AN ALTERNATIVE SCIENCE

1   Tomas, Andrew. *Shambhala: Oasis of Light*, Sphere Books, London, 1976, p. 39.

2   Ossendowski, Ferdinand. *Beasts, Men and Gods*, Edward Arnold, London, 1923, p. 303.

3   Roerich, Nicholas, quoted by Andrew Tomas, op. cit., p. 39, from an article written in Central Asia in 1935.

4   Tomas, op. cit., p. 64.

5   Scott, Ernest. *The People of the Secret*, Octagon Press, U.K., 1983, pp. 202-16.

6   Allione, Tsultrim. *Women of Wisdom*, Routledge & Kegan Paul, Arkana ed., London, 1986, p. 135.

7   Ibid., p. 144.

8   Sheldrake, Rupert. *The Rebirth of Nature*, Rider, London, 1993, p. 86.

9   Brenner, Sydney. Quoted by R. Lewin, "Why is Science So Illogical?" *Science* 224.

10   Sheldrake, op. cit., p. 131.

11   Bateson, Gregory. Cited by Fritjof Capra in *Uncommon Wisdom*, Fontana, London, 1988, p. 216.

12   Heisenberg, Werner, cited by William Irwin Thompson in *Passages About Earth*, Rider, London, 1974, pp. 89-90.

13   Bennett, J. G. *The Masters of Wisdom*, Turnstone Books, London, 1977, pp. 30-79.

14   Palmer, E. H. *Oriental Mysticism*, Octagon Press, London, 1974, p. 65.

15   Scott, op. cit., p. 39.

16   Heer, Friedrich. *The Medieval World*, Weidenfeld & Nicholson, London, 1961,

pp. 125-26.

17   Lama Yeshe. *Introduction to Tantra*, Wisdom Publications, London, 1985, p. 139.

18   Jones, William. *On the Philosophy of the Asiatics*, quoted by Ernest Scott, op. cit., p. 218.

19   Allione, op. cit., p. 259.

20   Ibid.

21   Beings of light as spiritual teachers and guides are also mentioned as being present in modern near-death experiences, and are evidently of the order of discarnate Bodhisattvas. "By my side there was a Being with a magnificent presence," says one such account. "As this loving yet powerful Being spoke to me, I understood vast meanings, much beyond my ability to explain. I understood life and death. The Light Being, pure, powerful, all-expansive, was without form and it could be said that great waves of awareness flowed to me and into my mind. . . As I absorbed the energy of the Light I sensed what I can only describe as bliss." *Heading Towards Omega*, Kenneth Ring, William Morrow, New York, 1984.

22   Allione, op. cit., pp. 25 and 29.

23   The method of potentiated visualization is said to lead the yogi eventually into a state of *mahamudra*, the great cortical bliss that is likened to the ecstasy of sexual orgasm. The unconscious psyche is opened up and visions of the wisdom deity occur. Thus in Keith Dowman's *Sky Dancer*, the yogini Yeshe Tsogyel has a vision of a naked red woman, a beckoning dakini, of whose copious flow of menstrual blood she drinks deeply. "My entire being was filled with health and well-being, the saint recounts of this psychic exchange. I felt as strong as a snow-lion, and I realized profound absorption to be inexpressible truth." *Sky Dancer: The Secret Life and Songs of the Lady Yeshe Tsogyel*, K. Dowman, Routledge & Kegan Paul, London, 1984, p. 71.

     Similarly, Allione recounts a vision she had of the subtle luminous spiritual en-ergy of the *vajra* body in the form of a wild-looking old woman with bright eyes and grey hair streaming up from her head who suddenly appeared before her. She was naked, with dark golden-brown skin. Her breasts hung pendulous ly and she was dancing. . . She was inviting me to join her dance. Through the medium of dreams, this old wise woman was the means whereby Tsultrim re-ceived inspiration and guidance for writing her book on great Tibetan woman saints. *Women of Wisdom*, pp. xxix and 34.

24   Fortune, Dion. *The Mystical Qabalah*, The Aquarian Press, London, 1987, pp. 240-41.

25 Ibid., p. 241.

26 Irish legends about the Tuatha de Danaan, a beautiful and noble race descended from the goddess Dana (the goddess of poetry and knowledge, counterpart of Gaia and sometimes called Anu), whose kings ruled Ireland until they were displaced by the Celts and became the fairy people, may conceivably suggest that the two kingdoms, the fairy and the human, were once one until they diverged along different paths of evolution. These Celtic legends have their roots in the far older pre-Druidic Hyperborean teachings of deep prehistory and so may well contain long-forgotten truths. *The Masks of God*, vol. 3, Joseph Campbell, Penguin, Harmondsworth, 1983, p. 40.

27 Allione, op. cit., p. 42.

28 Roerich, op. cit., p. 28.

29 Tomas, op. cit., p. 75.

30 Vallee, Jacques. *Revelations*, Ballantine Books, New York, 1991, p. 237.

31 Spencer, John. *The UFO Encyclopaedia*, Headline Books, London, 1991, p. 10.

32 Vallee, op. cit., p. 237.

33 Ashe, Geoffrey. *The Ancient Wisdom*, Sphere Books, London, 1977, p. 186.

CHAPTER FOURTEEN:
A SIGN FOR THE NEW MILLENNIUM

1   Eliade, Mircea. *Myths, Dreams and Mysteries*, Harper & Row, New York, 1975, p. 237.

2   Seward, Desmond. *The Dancing Sun*, MacMillan, London, 1993, p. 100.

3   Ibid., p. 100.

4   Quoted by John Spencer in *The UFO Encyclopaedia*, Headline Books, London, 1991, p. 251.

5   Ibid., p. 107.

6   Ibid., p. 251.

7   Ibid., p. 298.

8   Yates, Frances A. *The Rosicrucian Enlightenment*, Routledge & Kegan Paul, London, 1986, p. 39.

9   Ibid., p. 30.

10 Wilson, Edgar. "In Search of the Elusive Chi," *Newsletter of the International Society for the Study of Subtle Energies and Energy Medicine,* 1 (1990).

11   Brennan, Barbara Ann. *Hands of Light*, Bantam Books, New York, 1988, p. 19.

12   Ibid., p. 16.

13   Ring, Kenneth. *The Omega Project*, William Morrow, New York, 1992, pp. 32 and 91.

14   Ibid., pp. 156, 236 and 240.

15   Ibid., p. 235.

16   For example, Michael Grosso's work in *The Final Choice*, N. H. Walpole, Stillpoint, 1985. His definitive description of the evolutionary agency he calls Mind at Large, a kind of transpersonal Overmind that can interact with matter, corresponds in every particular with Shambhala.

17   White, John. *The Meeting of Science and Spirit*, Paragon, New York, 1990, p. 172.

18   Grey, Margot. *Return From Death*, Arkana, London, 1985, p. 168.

19   Campbell, Joseph. *The Masks of God*, vol. 1, Penguin, Harmondsworth, 1984, p. 471.

20   Wilber, Ken. *Up From Eden*, Shambhala Publications, Colorado, 1981, p. 79.

21   Jones, William. *On the Philosophy of the Asiatics*, quoted by Ernest Scott, *The People of the Secret*, Octagon Press, London, 1983, p. 218.

22   Kramer, S. N. *History Begins at Sumer*, Thames & Hudson, London, 1958, p. 196.

23   Bernbaum, Edwin. *The Way to Shambhala*, J. P. Tarcher, Los Angeles, 1989, p. 258.

24   Bennett, J. G. *The Masters of Wisdom*, Turnstone Books, London, 1977, p. 69.

25   Scott, op. cit., p. 39.

26   Ling, David. *The Buddha*, Temple Smith, London, 1985.

27   Roerich, Nicholas. *Shambhala*, Inner Traditions International, Rochester, Vt., 1990, pp. 11, 31.

28   Ibid., p. 16.

29   Tomas, Andrew. *Shambhala: Oasis of Light*, Sphere Books, London, 1976, p. 172.

INDEX

Isaiah, 66
Isis, 63, 168-73, 285n. 28
Islam, 238-39

Jachin pillar, 176
Jacob's Ladder, 82-86, 113
Jeans, Sir James, 98
Jesus Christ, 133, 159, 265
Jewish Encyclopedia, 82
John of Patmos, 266
Johnson, Raynor, 106
John the Baptist, 138
Jones, Sir William, 240
Josephus, 149
Journeys. *See* Expeditions; Spiritual journeys
Judaeus, Philo, 229
Judaism
  founding of, 277n. 10
  metaphysical teachings of, 82-84
  transformation of into world religion, 137

Kailas, Mount, 46-47, 53, 89
Kalachakra Tantra
  cycles of time and, 119-24, 129-31
  instruction in, 114-16
  prophecies of Shambhala in, 119, 124-28, 268
  Shambhala as source of, 7, 8, 15, 23-25
  three levels of, 116-18
  yogic practice and, 32, 53
Kalapa, 24, 30
Kali, 94, 161
Kali Yuga, 14, 121, 125-26, 130, 163, 239
Kalki Avatara, Sri, 9, 125-26, 129, 281n. 21
K'am-trul Rinpoche, Garje, 5
Khamtul Rinpoche, 33-37, 105, 166
Khwajagan, 139
King, Peter, 52, 53
Kings of Shambhala, 23-25, 268-70
Kirghiz people, 53
Knights Templar, 55, 216, 217
Koran, 238
Krishna, Gopi, 94, 258
Kriyas, 261
Kuan Yin, 19
Kumbum Lamasery, 114

Kundala Shakti, 24, 104
Kundalini Age, 262
Kundalini shakti
  contemporary awakening to, 257-60
  as Light, 239
  medicine wheel and, 74-75
  mystical geography and, 102-6
  spiritual evolution and, 234-37, 265
  as unitive principle, 233-34
  See also Chakric system; Terrestrial kundalini
Kundalini yoga
  chakric system and, 29, 69-71
  contemporary revival of, 95-96
  Jacob's Ladder story and, 82-86
  Kalachakra Tantra and, 15, 28, 116, 117
  new schools of, 278n. 1
  sexual initiation and, 202-3, 289n. 26
  shamanism and, 257, 258, 260, 261-62
  Shambhalic tradition and, 28-33
  See also Yogic tradition
Kunlun mountains, 19, 20, 22, 41, 46
Kurma Purana, 78

Landscape, Shambhala, 23-27, 30, 31
Lao-Tzu, 8, 46
Law of correspondence, 58
Leigh, Richard, 55, 216
Le Roi du Monde (Guénon), 13
Leto, 197, 203
Lhasa Oracle, 118
Libra, 136
Light, transcendental, 238-44
Light-body, 239-42
Lincoln, Henry, 55-57, 60, 216
Linear time, 122-24
Ling, David, 266
Lissner, Ivan, 45, 67, 111-12, 167
Lives of a Cell, The (Thomas), 86
Longing, 262-63
Lost Horizon (Hilton), 8
Lotus blossom, 30
Lovelock, James, 88, 90-91
Lully, Raymond, 236-37
Lung-ta, 228
Luz, 83, 84-85

Twilight of the Gods, 163
Two pillars, 176

UFO Research Association, 249
Unidentified flying objects (UFOs), 11,
    245-50, 257, 258
Unified Field Theory, 91, 92-94, 230, 234
Unitive principle
    contemporary increase in, 234-35, 265,
        266
    evolutionary growth and, 234-37
    light and, 238-44
    longing for, 264-66
    new world model and, 266-68
    scientific theory and, 230-33
    in spiritual traditions, 233-34
Universal Energy Field, 100-102
Upanishads, 101-2
Up From Eden (Wilber), 261
Uplifting of the Soul of the Horse, 171
Ursa Major, 65, 67, 276n. 13

Vajra body, 69, 91, 183, 225, 238
Valentinus, Vasilius, 87
Vallee, Jacques, 246, 249
Valleys, hidden, 44
Vanaratna, 115
Versailles, 54
Virgil, 179
Virgin Mary, 251-52
Vishnu, 125-26, 281n. 21
Vishnu Purana, 125, 126
Voluspa, 160, 161
Volute, 174-76, 205
Vril, 89

Watson, Lyall, 89
Way of Shambhala, The (Bernbaum), 17
Western Shambhalic traditions, 8-15
Wheel of Time, 114, 120, 121, 124-28
White, John, 259
White Island, 78
Wilber, Ken, 261, 264
Wilson, Colin, 98
Wirth, W., 176
Woodroffe, Sir John. *See* Avalon, Arthur

World Axis
    cyclic time and, 186-87
    direct path to God along, 111
    explained, 80-86
    Gaia principle and, 187-89
    initiate Hierarchy and, 150-51
    location shifts of, 182-86
    pillar religion and, 179-82, 187
    terrestrial kundalini and, 68-74
World initiation
    contemporary signs of, 255-62
    as increase in unitive force, 234-35, 265,
        266
    as millennial theme, 251
    prophecies of, 129-31
World model, revising, 266-68
World Mountain, 62
World Parents, 157
World Pillar, 156, 160-61, 174, 177-80, 194,
    219
World Soul, 232
World Tree
    illustrated, 109
    initiation and, 158, 164-66
    shamanism and, 111-13, 257
    volute design and, 174-76
    See also Tree of Life

Yang-Ti, 240, 241-42
Yates, Frances, 139, 218, 225
Yearning, 262-63
Yellow Hat sect, 31, 33
Yeshe, Lama, 239
Yeshe Tsogyel, 44, 244, 294n. 23
Yggdrasil, 161, 162, 163, 164, 176, 205,
    275n. 2, 284n. 10
Yin-yang forces, 87, 89, 218
Yoga Tantra, 94, 202
Yogic tradition
    physiological symbology in, 31, 37-38
    sexual initiation in, 202-3, 289n. 26
    unitive energy in, 240-41
    use of mandalas in, 22, 23, 31-32
    See also Kundalini yoga
Yugas, 124-25

QUEST BOOKS
are published by
The Theosophical Society in America,
Wheaton, Illinois 60189-0270,
a branch of a world organization
dedicated to the promotion of the unity of
humanity and the encouragement of the study of
religion, philosophy, and science, to the end that
we may better understand ourselves and our place in
the universe. The Society stands for complete
freedom of individual search and belief.
For further information about its activities,
write or call 1-800-669-1571.

*The Theosophical Publishing House
is aided by the generous support of
THE KERN FOUNDATION
a trust established by Herbert A. Kern
and dedicated to Theosophical education.*